Presidentialism

Presidentialism

Power in

Comparative

Perspective

Michael L. Mezey

LYNNE
RIENNER
PUBLISHERS

BOULDER
LONDON

Published in the United States of America in 2013 by
Lynne Rienner Publishers, Inc.
1800 30th Street, Boulder, Colorado 80301
www.rienner.com

and in the United Kingdom by
Lynne Rienner Publishers, Inc.
3 Henrietta Street, Covent Garden, London WC2E 8LU

Library of Congress Cataloging-in-Publication Data
Mezey, Michael L.
  Presidentialism : power in comparative perspective / Michael L. Mezey.
    pages cm
  Includes bibliographical references and index.
  ISBN 978-1-58826-892-1 (hc : alk. paper) 1. Presidents—United States.
2. Presidents. I. Title.
  JK516.M475 2013
  352.23'50973—dc23
                                                              2013006137

British Cataloguing in Publication Data
A Cataloguing in Publication record for this book
is available from the British Library.

Printed and bound in the United States of America

The paper used in this publication meets the requirements
∞ of the American National Standard for Permanence of
Paper for Printed Library Materials Z39.48-1992.

5 4 3 2 1

For
JFM, JHM,
and as always,
SGM

Contents

Preface

I began work on this book shortly after Barack Obama was elected as the forty-fourth president of the United States. As an enthusiastic supporter of the Obama campaign, this was a thrilling moment for me. On election night, I was in Grant Park in Chicago with thousands of others to hear the president-elect's victory statement and to share in the joy of this electoral affirmation of my political values, as well as this historic landmark in the long struggle against racism. But in addition to being a supporter of the president, I was also a student of the presidency. I had taught a college course on the US presidency for more than thirty years and had written a book exploring the relationship between the president and Congress and how that relationship affected public policy. Among other things, that book discussed the daunting challenges that the US constitutional system poses for its presidents as they seek to deliver on their campaign promises. That theme tempered to some extent the elation that I felt in Grant Park on that November evening in 2008. I was struck, in other words, by the tension between the unbridled optimism that accompanied Obama's election and my knowledge as a political scientist that these great expectations were likely to be disappointed.

This disconnect between campaign hope and the challenge of governing was nothing new for students of the US presidency and, I thought, hardly worth another book-length discussion. But when considered in the light of another long-standing interest of mine, a different perspective presented itself. Specifically, I had often been frustrated by the tendency of those who study US political institutions to look at those institutions as sui generis and to seldom if ever compare them to institutions in other parts of the world. Although I well understand and value the unique characteristics of the governing arrangements of the United States, I also think that we too often ignore the similarities between our institutions and those in other countries. This chauvinism narrows our view of the world and does little to help us develop a more general understanding of how political institutions operate. My first book, *Comparative Legislatures,* aimed to counter this narrow perspective by discerning similarities and differences among the world's legislatures and thus developing a comparative context for understanding the US Congress. This present volume seeks to do something similar for the presidency.

It seems to me that in every nation that has a president, increased public attention and often inflated public expectations are focused on the person who holds that office. Over the years, increased political power has flowed toward the presidency and away from other political institutions, particularly legislatures. This movement toward presidentialism is driven by three forces: the expanding role of government in the lives of citizens, which has led to an increase in the size and prominence of the executive branch of government; the globalization of public policy issues to the point that there are fewer purely domestic issues and more policy issues that are international in nature, which are more likely to be dominated by the executive branch; and democratization and modern electronic media, which have combined to create an increasingly intimate bond between presidents and their people. In this book, I look at the way these forces have affected presidencies around the world and, in doing so, I place the US presidency in a comparative context.

* * *

I have a number of debts to acknowledge. My information on presidencies is drawn from the work of scholars who have studied the many countries that I discuss. I have extensively and shamelessly mined the literature that these colleagues have generated, and my intellectual debt to them is reflected here in my citations and extensive bibliography. I am grateful to DePaul University for a research leave that helped me to begin this project. Thanks also go to DePaul's excellent library system and to Jennifer Schwartz in the reference section, who helped me track down some of the more obscure source material. Rose Spalding, my colleague at DePaul and an expert on Latin America, was an important source of information and advice as I tried to understand the presidencies of that region. Another of my colleagues, Catherine May, helped me to refine some of my ideas for Chapter 6.

At different stages of this process, I had the opportunity to present portions of my argument to various audiences. In December 2009, Manuel Alcantara Saez and Mercedes Garcia Montero invited me to participate in the Seminar on the Legislative Branch in Latin America in Comparative Perspective, held at the University of Salamanca. In May 2011, Olivier Rozenberg asked me to speak at his graduate seminar at the Institut d'études politiques de Paris. In August 2011, in conjunction with the annual meeting of the American Political Science Association, I presented my ideas at a workshop on comparative executive power, organized by Wayne Steger for the section on Presidents and Executive Politics. And in April 2012, I spoke at the Center for International Development at the State University of New York at Albany, at the invitation of Mark Baskin. The comments and questions that I received from these different audiences were of immense help to me as I worked through the details of the book.

Similarly, I owe a great deal to the anonymous reviewers who read and commented on the manuscript. Although I do not know who these fellow scholars are, should they read this book, they will find their suggestions, corrections, and insights reflected throughout. Nonetheless, when one discusses so many countries around the world and tries to take a broad comparative view, errors of omission and commission are certain to occur, and for these I take full responsibility.

I want to thank the good people at Lynne Rienner Publishers, especially Jessica Gribble and Lynne Rienner, who saw the promise of this project and were willing to take a chance on an idea-driven, "big picture" book. Jessica handled the review process in a thoroughly professional and expeditious manner, and Karen Williams and her copyediting staff respected my authorial voice while at the same time saving me from countless errors of syntax.

Finally, I owe more than I can say to my family. My wife, Susan, has been a constant source of love and support for more than four decades. She is as well an indefatigable scholar whose dedication to the craft of research has been a model for me. She, along with our children, Jennifer and Jason, their spouses, Jonathan and Deirdre, and the five marvelous grandchildren that they have generated (Rebecca, Norah, Paul, Benjamin, and Daniel) are the lodestars that orient and give meaning to my life.

1

An Introduction to Presidentialism

On January 20, 2009, Barack Obama took the oath of office as the forty-fourth president of the United States. At that moment, the country was in what could only be described as terrible shape. The United States was confronting its worst economic crisis since the Great Depression. Unemployment was climbing toward double digits, major financial institutions were requiring huge investments by the government in order to avoid collapse, hundreds of thousands of people were about to lose their homes to foreclosure, and the domestic automobile industry was on the verge of bankruptcy. Internationally, the country's soldiers were fighting wars in Iraq and Afghanistan, the Middle East was once again in flames as Israelis and Palestinians confronted one another in Gaza, failed states in Africa and South Asia were sliding toward chaos, Iran and North Korea were hard at work on nuclear programs, and a new cold war with Russia seemed to be brewing.

Yet when polled a week before inauguration day, overwhelming majorities said that Obama would be a good president, that he would bring real change to Washington, and that he would make the right decisions on the economy, Iraq, dealing with the war in the Middle East, and protecting the country from terrorist attacks. More than 80 percent of the public believed that their new president would work effectively with Congress and that he would manage the executive branch wisely; 79 percent pronounced themselves optimistic about the next four years, and 78 percent said that they had a favorable opinion of the president-elect. Only 18 percent reported an unfavorable opinion.[1] All of this was particularly remarkable given the fact that he had prevailed in a tough, often bitter election campaign, winning just under 55 percent of the popular

1

vote. Equally remarkable was that the popular belief in Obama's abilities to deal with all of these challenges seemed to be largely a matter of faith rather than a reasoned assessment based on past performance. After all, Obama had served only four years in the US Senate, two of which had been devoted more to running for president than legislating, and before that his only government experience had been as a rank-and-file member of the Illinois state legislature.

One year after his election, however, things had changed. Although the economic free fall that he had inherited had been stopped—in large measure because of a huge economic stimulus program, government support for the automobile industry, and various initiatives to bolster the housing sector, all of which the president championed—unemployment had soared to 10 percent, home foreclosures were continuing, and, although Obama had begun to wind down the country's military commitment to Iraq, continued violence there and uncertain steps toward democracy called into question his ability to actually withdraw US troops. At the same time, he had escalated the country's commitment of troops to Afghanistan and expanded the air campaign against Taliban and al-Qaeda forces in Pakistan. In Washington, partisanship had intensified, his signature healthcare initiative was bogged down and losing public support, and deficit spending had reached alarming proportions as tax revenues declined and the countercyclical expenditures necessary to stop the recession increased. The public mood began to sour; Democrats lost the off-year gubernatorial elections in New Jersey and Virginia along with several special elections including, shockingly, the election to replace Senator Ted Kennedy of Massachusetts. Anti-Washington sentiment was on the rise, directed for the most part at the Democrats, who were in control of the presidency and both houses of Congress. Obama's job approval rating fell below 50 percent, his support among independent voters, who had provided him with so many votes a year earlier, sharply eroded, and the country's confidence that the president could deliver on his promise of change moved toward the vanishing point. The midterm elections of 2010 saw the Democratic Party lose its majority in the House of Representatives while barely clinging to its majority in the Senate, and according to public opinion polls, more voters disapproved than approved of the president's performance. In the view of many commentators, Obama seemed well on his way to becoming a one-term president. Nonetheless, in November 2012 he was reelected to a second term, although by a narrower margin than in 2008, a victory that may well have had more to do with the weaknesses of his opponent and the Republican Party than with widespread satisfaction with his first-term performance.

Some may attribute Barack Obama's first-term problems to his inexperience, mistakes, and misjudgment; others will cite the intractability of the problems that he confronted, many of which he inherited from his predecessor, as well as the unrelenting hostility of the Republican opposition to his agenda and to him personally. Although there is something to be said for these factors, such an analysis misses the point that Obama's experience tracks to a great extent the experiences of many if not all recent US presidents. Typically, presidents score their highest job approval rating at the moment that they take office and then experience an erosion of public support as their term progresses. There are, to be sure, short-term ups and downs, depending upon the events that dominate the news, but the long-term trend is toward lower levels of public support. In other words, all US presidents begin their terms with the high hopes and good wishes of the American people and end their presidencies seeming to have fallen short of meeting these expectations. More often than not, they leave office frustrated that they have accomplished less than they had hoped, angry about the things that got in their way, and already drafting the inevitable memoir, replete with self-justifications and score-settling.

Interestingly enough, this pattern of very high expectations that go unmet is not an exclusively US phenomenon. This point is typically missed by US voters as well as scholars, who fail to ask to what extent the experiences and practices of their political leaders and institutions compare to those in other countries. Such a comparative perspective can serve to move us away from idiosyncratic explanations for the success or failure of specific presidents and toward the structural and systemic issues that apply to all presidential systems. A brief review of recently elected presidents in France and Bolivia suggests that Barack Obama's experience during his first years in office was in many ways similar to that of other presidents.

In May 2007, a year and a half before the Obama victory, Nicolas Sarkozy was elected president of France, replacing Jacques Chirac, who had served in that office for twelve years and who in the minds of many had come to represent an aging, complacent, elitist, and distant political class (Smith 2007). Sarkozy won with 53 percent of the vote against his opponent, the Socialist candidate Ségolène Royal. It was a hard-fought race, turning in part on explosive issues such as immigration and French identity as well as more traditional concerns about the economy, corruption, and, like the Obama campaign, the need for "change." Sarkozy had made his reputation as a tough-minded minister of interior who took a particularly hard line against immigrants and the urban unrest with which they had been associated. Some three weeks after his election,

Sarkozy had a job approval rating of 65 percent, prompting one journalist to say that "not since de Gaulle returned to office in 1958 had a French leader enjoyed such popularity." He concluded that "a large number of French people seem to be ready to give M. Sarkozy a chance to push through his promised whirlwind program of fiscal, labor, education and criminal justice reforms" (Lichfield 2007).

But the Sarkozy honeymoon did not last any longer than Obama's. By May 2008, the same journalist was reporting job approval ratings for the president "between 28 and 35 percent, the "lowest for any year old presidency since the launch of the 5th Republic" (Lichfield 2008). By early 2009, Sarkozy's numbers had rebounded somewhat, but his job approval rating was still hovering at around 40 percent. The recession with which President Obama was trying to cope also had hit France and the rest of Europe, resulting in rising unemployment, threats to the stability and even survival of the euro, and severe fiscal challenges for the government as it sought to deal with mounting imbalances between revenues and expenditures. Sarkozy's efforts to curb budget deficits and to reform the expensive French pension system, together with a series of appointments that to some suggested cronyism and even nepotism, and several scandals involving members of his administration, had created in the minds of many an image of arrogance and detachment from public opinion and a view that the promised change either was not going to happen or was not going to be as popular or as painless as the public had been led to believe.[2] By the summer of 2011, less than a year before the 2012 presidential election, Sarkozy's disapproval ratings were approaching 80 percent (Gourevitch 2011), and other polls indicated that he was "deeply disliked" by some 60 percent of French voters.[3] Unlike Barack Obama, Sarkozy was narrowly defeated for reelection in May 2012, by Socialist candidate François Hollande.

In December 2005, Bolivia elected as its president Evo Morales, leader of the Movement Toward Socialism party. He was the first presidential candidate in recent Bolivian history to have received a majority of the popular vote (54 percent); as required by the Constitution, his predecessors had been selected by the Bolivian Congress when they failed to attain an electoral majority. Morales also was the first indigenous person to become president of Bolivia, and his election ignited joy among the poor and downtrodden of his country and fear among the landed elite, who were for the most part descended from the European immigrants who had for so long dominated the politics of the nation. His party also gained a majority of the seats in the Chamber of Deputies. His avowedly anti-US platform, his open affection for Hugo Chávez and

Fidel Castro, his pledge to nationalize leading industries, and his opposition to US-inspired policies aimed at eradicating cocoa cultivation set off alarms in Washington. However, a public opinion poll conducted shortly after Morales's election found that 65 percent of the population approved of the president-elect, 67 percent believed that his administration would be positive for Bolivians, and 45 percent said that they felt confident about the new president.[4] One month into his term, his approval rate had risen to nearly 80 percent.

Once in office, however, Morales faced strong opposition from the Senate, where his party lacked a majority, as well as from the wealthier eastern provinces of the country, whose leaders organized a constitutionally questionable referendum endorsing secession. He responded by scheduling a special election that would ask the people to vote on whether or not to recall him, his vice president, and the provincial governors, several of whom were opposition leaders. According to the rules, if he or the other officials were to retain their office, they needed not just a majority of the vote in the recall but a higher percentage of the vote than they had received in their initial election. Although seen by some as taking a risky gamble, Morales won a resounding victory, gaining substantially more support than he had registered in 2005, particularly in the poorer western part of the country, where he polled in excess of 80 percent. One observer suggested that the election results were less an endorsement of Morales and more a commentary on the dependence that Bolivians have on the presidency—"there is no alternative national leader, they only had a choice between Evo or a vacuum of leadership."[5] After his victory, he developed a new Constitution that would provide the basis for greater representation of indigenous people in the legislature, adopted a more aggressive approach to land reform, and sought a greater role for the government in regard to nationalization. He also proposed that the president be allowed to run perpetually for reelection, but, faced with resistance, backed off that proposal in favor of one allowing him an additional five-year term. Early in 2009, the new Constitution was approved, and at the end of the year Morales was reelected with 62 percent of the vote. The next year, he nationalized energy-generating firms and reformed the pension system, extending its benefits to millions of poor Bolivians. But he also suffered a major setback when he attempted to end government fuel subsidies; the resulting spike in gasoline prices caused violent street demonstrations and Morales was forced to back down.[6] His job approval ratings dropped to 32 percent at this point, compared with 70 percent at the time of reelection. By the end of 2011, things had not improved, with his job approval rating at 35 percent.[7]

What do these three presidencies, in three quite different countries—separated by language, geography, and culture—have in common? Each president was an atypical candidate in terms of his personal background—Barack Obama as the first African American president in US history, Nicolas Sarkozy as a descendent of Hungarian Jews who was baptized a Catholic, and Evo Morales as the first indigenous president in Bolivia's nearly 200 years of independence. Also atypical were the political careers of Obama and Morales prior to becoming president; while Sarkozy had more than twenty years of governmental experience at the local and national levels, both Obama and Morales had spent a good deal of time as "community organizers." Obama had served only four years in the US Senate, and Morales, a union leader and activist, had served only briefly in the Bolivian Chamber of Deputies. All three men were relatively young when elected—Morales forty-six, Obama forty-seven, and Sarkozy fifty-two—and each became somewhat of an instant celebrity. Sarkozy's marriage to a well-known model became fodder for the tabloids. One lost count of the number of times Obama and his family appeared on the cover of various magazines. And Morales's international travels were widely reported, while at home his opponents asserted that he, with the support of the country's media, was creating a cult of personality (Romero and Schipani 2009). All three presidents began their terms with public opinion polls suggesting widespread optimism about their prospects for success, optimism that would dissipate relatively quickly in the cases of Obama and Sarkozy, and a bit later in the case of Morales.

For Barack Obama, the hope was for a quick recovery from economic disaster and in the long term for a new kind of politics that would be more bipartisan and more transparent and put an end to what he called "business as usual." In the case of Nicolas Sarkozy, it was a return to law and order in the short term and a wide-ranging "modernization" of the French political system as well as the country's economy and society. For Evo Morales, it was the "overwhelming demand for change" in a political system dominated by traditional political parties and the promise that he "would open the political system to the indigenous masses" so as to achieve a more just distribution of the wealth of their nation (Gamarra 2008:130). In each case, these hopes were more easily articulated than realized. Obama faced opposition from an independent Congress and its obstructionist Republican minority; rather than the bipartisanship he had hoped for, his first term was characterized by an even more polarized and hostile political environment. Sarkozy faced opposition from an entrenched French political and economic establishment, and Morales from that portion of Bolivian society who had long held power and were not prepared to yield it willingly.

Each president had his successes. Obama saw his healthcare initiative enacted into law after a long struggle, Sarkozy played a central role in attempts to stabilize the euro during the Greek financial crisis, and Morales by all accounts strengthened the Bolivian economy while at the same time moving the country toward a more equitable distribution of its wealth. Despite their achievements, however, each failed to fulfill all the promises and to meet all the expectations generated by their election. Each failure was viewed by the media and the public as personal in nature—primarily as a failure of presidential leadership and less as an indication of systemic failures or of the resistance of a policy problem to simple, consensual, or pain-free solutions. The experience of each nation and each president, as different as they are, exhibits an outsized focus on the president—on one person who would bring about change, who would solve all of the country's problems. This personalization of governance, focusing intensely and almost exclusively on the president, is the heart of *presidentialism,* the central theme of this book.

Presidentialism

In presidential systems, the executive (that is, the president) and the legislature are elected separately and directly by the voters. The legislature has no primary role in the selection of the president; his tenure in office is fixed; and policy failures, popular discontent with his leadership, or adverse votes against his policy preferences in the legislature cannot drive him from office prematurely.[8] He can be forced to leave office before the end of his term only with extraordinary actions—for example, impeachment in the United States, a combination of impeachment and popular uprisings in Latin America (Pérez-Liñán 2007), or coups in those countries with militaries disposed to take such steps. Legislative terms are similarly fixed; only in a few instances can a president make the unilateral decision to dissolve the legislature and call for new elections (see Linz 1994:6; Lijphart 1994:99–100; Shugart and Mainwaring 1997:14). José Antonio Cheibub (2007:35) summarizes this arrangement succinctly by saying that, in presidential systems, the executive does not require the support of a parliamentary majority to exist and persist in office. David Samuels and Matthew Shugart (2010:4) describe the situation simply as "separate origin and separate survival" for both the legislature and the executive. In presidential systems, the president serves as both head of state and head of government. In the former capacity, he symbolizes the unity of the nation and, along with other national symbols, evokes a sense of patriotism among citizens. As head of government, he is the political leader of the nation, charged with a leading role in the policy decisions that the country takes.

In parliamentary systems, in contrast, the voters, rather than electing the executive, elect legislators who in turn select a cabinet that constitutes the executive. The cabinet—sometimes referred to as "the government"— is composed of legislators from the party or parties that make up the majority in Parliament, and is headed by a prime minister (or a premier) who serves as head of government or chief executive. The prime minister is not the head of state; that position and its symbolic functions belong to either a constitutional monarch, or to a typically nonelected and relatively powerless president in those parliamentary systems that do not have a monarch. The government is accountable to the legislature; this means that the prime minister and cabinet can be removed prior to scheduled elections if they lose the support of their legislative majority. Reciprocally, in many parliamentary systems, the government holds the power to dissolve the legislature and schedule new elections. In other words, in parliamentary systems, the executive is selected by, and serves at the pleasure of, the legislative majority (see Samuels and Shugart 2010:26–27).

A third category of constitutional arrangements combines aspects of parliamentary and presidential systems. In semipresidential (or mixed) systems, executive power is shared between a president who is directly elected by the voters, serves a fixed term in office, and enjoys independent powers, and a prime minister and cabinet who are dependent on a parliamentary majority for their survival in office. The president is the head of state and serves jointly with the prime minister as head of government (see Linz 1994:48ff.; Cheibub 2007). The discussion in this book includes both presidential and semipresidential political systems. As compared with parliamentary systems, presidential and semipresidential systems together constitute a majority of the democratic political systems worldwide, with slightly more semipresidential than purely presidential systems (Samuels and Shugart 2010:6).[9]

These distinctions among parliamentary, presidential, and semipresidential systems rest upon the wording of a nation's constitution.[10] But the theme of this book is that presidentialism is more than simply a constitutional category; it includes a set of public perceptions, political actions, as well as formal and informal political power arrangements that to a greater or lesser degree characterize all countries that have presidential or semipresidential constitutions.

In the first instance, presidentialism is characterized by a broadly shared public perception that places the president at the center of the nation's politics and views him (or her) as the person primarily responsible for dealing with the challenges before the country. One leading scholar of Latin American politics summarized this phenomenon in the following terms: "The president is taken to be the embodiment of the nation and the main custodian and definer of its interests." The president is thought to be "the individual who is most fit to take responsibility for the destiny of the nation" (O'Donnell 1994:59–60). Popular expectations for the welfare of the nation and for the satisfactory performance of its political system focus on the presidency, often to the exclusion or at least the marginalization of other public officials and political leaders. These lofty expectations mean that policy failures as well as successes, whether or not they are the result of the actions or inactions of the president, are nonetheless attributed almost exclusively to him.

Second, presidentialism is characterized by the efforts that presidents and others make to increase the power and authority of the presidency so that the occupants of the office will have the capacity to meet the expectations that the public holds for them, or simply because it is in the nature of an office holder to seek to aggrandize his power. Presidents use their rhetorical skills to encourage popular support both for their policies and often for enhanced presidential power. They argue implicitly and often explicitly that because they are elected by all of the citizens, their plans and proposals embody the will of the people and therefore that deference to the president and to his agenda is required if his, and by extension the people's policy goals, are to be achieved.

Third, presidentialism refers to the actual movement of power and authority in the direction of the president. Although this process can take place quickly, it more typically occurs over an extended period of time, decades perhaps; in the short term, presidential power can wax or wane in a particular country, but the long-term trend is toward the accumulation of more power in the hands of the president. This takes place either through usurpation of power by the incumbent or the voluntary ceding of power to the president by other political institutions, particularly the legislature, or more typically by a combination of both factors. This is justified either as an appropriate response to the public expectations that focus on the president or as an unavoidable necessity given the realities of leading and governing the modern nation-state.

Whatever the process or its justification might be, presidentialism reflects the fact that presidents around the world have, over the years, come to enjoy an increased capacity to determine public policy. At first glance, this assertion seems to fly in the face of the policy failures and disappointments that so many presidents experience in their time in

office. In the United States, President Obama and all of his recent predecessors have been unable to gain approval for some of their highest-
priority policy initiatives. But such failures indicate that while the power
of the US president has increased, the expectations that people have of
him have increased at a faster rate, so that despite the increased power of
the office, the gap between what is expected of him and what he can
deliver has grown. On the other hand, in some countries, presidential
power has increased at a rate comparable to the increase in public expectations, so that the gap, if it exists, is substantially smaller. Arguably, this
has been the case with Bolivia's President Morales.

Presidentialism thus incorporates a state of mind of a public disposed
toward connecting themselves and their political fate to the personality
and policies of a single leader, to the efforts of presidents to exploit that
state of mind in order to generate popular support both for their policies
and for their own more central role in determining public policy, and to a
tendency, more fully realized in some nations than in others, to allocate
state power in a way that conforms to this state of mind.

Personal vs. Collective Leadership

Presidentialism emphasizes the personal leadership of a singular leader,
while parliamentary systems are characterized by collective leadership.
In presidential systems, the president alone is responsible for administering the nation's executive power. He may choose to consult with others as he exercises his power, or delegate responsibilities to others who
report to him, but he sits atop the executive hierarchy and has the final
say on all executive decisions. He need not conduct a vote among his
advisers or cabinet members prior to taking action; he can simply act.

In parliamentary systems, policymaking power lies in the hands of the
leaders of the majority party or coalition. The prime minister, functioning
as head of government, works in close consultation with individual legislators, particularly members of the governing party or the parties that
compose the governing coalition, as well as with a cabinet that reflects the
majority in the legislature. The prime minister typically does not have the
unilateral power to act; cabinet votes or at least discussions authorizing
such actions take place prior to major executive decisions, especially in
those cases when the government is composed of a coalition of political
parties. Thus, in parliamentary systems, major political actions and public
policy decisions or initiatives are more likely to be attributed to political

institutions (as in "the government proposed the policy") than to an individual (as in "the prime minister proposed the policy"). In presidential systems, executive actions are attributed to the president, usually by name (as in "Sarkozy proposed the policy").

Parliamentary systems tend to be characterized by strong political parties that play a significant role in providing policy cues to voters, identifying who will hold political power, and determining the content of public policy. In contrast, presidential systems tend to emphasize the personality and policy priorities of the president and de-emphasize political parties as well as other political institutions. While executive leaders in parliamentary systems are members of, and therefore inextricably bound to their legislative bodies, presidents can distance themselves from their legislatures, or even attack the legislature as an institution. For example, President Luiz Inácio Lula da Silva of Brazil frequently indicated that he held members of Parliament in relatively low esteem and, toward the end of his first term in office, according to one analyst, "increasingly sought to rely on his personal charisma rather than on the party organization for support" (Samuels 2008:174). US presidents have regularly sought to depict themselves as standing above the partisan conflict that characterizes Congress. President Bill Clinton, after his party lost control of Congress in the 1994 midterm elections, practiced a policy of "triangulation"—depicting himself as the moderate and sober leader standing apart from the Republican conservatives who controlled the House and the Senate as well as from his own ostensible allies in the Democratic Party. President Obama, during his reelection campaign, frequently criticized Congress for blocking his initiatives, usually failing to distinguish between its Democratic and Republican members. President Rafael Correa of Ecuador characterized his Congress as a "sewer" of corruption, and his party, to demonstrate its disdain for that institution, ran no candidates for legislative seats during Correa's election campaign (Hayes 2006).

Writing about Latin American presidencies, but in terms that are more generally applicable, Guillermo O'Donnell remarks that presidents tend to "view themselves as above both political parties and organized interests," that they seem to view other institutions such as legislatures and courts as "nuisances," and that they depict themselves as standing alone as the sole representatives of the people as a whole. "Since this paternal figure is supposed to take care of the whole nation, his political base must be a movement, the supposedly vibrant overcoming of the factionalism and conflict associated with parties" (1994:60).

Presidential Visibility

To the citizens of presidential nations, the president is by far the most visible domestic political actor. Today, the president of the United States is the dominant figure in the political consciousness of the American public. Nearly every person in the country older than the age of six knows the president's name, and no other political leader is as widely known. US history is recounted in terms of presidential administrations—the Age of Jackson, Lincoln and the Civil War, Roosevelt and the New Deal, the Reagan years. Highways and airports are named after past presidents, the faces of the greatest adorn the nation's currency, and monuments are built to commemorate them. The quadrennial presidential elections attract more media attention and more voters than any other election, and many citizens vote only in presidential elections. Once he is in office, the nation's politics tend to revolve around the president. His words and actions dominate the news, and citizens as well as Congress look to him for leadership and policy initiatives on major issues.

Similarly, virtually every French citizen knows that their president's name is François Hollande; fewer, I suspect, know that the prime minister is named Jean-Marc Ayrault, and even fewer could name key members of the National Assembly. The name of Charles de Gaulle, four decades after his death, still resonates with the French people. The country's main airport is named after him and a magnificent Parisian museum bears the name of his successor, Georges Pompidou. Before the death of Hugo Chávez, one could not speak of Venezuela without focusing on its colorful and controversial president. Few people outside Venezuela and only a few more inside the country would have been able to name another major government leader. Indeed, presidential dominance is a common theme throughout Latin America. President Evo Morales's preeminent role in Bolivian politics is comparable to the roles that Presidents Cristina Fernández de Kirchner in Argentina, Lula da Silva in Brazil, and Rafael Correa in Ecuador play in the political lives of their nations. In Africa, President Robert Mugabe has controlled Zimbabwe since its independence, often with an iron fist, and in the more democratic South Africa, presidents such as Nelson Mandela and his successors, Thabo Mbeki and Jacob Zuma, have been at the center of public attention and the policymaking process. The founding presidents of postcolonial Africa—Banda, Nkrumah, Senghor, Nyerere, Kenyatta—have the same meaning to the people of their countries that George Washington has to Americans. These leaders constantly blurred the distinction between themselves and the state as each moved to expand his power and control his country, and each remains a major historical figure nationally and on the continent as a whole. And just as Americans tend to recount their history in terms of presidential administrations, one student of francophone Africa says that it is "hardly accidental that regimes in Africa and elsewhere tend to be denominated by the names of their leaders—the Wade regime [in Senegal], the Biya regime [in Cameroon], the Bongo regime [Gabon], and so on" (Le Vine 2004:292). Similarly, as Russia moved in recent years from authoritarianism to an ostensibly more democratic system, the presidency, first with Mikhail Gorbachev and Boris Yeltsin and then with Vladimir Putin, became the primary focus of public attention and virtually synonymous with governmental power.[11]

The President and the People

Presidents have a unique relationship with the citizens of their countries, a relationship derived in part from the fact that presidents are the only political leaders elected by the population as a whole and in part from their role as head of state. It is a relationship that presidents are inclined to cite when their policies are questioned or when they are perceived as having overstepped the constitutional limits of their power.

In the United States, almost from the beginning of its constitutional history, its presidents have justified the expansion of their powers in democratic terms—in terms of their connection with the people. Thomas Jefferson argued that when as president he needed to use discretionary power beyond the explicit terms of the Constitution, he would appeal to the people to judge whether he had acted appropriately or not. In his view, "governments are republics only in proportion as they embody the will of the people and execute it" (Bailey 2007:14). By the time that Andrew Jackson became president, the electorate had expanded significantly, and Jackson, who had arrived at the presidency over the opposition of the Washington elites, styled himself as "the people's" president. For him, the first principle of the United States was that "the majority should govern" (Meacham 2008:120). One student of his presidency suggests that Jackson wanted the power to act as freely as he could because he believed his judgment would serve the country well, for he made no distinction between himself and the broad idea of "the people" (Meacham 2008:250). Three decades later, Abraham Lincoln justified his expansion of presidential powers beyond its clear constitutional limits as being in response to the wishes and needs of "his rightful masters, the American people." Similarly, Theodore Roosevelt argued that the president's power could be restricted only by the specific words of the

Constitution, and that where the document was silent, he had discretion to act. When he acted, he did so as the "steward of the people, bound actively and affirmatively to do all he could for the people" (Pfiffner and Davidson 2009:44–45). And in the mid–twentieth century, as the nation moved toward universal suffrage and as modern methods of mass communication developed, the connection between presidential power and popular, democratic government became even stronger.

Presidents outside the United States have justified their actions in similar democratic terms. Like their US counterparts, they too are the sole leaders in their countries who are in office by virtue of the votes of a national electorate. Hugo Chávez, during his 2000 campaign for the Venezuelan presidency, adopted the slogan "with Chávez, the people rule" (Hawkins 2010:15). Evo Morales, on the eve of his election to the Bolivian presidency, declared in an interview with a Brazilian newspaper that "when elected, I intend to be the people's president."[12] When the new Constitution that Morales designed and championed—and that significantly expanded presidential power—was approved, he said that the vote to approve the document was "not a vote for the government; it is for the Bolivian people" (Partlow 2009). Chávez and Morales are often viewed as part of a new generation of Latin American presidents who have come to office as populist outsiders who present themselves, their policies, and their actions—and especially those actions that stretch the ostensible constitutional limits of their power—as a manifestation of the will of the people (Mainwaring 2006; Barr 2009; Hawkins 2010).

The president's ability to gain popular support for the expansion of his powers is abetted by the popular disposition to personalize politics— for individual citizens to attach themselves and their political priorities and aspirations to a singular leader rather than to a larger, more collective organization such as a political party or a legislative body, or to a particular set of ideological beliefs that transcends individual leaders. Such a disposition is encouraged by the fact that the president occupies a dual role; he is not only head of his government but also head of state. The role of head of state, although largely ceremonial, is intimately connected with the history and symbols of the nation. Presidential appearances are typically accompanied by the flags, the music, and the backdrops that arouse a sense of nationalism among a population. This allows presidents, if they wish, to blur the distinctions between support for them and their policies, and patriotic support for the nation, as they seek to justify their actions or expand their power.

The president of the United States may, in his role as head of state, lay a wreath at the Tomb of the Unknown Soldier in the morning, and then in the afternoon, in his role as head of government, may hold a press conference to announce a new economic initiative and denounce his opponents in Congress or in the opposition party. Although political scientists and other informed observers can distinguish these two roles, it is not clear that the American people always make this distinction. Presidents regularly use the trappings associated with their role as head of state to generate popular support for the policy initiatives that they undertake in their role as head of government. Presidential addresses to the nation are televised from the Oval Office of the White House, the very symbol of the US presidency, and the president's State of the Union address to Congress is accompanied by great fanfare and ceremony as both political supporters and political opponents greet him with handshakes and cheers, representing their support for the office of the presidency and his role as head of state, rather than their support for the political positions that the president is about to announce in his speech in his role as head of government.

In parliamentary systems such as the United Kingdom's, the positions of head of state and head of government are separate, so it is more difficult for the prime minister as head of government to marshal the nation's symbols in support of his political program. In England, the head of state is the queen. She is the one who evokes patriotic emotions among the citizens of England, and it is her appearances that are accompanied by the Union Jack and "Rule Britannia." Like the president of the United States, she appears on state occasions amid great pomp and ceremony, but unlike the US president she is the object of widespread public affection, and studiously avoids overt involvement in the political conflicts and contests of the day. Political attacks on the queen, although not unheard of, are generally considered a breach of proper behavior. The queen has few significant governmental functions. She receives the credentials of foreign ambassadors, officially asks the leader of the majority party in Parliament to form the government, offers advice to the prime minister, which of course he is free to accept or ignore, and at the opening of Parliament gives the speech from the throne, written for her by the government and outlining the policy positions and priorities of "her majesty's" government. The head of the queen's government is the prime minister, and he and his co-partisans in the parliamentary majority make the political and policy decisions for the nation. Little in the way of ceremony characterizes his public appearances, and support for him is based entirely on political and personal considerations rather than on any sense of patriotism. Unlike for the queen, attacks and criticisms directed at the prime minister are a staple of everyday political discourse in Great Britain.

The president's role as head of state in a presidential system should not be confused with the role of presidents who are heads of state in parliamentary systems that are not constitutional monarchies. In countries such as Israel, Italy, and Germany, the head of government is the prime minister, but each of these countries has a president who serves as head of state. Typically, the president is an elder statesman or stateswoman, and is usually selected by the legislature rather than by popular election. As head of state, he receives ambassadors from foreign nations and, like the queen of England, makes appearances on state occasions, standing above the political fray as a unifying and nonpartisan figure. Constitutionally, the president may be named as head of the armed forces, but the decisions about the governance and disposition of those forces are not made by the president. Just as British military decisions are made by "her majesty's" government and not by the queen herself, so too are Italian military decisions made by the Italian cabinet rather than the president. Presidents in these contexts may have the same formal responsibility as does the queen, of asking the majority-party leader to form a government, and these presidents may be able to exercise some informal influence on that process and on the resulting government itself, but no one would think of these presidents as heads of government.

In semipresidential systems, the president is popularly elected, has significant powers under the Constitution, and is recognized as the head of the state. However, he shares the role of head of government with a prime minister who, like his counterparts in purely parliamentary systems, is accountable to a parliament. In France, the president is an authority figure "who is abstract, impersonal, and removed from the people, yet at the same time embodies personal charisma." Charles de Gaulle personified such a leader, "because of his towering personality, his martial figure and background, his Resistance leadership, and his image as a prophet of legitimacy" (Safran 2009:235–236). So it is the president in France, as well as in other semipresidential systems, rather than the prime minister, who is best able to deploy the symbols of the nation in the service of his political and policy agenda.

Presidential Power: A Continuum

All presidential systems are characterized by an intense popular focus on the president, who tends to portray himself as a person above partisan and legislative conflicts, as the sole and true representative of his people, and as the embodiment and custodian of the nation's history and symbols. But when it comes to actual presidential power, there is much greater variation. In theory, as well as constitutionally, presidential systems require the president to act cooperatively with other autonomous decisionmakers such as independent legislators, professional bureaucrats, and members of the judiciary, all of whom can constrain or reject his initiatives. Although most presidential systems have such independent institutions with constitutionally designated powers of their own, the power and prerogatives of these institutions tend to decline as nations move in the direction of presidentialism, and those who hold positions in these institutions tend to defer to the president. In either event, the prerogatives of the president increase to the point where the checks on presidential power may become more apparent than real.

This last point suggests that presidentialism, to the extent that it refers to presidential power as it is practiced, is not an either/or phenomenon, but rather a continuum. Political systems may be presidential in the constitutional sense, but may be characterized by varying degrees of presidentialism when it comes to the ability of the president to actually control public policy. In some countries, the degree and pace of the movement of power toward the president have been uncertain and uneven, with episodes of presidential aggrandizement followed by reassertions of power by other political institutions, especially national legislative bodies. Periods of presidential dominance may be followed by periods in which the president is unable to achieve his major objectives and finds himself to a significant degree hemmed in by other political actors. Such has been the case in the United States, where presidents often find that their agendas are frustrated by congressional opposition, where the Supreme Court has, on occasion, invalidated presidential actions, and where bureaucrats can resist presidential efforts to control their actions. In such an environment of "constrained presidentialism," highly elevated public expectations are still directed at the president, he still dominates the political consciousness of the nation, and he still claims to speak for the people as a whole; however, he finds it difficult to meet the expectations that are focused on him because of the resistance that he faces from other political institutions and actors.

Although these systems of constrained presidentialism constitute a formidable guard against the danger of executive authoritarianism, other problems can arise from a mismatch between popular expectations and the president's ability to meet those expectations. In the short term, there is likely to be a decline in political support for the incumbent president, as Obama, Morales, and Sarkozy experienced. In the long term, there may be a decline in support for a political regime when its leaders consistently fail to deliver on the promises, implicit and explicit, that they make to their citizens, or fail to deal effectively with the challenges confronting their nation. When people believe that a new president will change their world, and then discover after the president has been in office for a while that their world remains essentially unchanged or even seems to have deteriorated, popular discontent, cynicism, and perhaps political instability can result. In systems where separate institutions really do share power, many political leaders have the ability to stop government action by saying no. Although such systems will minimize the likelihood of authoritarianism, an inability to act on pressing economic or social issues can contribute to instability either because unsolved problems can deteriorate into crises, or simply because citizens come to doubt the legitimacy and efficacy of a political system that cannot respond to their concerns (see Linz 1990, 1994; Haggard, McCubbins, and Shugart 2001). Ironically, such overly constrained presidencies can create conditions that are ripe for an authoritarian leader who promises to break the deadlock and address the problems of the nation in a forceful manner.

At the opposite end of the continuum from constrained presidentialism, one finds "hyperpresidentialism"—presidential systems in which there are very limited or no constraints on the president. Hyperpresidentialism implies "the systematic concentration of political power in the hands of one individual who resists delegating all but the most trivial decision-making tasks" (Bratton and van de Walle 1997:63; see also Rose-Ackerman, Desierto, and Volosin 2011). These extreme cases of presidentialism occur when presidents completely dominate their political systems through some combination of constitutional powers, a rigid and hegemonic governing party, and the extraconstitutional intimidation of opponents. The early presidents of postcolonial African states held office under constitutions that were "personally tailored to the needs of the ruler" in order to establish an "exalted and legally unencumbered presidential office" (Jackson and Rosberg 1982:269), and several countries currently have constitutions that allow for such presidential dominance.

These political systems, as well as similar ones outside of Africa, are of a different order than those constrained presidential systems that we are accustomed to thinking of as democratic, and some might argue that they should be considered part of a discussion of authoritarianism rather than presidentialism. On the other hand, authoritarianism may well be the logical outcome of the movement in the direction of hyperpresidentialism that one sees in ostensibly democratic nations, and suggests some of the worst aspects and greatest dangers of presidentialism—that is, as democratic presidencies acquire the powers associated with presidentialism, they may begin to take on some of the characteristics of more authoritarian systems. Hugo Chávez began his tenure in Venezuela as a more constrained president, but over the years he moved in the direction of greater presidential power to the point where some observers view his regime as more authoritarian than democratic (Human Rights Watch 2008).[13] On the other hand, although there are obvious dangers at this end of the presidentialism continuum, the examples of Evo Morales in Bolivia and Lula da Silva in Brazil suggest that strong presidents may be in a better position to achieve significant societal changes than their more constrained presidential counterparts.

In sum, systemic dangers as well as benefits can be found at each end of the presidentialism continuum. In terms of the former, at the hyperpresidential end lies the danger of authoritarianism; at the constrained end is the debilitating gap between public expectations and the president's capacity to deliver on these expectations, a gap that can lead to political alienation and instability. In terms of benefits, hyperpresidentialism can provide the opportunity to break the policy deadlocks that can characterize constrained presidential systems, but these constrained presidencies also provide a greater assurance that democratic institutions and civil liberties will be preserved.[14]

Although the actual ability of a president to control public policy may vary, during the twentieth century all presidential systems have been characterized by a steady enhancement of presidential power, an exponentially greater focusing of popular expectations on presidents, and a much stronger public disposition to hold presidents primarily or even solely responsible for public policy successes and failures. There are political, cultural, and technological forces that are global in nature that are driving political systems toward this increasing degree of presidentialism. These factors, to be explored in detail in the ensuing chapters, include the expanding role of governments in the lives of their citizens, the globalized nature of an increasing number of the public policy questions that these governments face, and the increasingly intimate relationship between the presidency and the people facilitated by the electronic mass media.[15]

Plan of the Book

As we will see in Chapter 2, one of the major goals of the Enlightenment period was to identify arguments and eventually mechanisms for constraining those holding executive power, in almost all cases kings, either benevolent or malevolent. This enterprise proceeded from the realization that while an executive function was an indispensable component of every political system of the world, it was also an office that throughout history had proven to be a source of tyranny. Machiavelli's Prince epitomized the executive in its most malevolent form. Written constitutions were developed as a means to formalize restraints on the executive; as political theorist Harvey Mansfield Jr. (1993) has suggested, the task was to "tame the prince." The US Constitution, based upon the teaching of Enlightenment philosophers such as Montesquieu and Locke and drawing upon the US Founders' understanding of Greece and Rome, provided a model of how that might be accomplished in the context of republican (as opposed to monarchical) government by creating the US presidency. Other nations that developed presidential systems were guided by some of the same theories that appealed to the US Founders; in addition, a presidential model proved to be congruent with the history and culture of a number of nations in Latin America and Africa where presidential systems came to be the dominant form of government.

As will be discussed more fully in Chapter 3, the US formula was not the only way to define and confine the constitutional power of presidents. Among the more democratic presidential systems, there are systems where the president dominates because he has the solid support of a highly disciplined legislative majority along with the veto power, the ability to issue decrees, and budgetary control. In Mexico during the period when the Institutional Revolutionary Party (PRI) was the dominant party in the country, presidents controlled the policymaking process by virtue of their role as the leader of the party (see Saiegh 2010:59). In other Latin American countries where presidents have not been able to count on support from the legislature or where presidents have confronted a highly fractionalized party system, they have relied on a range of formal and informal powers that have either allowed them to act unilaterally, or have been sufficient to allow them to cobble together temporary legislative majorities. This was the situation in both Chile and Brazil beginning in the last decade of the twentieth century and continuing into the first decade of the twenty-first after military governments ceded power to civilians. Earlier in the twentieth century, formal presidential powers as they were written down in constitutions often were supplemented by implicit support from the military establishment that enabled presidents to maintain and extend their power. Such systems were examples of hyperpresidentialism.

In the United States, even when the president's party has held majorities in both chambers of Congress, he has not always been able to count on the support of his co-partisans for his policy initiatives; but unlike some of his counterparts in the Southern Hemisphere, he has not relied upon the military to force his will upon the nation. US presidents also have a limited though significant arsenal of unilateral powers, and so their success has depended heavily on their ability to persuade others to support their policy initiatives. The US system as well as the hybrid semipresidential system that exists in France are characterized by a more balanced arrangement between the president and other political institutions, exemplifying the notion of constrained presidentialism. Despite these distinctions, all of these systems exhibit the constitutional, political, and psychological characteristics of presidentialism, although to a greater degree in some nations than in others.

One of the forces driving presidentialism is the increasing role that national governments have come to play in the lives of their citizens. As the permissible and expected scope of government actions has expanded, the expectations that citizens have for what the government—and therefore the president—could and should do for them have also expanded. And as government has done more, the result has been that the size of government, calculated in terms of the number of people in its civilian and military bureaucracy, the number of agencies that these people staff, and the cost of all the work that government does, has grown exponentially. More important than the growth of the bureaucracy in terms of size and cost, the jurisdiction and the discretionary power of these bureaucracies have also increased. Because national bureaucracies are part of the executive branch and because every president has the title of chief executive, an expanded bureaucracy has meant expanded presidential power. The role of the growth of government in the movement toward presidentialism will be explored in Chapter 4.

A second factor driving presidentialism is the inexorable movement toward the globalization of every nation's politics, whether one is talking about considerations of war and peace, or the interconnected financial and trade regimes that have such a huge effect on the economies of every nation in the world. Standing and often expansive military establishments exist in virtually every country, and expenditures on military equipment and personnel have become a major part, and in some countries even the largest single part, of the government's budget. Because the president is typically commander in chief of the nation's armed forces, and because the arguments for executive domination of policymaking have always been most persuasive in regard to military and diplomatic issues, large military establishments add significantly to the power of the president. But beyond questions of war, there is an international dimension to an increasing range of public policy issues. Trade, monetary policy, access to scarce natural resources, environmental questions, and agriculture policy are just a sampling of the issues that have both domestic and international dimensions. Because most political systems, either implicitly or explicitly, concede to their presidents broader prerogatives in regard to the nation's intercourse with foreign governments and institutions, the globalization of public policy issues has further enhanced the role of presidents. This will be the subject of Chapter 5.

Finally, and perhaps most important, democratization, with its imperative that political leaders must cultivate and depend upon popular support if they are to wield legitimate power, has driven political systems in the direction of presidentialism. The idea of popular support has developed a wider meaning in the modern age than it had when presidential systems were originally created. During the twentieth century, restrictions on the franchise that were in place during the nineteenth century and earlier began to wither away to the point that today, in almost every nation in the world where elections take place, all adults, with only a very few restrictions, are eligible to participate. This has encouraged and in some ways required presidents and presidential candidates to appeal to a broad and extensive mass public with variable interest in and information about politics and public policy. In addition, the transformative role of the electronic media has provided sitting and aspiring presidents with direct and continuous access to that public. This has had a significant impact not only on the way in which presidents are selected but also on the way in which they seek support for their policies and on the manner in which they choose to govern. A combination of democratization, the electronic mass media, the psychological need of voters to commit themselves to a singular leader, and the weakening of both party structures and overarching ideological commitments has moved politics in the direction of personalism, with its emphasis on the individual leader, and away from political institutions, with its emphasis on collective decisionmaking processes involving multiple political actors. This will be the subject of Chapter 6.

The argument of this book is that the movement toward presidentialism, driven by these three forces—the expanding role of the state, the globalization of multiple policy areas, and what some might call hyperdemocracy—is to a great extent inexorable. In fact, some of the same forces driving countries with presidential offices in the direction of presidentialism have been seen by some as contributing to the "presidentialization" of political systems with parliamentary structures. Thomas Poguntke and Paul Webb (2005:13–17), for example, cite the internationalization of politics, the growing role of the state, the changing structure of mass communication, particularly in regard to the role of television, and the weakening of political parties due to the erosion of a politics based on traditional social cleavages as forces leading to the increased personalization of parliamentary systems. Although still committed to collective decisionmaking, many of these systems are experiencing an increased focus on the singular head of government. We will not be concerned with this evolution of parliamentary systems in this book, but the appearance of aspects of this phenomenon in nonpresidential systems strengthens our confidence that we have correctly identified the universal driving forces of presidentialism.

The seeming inevitability of presidentialism carries both risks and rewards for political systems. Although it is clear that dominant presidents can and often have done good and even essential things for their countries—things that collective institutions such as legislatures have not been able to achieve—there are several critiques of presidentialism: the danger that hyperpresidentialism will lead to authoritarianism; in situations of constrained presidentialism, the perils of a widening gap between what is expected of presidents and what they can deliver; the implications of presidentialism for democracy and political stability; the effect of presidentialism on the quality of governance as well as the quality of presidents; and the specific implications of presidentialism for issues of war and peace. These critiques will be assessed in Chapter 7.

Some of these critiques will bring us back nearly full circle to the issues discussed in Chapter 2, which identifies the restriction of executive power as one of the primary goals of constitutionalism. The strength of the forces driving presidentialism is such that they raise serious questions about the extent to which political systems can succeed in constraining the power of the president. It may be that Machiavelli's Prince cannot be tamed, or at least that the realities of the modern nation-state mean that the older mechanisms for constraining executives are no longer up to the task. Alternatively, if the powers of the president can be constrained, but the expectations of the mass public continue to focus disproportionately on the president, a president's inability to meet popular expectations can jeopardize popular support for the regime and perhaps invite instability. In other words, an overriding commitment to guard against the danger of authoritarianism may come at the expense of effective government that meets the needs and expectations of its citizens.

Notes

1. Gallup Poll, January 16, 2009, www.gallup.com/poll/113824/Obama-Wins-83-Approval-Rating-Transition.aspx; Nagourney and Connelly 2009.

2. "Le roi s'amuse," *The Economist,* January 28, 2010.

3. "François Hollande, Challenging Sarkozy, Calls for Change," *New York Times,* January 22, 2012.

4. "Bolivian Survey Shows Morales with 65 Percent Approval Rating," *La Razon, La Paz* (in Spanish), January 16, 2006, BBC Worldwide Monitor.

5. "Evo's Big Win," *The Economist,* August 16, 2008.

6. "Profile: Bolivia's President Evo Morales," January 12, 2011, www.bbc.co.uk/news/world-latin-america-12166905.

7. IPSOS/Apoyo polls reported at http://incakolanews.blogspot.com/2011/12/bolivia-evo-morales-ends-year-with-35.html.

8. In some systems, the legislature becomes involved in presidential selection in extraordinary circumstances. In the United States, the House of Representatives selects the president if no candidate receives a majority of the electoral votes, and in Bolivia, Congress selects the president if no candidate receives a majority of the popular vote.

9. In practice, these distinctions among parliamentary, presidential, and semipresidential systems are not always easy to make. For example, in Botswana the president is selected by the legislature and is accountable to that body as well, so the system operates in a parliamentary manner. In contrast, in South Africa the president is selected by the legislature, but once he is designated, he is not accountable to that body, and so, despite the manner in which the executive is selected, the country operates presidentially. In terms of semipresidential systems, there are instances where a popularly elected president serves with a prime minister, but the prime minister is not accountable to the legislature (Guyana, South Korea, Sri Lanka), as well as the more common arrangement of a popularly elected president and a prime minister who is accountable to the legislature (see Siaroff 2003).

10. Alan Siaroff (2003) rejects the semipresidential classification is favor of what he believes to be the more precise "parliamentary systems with a presidential dominance" and "parliamentary systems with a presidential corrective." Matthew Shugart and John Carey (1992) divide semipresidential systems into "premier presidential" and "president-parliamentary," with the latter implying greater presidential power than the former.

11. In parliamentary systems, the prime minister also may be the most visible political actor in the nation, and British prime ministers such as Margaret Thatcher and German chancellors such as Angela Merkel have dominated the political systems and political cultures of their nations in a manner not dissimilar to that of presidents. Nonetheless, these leaders remain part of a collective government, accountable to their co-partisans, and it is therefore less likely that citizens of these countries will view such leaders as indistinguishable from the state.

12. *Correio Braziliense* (in Portuguese), August 1, 2005, BBC Monitoring Latin America–Political.

13. Freedom House classified Venezuela as only "partly free" in its 2010 report; www.freedomhouse.org/template.cfm?page=505.

14. On the other hand, Sebastian Saiegh (2011:89) finds that presidents whose parties do not have majority support in the legislature—the equivalent of constrained presidencies—have only slightly lower success rates for their legislative initiatives than those presidents whose parties command a legislative majority.

15. The first two factors—the expanded role of government and the increasing prominence of international issues—no doubt have contributed to an enhanced focus on executives in all political systems, both presidential and parliamentary. But our concern here is only with their impact on presidential and semipresidential systems.

2
An Intellectual History of Executive Power

The term "president" did not enter the vocabulary of government and politics until 1787, when the authors of the US Constitution created the US presidency. However, many of the essential functions and responsibilities of that office appeared in various forms and under various titles even in the most ancient political systems. Whether using the title of king, emperor, consul, or caesar, governments throughout history have had an executive office with the power to perform specific administrative tasks and endowed as well with the more ambiguous responsibilities associated with the concept of national leadership.

What Is Executive Power?

The fundamental meaning of the term "executive power" can be derived from the verb "to execute," or the power to carry out. Every state requires a person or a group of people responsible for implementing and enforcing its laws. The need for an executive in this sense is universal, no matter if the laws are developed through a broadly democratic process or are the result of a decree by an absolute ruler. A decision to build roads can be taken by a representative assembly or by a benevolent despot, but the tasks associated with the actual building of the roads—the hiring of the workers, ensuring their safety, the purchase of the supplies, and the assurance of quality control—devolve upon a smaller group of people generally classified as administrators.

In a more general sense, most laws regulate or restrict the freedom of individual citizens. As John Locke instructed, individuals, as members of civil society, cede a portion of their freedom to the government in return for the security and stability that the government can provide. But not everyone is going to be willing to comply with the restrictions that governments place on their freedom. No matter how a state decides to set its tax rates, taxes need to be collected, and to do that, machinery in the form of tax collectors and record keepers needs to be established. And, because resistance to taxation is as old as civil society, those who resist paying taxes may need to be coerced into doing so, and those who refuse need to be sanctioned. In sum, all states need an executive capacity that is able to implement its policy decisions, ensure compliance with the law, and impose sanctions on those who choose to break the law.

But executive power refers not just to the ministerial work of implementing and enforcing laws. Executive power is also associated with the concept of leadership—the capacity to provide direction for a nation and its citizens, to motivate and guide other policymakers or the public at large, to move the polity toward agreement on important decisions. At their best, leaders unify a diverse people behind a common cause, or a shared set of symbols that embody the nation and its collective interests. One scholar of the US presidency refers to presidential leadership as the ability to "understand, cope with, and ultimately master the changing political environment, and to reshape it more closely toward desired ends" (Burns 1973:195). The tools of leadership can include rhetoric and persuasion as well as command and coercion. Sometimes the work of leadership is to organize majorities, and sometimes it involves decisive, unilateral action. Great leaders are able to steer their countries safely through crises and in more normal times move them in directions that promote the general welfare of their citizens or aggrandize the power of the nation in the international arena.

The concept of leadership is central to the way in which we think about politics and the way in which we recount national histories. Bad times for a people or a country are often attributed to poor leadership, and national success and prosperity, particularly in the face of great challenges, are often attributed to good and sometimes great leadership. From Caesar Augustus to Joseph Stalin, from Simón Bolivar to Nelson Mandela, from Abraham Lincoln to Franklin Roosevelt, from Charles de Gaulle to Mao Tse-tung, the fate of nations and sometimes the world, for good or ill, is traced, almost reflexively, and of course simplistically, to the skills and failings of individual leaders. And it may not be simply a matter of perception and reflex. Although we cannot know what course Latin American history would have taken without Bolivar, or what would have happened in the United States if someone other than Lincoln had been president during the Civil War, we can, with confidence, say that things would have been different absent such unique and gifted leaders.

In terms of governmental structures, the focal point for such leadership is the executive. Leadership after all is a singular quality; it is much less likely that a collective body such as a legislature, a central party committee, or a military junta will provide leadership. Certainly, all of these bodies are capable of acting, but it isn't clear that any are capable of persuading. While executive leadership is ubiquitous, how leaders are selected and the form that leadership takes depend upon cultural and political factors. In traditional societies, individuals, and sometimes councils, typically selected on the basis of ascriptive characteristics such as age or heredity, led with greater or lesser levels of consultation, and ordinary subjects complied, sometimes because they were coerced, and more often because obedience was a cultural imperative and resistance was likely to be futile. In modern nations that have no commitment to democratic processes, tyrants, or absolute rulers, lead by edict, rarely consult, and rely heavily on violence and coercion to deal with those who might resist or dissent from their decisions. Executive leaders who operate in a more democratic context, while occasionally utilizing unilateral powers delegated to them by constitutional or statutory instruments and employing coercion as necessary, for the most part draw upon their legitimacy as elected leaders to evoke compliance. To accomplish specific goals, they rely primarily upon their political and rhetorical skills and their powers of persuasion to move a people and its elites in the direction that they prefer.

This link between executive leaders and their people points to a personal dimension of leadership that exists in more authoritarian as well as more democratic systems. Simply put, leadership implies the existence of followers who support the decisions, or follow the directions, of the leader, and therefore effective leaders, especially those whose ability to command is limited, must possess a set of characteristics that encourage others to follow them. These characteristics may include a history of heroic accomplishments on behalf of the state, superior oratorical skills, a charismatic ability to connect with deeply and widely felt emotions, or religious, ethnic, or familial connections with past leaders. Whatever the particular combination of characteristics, they all emphasize a popular commitment to the personal leadership of a specific individual. In other words, the commitment is in the first instance to an individual rather than to a collective body such as a political party or legislature, or to something more abstract such as a political ideology. Leaders, in turn, can exploit that commitment by translating it into support for their policy proposals, for the expansion of their own authority, and in some instances as justification for the assumption and exercise of arbitrary power.

Restricting the ability of executive leaders to use arbitrary power to compel others to acquiesce in decisions that they take largely on their own is the great and continuing challenge that confronts all political systems that wish to avoid authoritarianism. Doing so depends in part on constitutional provisions but also on the times and issues that a nation confronts. The case for relatively unconstrained executive leadership has always been strongest at times of crisis, particularly during war or domestic unrest, and it is at such times that attempts to rein in executive power are unlikely to be made and, if they are, seldom succeed, often notwithstanding constitutional provisions. Joseph Nye Jr. (2008:10) notes that for the Greeks, the verb "to lead" was originally a military term meaning "to be general of soldiers." When a nation's military forces are in the field, whether fighting in defense of the nation or in service to an aggressive imperial agenda, executive power, often in its most extreme form, typically receives its highest level of public support. Times of crisis, emergency, or war afford executives the opportunity to tie their exercise of extraordinary powers to the broadly felt desire for national survival as well as to the nationalistic and patriotic sentiments that usually come to the fore at such moments. At times like these, the people call for heroes, and presidents are the ones from whom heroic leadership is expected. And more practically, dealing with an emergency or with a dangerous situation assumes the need for a system of centralized command and control, and implies a hierarchical structure with a single person ultimately in charge.

On the other hand, in the case of domestic policy issues, especially relatively minor ones, executive power is more easily constrained, either because executives do not care to spend their time on such issues, or because the number of issues is so large that decisionmaking power needs to be delegated to others, or because there is less popular support for arbitrary executive power on such matters. But, of course, there are also times of domestic crisis—economic collapse, insurrections—that raise the same sorts of fears that arise during international crises, and will cause a people to support extensive powers for the singular leader who, they expect, can lead them safely through troubled times. At times of domestic instability, those in executive positions are expected to take the necessary steps to restore law and order, steps that may well transcend the normal bounds of constitutional behavior.

In sum, there are three components to executive power that both justify its existence and explain the extent to which it can dominate a political system. The first is the need for administration. As the functions of the state increase, the job of administering its affairs expands, and such an administrative role is at the heart of executive power. The second is the need for leadership. In any sort of collective arrangement, whether a garden club or a nation-state, there must be some person who can articulate a vision and direction for the group, who can set the agenda, bring important issues to the fore for collective deliberation, motivate participants to choose wise collective action, and speak authoritatively to others on behalf of the group. People need and expect such leadership, especially in challenging times, and this is a function that falls to those who hold executive positions. The third is the capacity to act unilaterally, particularly in regard to international issues or in response to other emergencies. On international issues, the nation is expected to speak and act as one, and it is the executive who is capable of meeting that expectation. This is particularly the case when these issues involve the use of military force, but it is also the case when domestic problems rise to an emergency level.

The Greeks and Romans

These three strands of executive power—the bureaucratic responsibility for executing laws, the responsibilities associated with national leadership in normal times, and the extraordinary responsibilities of leadership that characterize times of crisis—were already apparent in both ancient Greece and ancient Rome. The Greeks were concerned with the means of achieving popular government, and the short story of Athens is one of oscillation between larger and smaller decisionmaking bodies. These were the two poles that Aristotle identified as democracy and oligarchy, and ultimately he endorsed a mixture of the two as the best structure for government. Aristotle also identified three elements in every constitutional arrangement: the deliberative, the magistracies (the executive), and the judicial. But this classification of functions should not be taken as equivalent to our current understanding of legislative, executive, and judicial powers and especially not as an equivalent of the three distinct branches of government that characterize most modern nation-states. A better interpretation is that Aristotle saw these as essential functions in all regimes, functions that could be discharged by one person in a monarchical situation or by different people in different offices in democratic or oligarchic regimes (see Mansfield 1993:51ff.).

In terms of executive power or responsibilities, what Aristotle actually sketches out in Book VI of *The Politics* is the equivalent of the modern bureaucracy.[1] He begins with a list of six "indispensable" offices that sound a great deal like the administrative structure of a modern city. These offices are charged with such functions as overseeing the marketplace by supervising contracts and ensuring good order; the superintending of public and private property in the city, including the maintenance and repair of buildings and roads; a similar position for the agricultural areas of the state; an office assigned to receiving, holding, and paying out the public revenues; an office responsible for the registration of contracts, court decisions, and indictments; and an office that deals with the execution of sentences on offenders, the custody of prisoners, and the recovery of debts due the state.

Aristotle moves next to four offices that might be equivalent today to positions of national leadership and that require for those who hold them "a large experience and a high degree of fidelity." These include an office charged with the defense of the city and usually held by people "called generals and commandants"; an office of finance that "receives and audits the accounts of other offices"; and an office that introduces public policies and presides over the popular assembly, if there is one. Finally, there is an office "which is concerned with the cult of the civic deities" that is filled by priests and custodians of temples. Aristotle also suggests that different states might create other, additional offices—for example, one charged with the supervision of children, or the supervision of athletic or dramatic contests (Barker 1962:273–277).

In Athens, standing astride these offices was a body called a "Council," which functioned as a sort of executive committee to check the power of the citizens, who were represented in an "Assembly." The size of the Council varied, but for most of the period of Athenian democracy it was composed of 500 members, with 50 a month acting as councilors. Nothing was to be brought before the Assembly without an initial resolution by the Council. The Council also had some judicial functions, summarized by Aristotle as the authority to "safeguard the laws" and to conduct state prosecutions and public audits. There is also evidence that the Council was involved in what we could call today the conduct of foreign policy, justified in part by its smaller size, when compared with the Assembly, and its superior ability to keep secrets by conferring in private. And, as suggested earlier, in times of international crisis, the number of decisionmakers became even smaller, with power apparently devolved upon a small group of "elders" or "preliminary councilors" who took over many of the responsibilities formally belonging to the Council, including funding the navy, enforcing order, and appointing ambassadors. The gradual replacement of the Council, whose members were selected by lot, by these preliminary councilors presaged, in the view of both Aristotle and Thucydides, the end of Athenian democracy.[2]

In the case of Rome, the original city-state was ruled by a succession of kings who, combining both civil and religious leadership responsibilities, acted as absolute rulers. When the monarchy was deposed and replaced by the Republic, the Senate, a body of 300 members, dominated for the most part by the aristocracy (or patricians), ruled. The Senate was the place where the great public issues of the day were debated and decided. What we would think of today as the executive power in the Republic was divided among a number of different "magistrates." The most important of these were the Consuls, usually two in number, who were selected by the Senate and served for one-year terms. The Consuls controlled the military, and had authority over wars, the state's finances, and the administration of justice. Although the Consuls had enormous power, they also were constrained by the brevity of their terms and the fact that there were always two of them, neither of whom could act without the approval of the other.

As the Consuls came to occupy themselves primarily with foreign and military matters, some of their "domestic" responsibilities were delegated to other executive officers. The Praetors, for example, had the function of administering justice, and as the size of the Republic expanded, both geographically and in terms of population, the number of Praetors, along with their responsibilities, increased; eventually, they came to perform a role akin to that of regional or local governors. The Censors, another group of executive officers, had three primary duties: to perform a census of the people, to oversee their conduct, and to commission public works such as roads and aqueducts. The census involved taking an exact tally of each citizen's possessions and estates for taxation purposes as well as for determining their military rank. The Censors also had the power to judge the morality of individual citizens and to mete out punishment for misbehavior, often to the extent of depriving a person of the right to vote. The Aediles were the minor functionaries in charge of such things as weights and measures and the maintenance of public buildings, including temples, theaters, and baths. The Aediles also acted as judges in cases involving the sale and exchange of estates and had the added responsibility of providing entertainment (circuses) for the population. Ultimately, as the Republic expanded and yielded to the Empire, the power of the Senate ebbed, and the dispersed executive authority that had characterized the Republic came to be concentrated in the hands of emperors ranging from the wise and consultative (Augustus) to the mad and tyrannical (Nero).[3]

In terms of executive power, then, the Greek and Roman experiences tell us of the need, felt even then, for what we would call today a bureaucracy charged with the various administrative chores of the state. Some of these are quite familiar to us, such as the census, supervision of weights and measures, and in the case of Aristotle, the maintenance and repair of public buildings and roads, the supervision of public funds, and the administration of prisons. Others are less familiar, such as judging the morality of individual behavior and providing entertainment for the masses. Other functions suggested a combination of what we would call today executive and judicial functions, such as the administration of justice.

Beyond administration, however, Greek and Roman practices only hinted at a need for broader political leadership. It seems clear that when Athenians and Romans, at least under the Republic, thought of a single individual in charge, they thought of absolute rule by a king, or an emperor, an arrangement that in general they wished to avoid. Although they recognized the occasional need for such rulers in times of crisis, particularly international crises, they were suspicious of placing too much power in too few hands; their preference seemed to be for collective executive leadership—from the 500-member Council of Athens, to the Senate and the dual Consuls of Rome along with the lesser administrative officers with whom they shared executive power. As Harvey Mansfield Jr. (1993) observed, Aristotle always referred to the executive in the plural, even though he was well aware of the singular executive in the person of the king, which is the subject of an extended discussion in Book III of *The Politics*. The suspicion of absolute power was so great in Rome that the two Consuls served only a brief term in office, and although they recognized the need for a singular leader to exercise more centralized power in times of national emergency, such episodes were limited to a six-month period. In more normal times, it was the expectation that the power of these executives would be checked to a greater or lesser degree by other larger and more popular institutions.

But these practices designed to restrict executive power were consistently challenged and often nullified by advocates of despotism and the absolute governance of caesars and kings. Particularly when military concerns came to the fore—either in defense of the state against foreign attack or in support of military adventures against foreign powers—Rome turned to singular leadership. Such adventures were the primary occupation of the Roman Empire. The task of subduing a far-flung set of people and nations through the might of the Roman legions and governing these provinces once subdued meant that the Empire would be associated with strong, nearly absolute leaders. And when the Empire fell, government by absolute leaders remained, usually in the person of emperors or kings, some of whom, with the emergence of the Church of Rome, claimed that they ruled by divine right.

Machiavelli

Absolute rule by kings and emperors was the norm during the first millennium of the modern age, and the nature of executive power was not much commented upon or examined. During the Middle Ages, commentaries on government by various writers tended to focus on what we would think of today as administrative powers, with judicial powers and the notion of lawmaking itself not well developed. Laws were thought of as relatively fixed, either a matter of custom or divinely inspired, and given this, no lawmaking function seemed really necessary. In any case, the monarch would determine the content of the law. Only in judging whether the law had been violated was the monarch expected to abide by the law. The executive power, in the view of one scholar, meant "either the function of administering justice under the law, or the machinery by which the law was put into effect" (Vile 1998:32). In either form, however, this was to be the job of the king. It was not until the Enlightenment period that the idea emerged of an institutional locus for the making of laws that did not emanate from the king, but that the king was still required to implement or enforce.

But before that was to occur, the prevailing view of the executive was articulated by Nicolo Machiavelli early in the sixteenth century. In *The Prince,* Machiavelli develops a model of a strong, sometimes brutal, often amoral executive whose mandate to rule is not based on a theory of divine right but rather on the force, or sheer power, at his disposal.[4] He rules, in brief, because he has superior power, and that power is to be used to successfully fight wars and to maintain domestic order. Machiavelli instructs his Prince that he "ought to have no other aim or thought, nor select anything else for his study, than of war and its rules and discipline; for this is the sole art that belongs to him who rules" (111). The Prince's second obligation is the maintenance of the state. In dealing with the possibility of domestic unrest or resistance to his rule, Machiavelli advises the Prince to use fear in order to gain compliance. While it might be nice to be loved as well as feared, Machiavelli's view was that this was unlikely to happen. So given the choice between the two, there is "greater security in being feared than in being loved," because "fear is supported by the dread of pain, which is ever present" (130–131). Fear, in other words, produces obedience, and fear in turn is produced by the overwhelming and superior power in the hands of the Prince. Machiavelli's leadership lesson to the Prince is to be flexible in his approach so that he can do whatever is necessary to achieve the goals of the state. He should do good if he can, but he must prepare himself to commit evil as well, because inevitably he will need to do just that.

Although Machiavelli's discussion of the Prince is congruent with the state of executive power at the time that he wrote, there also are elements in Machiavelli that are as relevant today as they were 500 years ago. The two tasks of prosecuting wars and keeping the peace domestically would be prominent items on the job description of any modern executive. And certainly, the fear of the power of the state to punish is one of the reasons why citizens obey the law and in some states it is the only reason for compliance. But as we now know, citizens obey the law for other reasons besides the fear of state sanctions. And most executive leaders feel compelled to offer a normative justification for their actions using some formulation of the public good. But the most important difference between Machiavelli's Prince and the modern executive is that the former is unconstrained, not just in international matters of war and peace, but on all matters. He can do whatever his power allows him to do, and he can employ whatever techniques he chooses in order to accomplish his ends. The goal of modern political philosophy as it speaks to the structure of government is to retain the essential functions of the executive while restraining the unilateral powers of such leaders—in other words, to develop a theory of government that would "tame the prince." It is to two of those theorists, Locke and Montesquieu, that we now turn.

Taming the Prince: Locke

John Locke is probably the most influential of the Enlightenment thinkers for those who study the structure of government, and his *Of Civil Government* represents a sustained attempt to reconcile the need for executive power with the need to protect the polity against the arbitrary actions and potential evils of Machiavelli's Prince.[5] Writing in the mid–seventeenth century, he begins with a discussion of the state of nature, where men enjoyed complete but ephemeral freedom. In the state of nature, each person was the judge of what was right or wrong, and each person was free to execute his own vision of himself. However, this freedom could not be enjoyed because one's life and property would be endangered by those who were strongest. In order to avoid the perils and uncertainties of the state of nature, men formed civil society and in the process gave up some of their freedom. In doing so, they surrendered the right to do whatever they saw fit in return for regulation by the law, and they gave up their individual power to punish others by creating a power to enforce that law. In sum, they defined and created both a power to make law and a process for executing law.

It followed from this, argued Locke, that those who govern derive their right to do so from the consent of the governed—the ones who created civil society—rather than from divine right or from the force of their arms. Civil society for Locke depends upon the notion that man is "by nature all free, equal, and independent," and therefore cannot be "subjected to the political power of another without his own consent, which is done by agreeing with other men to join and unite into a community" (78). This leads him to the assertion that in what he calls a "well ordered commonwealth" the legislative power must be dominant; legislatures, composed of "diverse persons," have the "power to make laws for all parts and for every member of the society, prescribing rules to their actions" (120, 125). Laws, in other words, would be made by the representatives of those who were asked to abide by those laws.

Locke's next point is that because the laws that are made "have a constant and lasting force and need a perpetual execution . . . it is necessary that there be a power always in being, which should see to the execution of the laws that are made and remain in force" (121). Having defined the role of the executive ("a power always in being"), Locke then makes the distinction between what we would call today domestic affairs and foreign relations. He suggests that there exists a "federative power" encompassing "the power of war and peace, leagues and alliances, and all the transactions with all persons and communities without the commonwealth." The federative power cannot be assigned to the legislature because dealing with other nations is not a matter of making laws that govern the actions of citizens. Rather, such actions must be taken in reference to the "actions and variation of design and interest of foreigners" (122). Although Locke indicates that the executive power and the federative power are analytically separate, he argues that in fact both powers need to be in the hands of the same person, because both powers require "the force of the society for their exercise" and placing them in different hands "would be apt some time or other to cause disorder and ruin" (122–123). In Locke's world, the hands into which both these powers would be placed belonged to the monarch.

Locke struggles with the relationship between legislative and executive power, suggesting on the one hand that the legislature can at any time it wishes assemble and change the laws, thereby demonstrating its supremacy. On the other hand, Locke indicates that for the good of society, "several things should be left to the discretion of him that has the executive power" (135). He calls this the prerogative power, which he defines as the "power to act according to discretion for the public good, without the prescription of the law, and sometimes even against it" (136). Such discretionary power is necessary because the legislature is not always in session, because the law cannot anticipate "all accidents and necessities that may concern the public," and because executing the law with "inflexible rigor" may do harm (136). Locke takes pains here to challenge Machiavelli, because he is aware that the notion of prerogative might well be taken as endorsement of the absolute power of the Prince. His challenge turns upon the stipulation that the prerogative be used for the good of the people. Absolute monarchs as well as Machiavellian princes had exercised the prerogative to pursue their own interests or to promote "an interest distinct from that of the public" (139). Locke guards against this interpretation of the prerogative power, arguing instead that the people, through their legislature, can restrict the prerogatives of the executive if they determine that the executive is not acting in the public interest. If the executive resists such attempts to place limits on his prerogatives, and if he acts in a despotic manner, he stands in violation of the laws of nature and the people in turn have the natural right to resist the actions of the executive. Ultimately, the prerogative, in Locke's view, is only "the power of doing public good without a rule" (141).

Taming the Prince: Montesquieu

While Locke placed his faith in the natural right of the people to resist executive tyranny, the French thinker Montesquieu, writing about a century later, argued that other, stronger precautions against executive tyranny were necessary. In *The Spirit of the Laws,* Montesquieu identified three forms of government: republican, monarchic, and despotic.[6] Republican governments were controlled by larger or smaller numbers of people depending upon the strength of their commitment to aristocratic rule. Monarchies, in contrast, were characterized by the rule of one person. Monarchies were different from despotic states because the actions of the monarch, as Locke suggested, were constrained at least in part by laws as well as by parliaments, whereas there were no restraints on despots. But Montesquieu worried that when power was concentrated as it was in a monarchy, there was a tendency to move toward despotism.

This was especially so when monarchs indulged their taste for war. In Montesquieu's view, monarchs were obsessed by their need for the glory that was achieved on the field of battle, and such adventures usually ended badly for the nation, and inevitably threatened liberty. In a larger sense, Montesquieu was suspicious of the great leaders extolled by Machiavelli "who in pursuing their own glory transform the world around them" (Shklar 1987:51). Rather, says Montesquieu, the Prince "cannot impart a greatness which he has not himself; with him there is no such thing as glory." The Prince has "so many imperfections that they are afraid to expose his natural stupidity to public view" (Montesquieu 1949:58–59).

For Montesquieu, the most important value was individual liberty. He distinguished "liberty" from what he called "independence"; the latter meant doing as one pleased, while the former referred to the condition that causes people to feel that their person and property are secure. Liberty is threatened by the abuse of power, and government needs to be constituted so that "no man shall be compelled to do things to which the law does not oblige him, nor forced to abstain from things which the law permits" (150). Liberty is preserved in a political system characterized by "moderation" in its leaders, and moderation can be achieved only through limitations and constraints placed on the executive power (see Mansfield 1993:229). Such a political system requires the rule of law and a limited government whose various components would have an egalitarian rather than a hierarchical relationship with each other. The best system for this purpose is one of interlocking and mutually checking interests and powers (Shklar 1987:85–86).

On this reasoning, Montesquieu disaggregates the various functions that Locke had bestowed on the executive, especially the responsibility for judging violations of the law and the responsibility for decisions about going to war. He posits three governmental powers: "the legislative; the executive in respect to things dependent on the law of nations; and the judicial in regard to matters that depend on civil law" (151). When these powers are united in the same person or people, there can be no liberty, because people will fear the enactment and execution of tyrannical laws. Liberty is also imperiled if the judicial power is joined with the legislative and executive powers; in that case, the citizen would be exposed to arbitrary control because "the judge would be then the legislator. Were it joined to the executive power, the judge might behave with violence and oppression" (152). To avoid these failures, he advocated a separate and independent judicial power "exercised by persons taken from the body of the people at certain times of the year . . . in order to erect a tribunal that should last only so long as necessity requires" (153). As for military power, the legislature was to assemble the army and was to have the right to disband it when it pleased. However, "once an army is established, it ought not to depend immediately upon the legislative, but on the executive power" (161). There were two reasons for this. First, the function of the army consisted "more in action than in deliberation," and action is associated with the executive. Second, the army will not respect members of the legislature who are likely to place a premium upon prudence rather than action and on deliberation rather than strength; inevitably, they will view legislators as "cowards, and therefore unworthy to command them." Should legislators try to command the military, the military will prevail, and a "military government" would ensue (161).

In regard to lawmaking, the only role that the executive should have was the power to reject proposed legislation, especially in defense of its own prerogatives; otherwise, if the executive was "to have a part in the legislature by the power of resolving, liberty would be lost" (159). The executive was not even to play a role in suggesting legislation or advocating for particular funding priorities. "Were the executive power to determine the raising of public money, otherwise than by giving its consent, liberty would be at an end," because the executive would in essence become the legislature (160). Finally, although the legislature could not veto the actions of the executive, it could check the executive by examining "in what manner the laws it has made have been executed" (158).

Montesquieu was not blind to the virtues of executive power. He thought that there were situations in which it would be advantageous for the affairs of the state to be "conducted by a single person" whereby "the executive power is thereby enabled to act with greater expedition" (54). He did not wish for his executive to be dependent on or distracted by the legislature and advised therefore that the legislature not be in constant session, which would oblige the executive "to think only of defending its own prerogatives and the right it has to execute" (157). The executive also would have the power of calling the legislature into session, and of regulating "the time of meetings, as well as the duration of those assemblies" (157). The legislature would be barred from threatening or deposing the executive: "his person should be sacred, because as it is necessary for the good of the state to prevent the legislative body from rendering themselves arbitrary, the moment he is accused or tried there is an end of liberty" (158). In sum, despotism, in Montesquieu's view, could arise from too much power in the hands of either the legislature or the executive.

Inventing the Presidency: The United States

Those who designed the US Constitution derived from Locke their commitment to liberty and to the principle that the primary purpose of government was to create an environment in which the liberty as well as the property of its citizens would be protected. This is reflected in the famous opening sentences of the Declaration of Independence as well as in the various justifications that would be offered a decade later for the new Constitution. As James Madison noted in the 37th Federalist Paper, "among the chief blessings of civil society" was the "repose and confidence" that it established in the minds of its citizens (37:226).[7]

Also from Locke, the US Founders derived their commitment to republican government, a government in which the legislative power must dominate. In fact, under the Articles of Confederation, the first governing document for the newly liberated colonies, all there was at the national level was a Congress, composed of representatives from each of the states with each state delegation having one collective vote. There was no executive, save for the person who presided at meetings of Congress; although the term "president" probably originated from this position as "presiding" officer, the responsibilities of the position, which rotated among the representatives of the various states, consisted almost entirely of keeping order at the meetings. In the former colonies, now independent states, where most of the governing in the new nation took place, nearly all power was in the hands of state legislatures Not wishing to re-create the abusive office of royal governor that existed prior to the Revolution, the new constitutions of these states, with the exception of New York, were characterized by governors with little in the way of power, in some cases appointed by the legislature, typically serving only a brief term in office, and in some instances required to act in concert with a council.[8]

When the Constitutional Convention met in Philadelphia, the primary goal of the Framers was to establish a national government that was stronger than the very weak one that existed under the Articles of Confederation. Under the Articles, Congress required the agreement of nine of the thirteen states in order to act, and states were able to ignore the actions of the central government. Although strengthening the national government would seem to suggest a fortified executive branch, the hostility toward executive power abroad in the land was so strong and the commitment to republican government (to which a strong executive was viewed by many as antithetical) so firm, that to establish a powerful executive might well have torpedoed the enterprise at the outset. Thus, the first branch of government listed in the new Constitution is Congress, in which "all legislative powers" are vested. Among the legislative responsibilities for the new Congress were all of the key policy areas that would require action by the new government: the power to raise revenue and decide upon what it would be spent, the power to raise and support military forces, the power to declare war, govern the size of the military, and determine the rules under which it would operate, along with a whole range of other responsibilities in regard to interstate commerce, the coinage of money, and the building of roads.

The elevation of Congress to the role of first branch of government was in part a reaction to the colonial experience and in part a matter of political calculation. The break from Great Britain was precipitated by the arbitrary acts of the king of England, whose representatives in the colonies were his appointed (and widely detested) governors. In opposing the king and his governors, the colonists found their voice in the colonial assemblies, and at the national level in the continental congresses. So as they thought about a new Constitution, the Founders had both a strong bias against executive power, and no handy models for an executive power that would be stronger than what had existed under the Articles, but that would not be so strong that it would threaten to replicate their experiences under the Crown. And politically, there was the need to get the new Constitution ratified in the face of antimonarchical sentiments that were even stronger among the population than they were among the Constitution's authors.

Nonetheless, an executive power was necessary both to carry out the laws passed by Congress and also to check the legislative branch, which in the view of many of the Founders, its republican virtues notwithstanding, had come to abuse its powers at the state level. Here, Montesquieu's idea that liberty was threatened when any single institution had too much power was taken to heart. Madison critiqued the state legislatures for "extending the sphere of its activity and drawing all powers into its impetuous vortex" (48:309) and castigated its disposition to "sacrifice the aggregate interest to the local views of their constituents" (10:77). Elbridge Gerry of Massachusetts said that "the worst men get into the legislature—men of indigence, ignorance, and baseness" (Farrand 1966, vol. 1:32).

And so Article II created a potentially strong president who would have the capacity to check the power of the legislature. This potential for presidential strength was suggested by a number of factors. First, the office would be held by one person rather than by a council, as was the practice in some of the states. Second, the president would be rendered independent of the legislature, because he would be selected by an Electoral College rather than by the legislature, as many at the Convention had advocated. Although he would serve only a four-year term (advocates of a strong presidency had suggested a much longer term), he would be eligible for perpetual reelection. Because Congress would have little to do with the selection of the president and because he could serve for an unlimited number of terms, he would be in a position to check the powers of the legislature by vetoing legislation that it passed. But the veto was conditional, capable of being overridden by a two-thirds vote in both legislative chambers. But more important, it was a negative power that the president could use to stop Congress from acting; what was much less clear was what, if any, affirmative powers the president would have.

The words of Article II are quite vague on the subject. It vests the "executive power" in the president of the United States, who is instructed to report to Congress "from time to time" on the state of the Union. He also is permitted (contrary to Montesquieu's advice) to recommend measures for Congress's consideration. He is empowered "by and with the Advice and Consent of the Senate," to make treaties with foreign nations, although such treaties needed to be approved by a two-thirds vote of the Senate. He also has the power to appoint administrative office holders, ambassadors, and judges, subject to confirmation by the Senate. And finally, he is the commander in chief of the armed forces, presumably directing their day-to-day activities in the event that Congress should declare war and decide to raise and support an armed force for the president to command.

The wording of the constitutional provisions that describe the powers of the president has been a subject of puzzlement and debate among scholars, especially when one compares the brevity of Article II with the long and detailed exegesis on congressional power contained in Article I. It is apparent that the most specific portions of Article II deal with comparatively trivial responsibilities—for example, reporting on the state of the Union, requesting information in writing from government officers, and granting reprieves and pardons. At the same time, what turned out to be the most important aspects of presidential power are written so vaguely that they literally cry out for definition. The Constitution vests the "executive power" in the president, but doesn't define that power. What does it mean to "faithfully execute the laws"? Is this simply an automatic ministerial function—doing exactly what the law instructs—or does it imply a degree of discretionary power in terms of interpreting the meaning of the law and acting accordingly? Does the treaty-making clause, combined with the power of receiving and appointing ambassadors, suggest a leading role for the president in foreign relations? Does the requirement to report on the state of the Union, along with the provision allowing the president to recommend measures for the consideration of Congress, amount to an expectation that the president should provide policy leadership to the legislature and to the nation? Does the role of commander in chief confer upon the president a broad unilateral role of committing the military to the protection of the nation against all enemies, foreign and domestic, or is it simply meant to say that at times of war, he is in charge of military decisions? Absent a declaration of war by Congress, does this role mean that the president simply has the power to defend the country against a sudden attack, or does it mean that he can deploy troops even in times of peace?

Some argue that the vagueness of the Constitution is attributable to the fact that the Founders, lacking established models for a republican executive, were uncertain about what they wanted from this new office, and were genuinely worried that extensive executive power posed a threat to liberty. Speaking at the Constitutional Convention, George Mason of Virginia said that while he accepted the idea that the executive's capacity for secrecy, dispatch, and energy was important for the new government, these attributes also were contrary to "the pervading principles of republican government" (Farrand 1966, vol. 1:112). Edmund Randolph, also of Virginia, agreed that "the turbulence and follies of democracy" that were on full display in legislative bodies needed to be checked, but he worried that a strong executive was "the fetus of monarchy" (Farrand 1966, vol. 1:51). Hugh Williamson of North Carolina added that such an executive would "spare no pains to keep himself in for life and then lay a train for the succession of his children" (Farrand 1966, vol. 2:101).

It may be that most if not all of the Founders were prepared to resolve these doubts in favor of a strong executive, but that the need to convince a nation that was at best skeptical about executive power to ratify the new Constitution militated in favor of the cautious and vague wording that they chose. From this perspective, they wrote in generalities in the hope that the ambiguities that they created would permit future presidents the latitude to interpret the language in a way that allowed them to meet the new and largely unknown challenges that they knew the nation would surely confront in the future. Scholars also have noted that the Founders designed the presidency with the certain knowledge that George Washington would be the first person to hold the office. They knew that the first decisions of the first president would set a precedent for those who would follow, and they were confident that Washington was both prudent and strong enough to make the right choices.

Taming the Prince: Hamilton

At the Constitutional Convention, Alexander Hamilton was the primary champion of a strong executive, arguing at one point for a president who would serve for life and who would have an absolute veto over all acts of Congress (Burns 1973:6–7). Such a vigorous executive would guarantee the strong national government that Hamilton viewed as essential to the future of the new nation. Although Hamilton's model was not adopted by the Convention, he assumed the task of explaining and defending to a skeptical public the presidential model included in the draft Constitution, and of assuaging the doubts of those who saw the office as a threat to republican liberty. Writing in the 9th Federalist Paper, he identified the challenge to the Convention as ensuring that "the excellence of republican government may be retained and its imperfections lessened or avoided" (9:72–73). The presidency, together with the new Constitution as a whole, Hamilton argued, was the way to address these imperfections of republican government and thus strengthen rather than weaken it.

The first problem that needed to be dealt with was how to choose the president. Existing executive arrangements faced no such problem; monarchs inherited their positions, and royal governors were appointed by the monarchs. But in a republic, the right to rule did not come from divine sources or through inheritance or appointment, but was derived from the people, from the consent of the governed. In the 68th Federalist Paper, Hamilton asserts that republicanism made it "desirable that the sense of the people should operate" in the process of presidential selection. However, it was equally important that steps be taken to ensure that a person of high quality be selected, that the selection process be free from "tumult and disorder," that it not be tainted by "cabal, intrigue, and corruption," and that it guarantee that the president be independent of the legislative branch (68:412–413).

The first two goals could not be achieved if the most republican option—having the people elect the president—were selected, but that approach never received serious consideration at the Convention. Most of the Founders were convinced that the people did not have the capacity to make a wise choice among presidential candidates. Roger Sherman, a delegate to the Constitutional Convention from Connecticut, thought that the people "will never be sufficiently informed of characters," and George Mason of Virginia suggested that referring the choice of the president to the people was analogous to referring "a trial of colors to a blind man" (Farrand 1966, vol. 2:29, 31). They also worried that a popular election would be marred by demagoguery, with candidates for the presidency appealing to the passions and emotions of the voters rather than to their reason and virtue. This is what James Madison had in mind when he warned against the "vicious arts by which elections are too often carried" (10:82). Just as distasteful would be the demagogue who flattered the people by telling them that they knew best; the role of the political leader, the Founders thought, was to do what he thought was in the national interest, notwithstanding public opinion to the contrary (see Ceaser 1979).

And the last two goals for the presidential selection process—avoiding corruption and guaranteeing the president's independence from the legislature—could not have been accomplished if the Convention had endorsed the most obvious alternative to popular election: selection of the president by Congress, along the lines of the parliamentary model then emerging in England. Madison reminded his colleagues at the Convention that one of the reasons why an executive was needed was "to control the National Legislature," which, like the state legislatures, could be expected to have a "strong propensity to a variety of pernicious measures." Certainly, a president selected by Congress would be unlikely to resist such "measures" (Farrand 1966, vol. 2:110), because Congress would take care to select someone who would do its bidding. And if a president selected by Congress wished to serve another term, he certainly would have a strong incentive to follow the direction of the legislature. As for the issue of corruption, it was feared that if the selection of the president were placed in the hands of Congress, candidates for the presidency might use unscrupulous means to secure votes, means that might include bribery or the promise of an administrative appointment. Gouverneur Morris, a delegate from New York, argued that a congressional selection process would "be the work of intrigue, or cabal, and of factions" (Farrand 1966, vol. 2:29).

But the Electoral College option—something that Hamilton had suggested early in the Convention but that was not accepted until almost the last minute—would speak to all four goals. Under such an arrangement, the president would be selected by a designated group of electors rather than by the people or by Congress. These electors in turn would be selected by the various state legislatures and thus the president would be chosen by a "small number of people selected by their fellow citizens from the general mass" who would, according to Hamilton, "possess the information and discernment requisite to so complicated an investigation" as judging the qualities of potential candidates. This process, Hamilton concluded, would avoid the "tumult" of direct election, guarantee to "a moral certainty that the office of president will seldom fall to the lot of any man who is not in an eminent degree endowed with the requisite qualifications," and make it most likely that the person chosen would be characterized by "ability and virtue" (68:414). Also, the electors would never assemble in one place; rather, each state's electors would meet in their home state, thus reducing the danger of bribes and corruption. And because Congress would only be involved in the selection of the president if no candidate received a majority of the electoral votes (in which case the House would select among the top five electoral vote-getters), the winner was likely to be independent of that body.

A second essential component of the electoral arrangement was the president's unlimited eligibility for reelection. This, according to Hamilton, would provide for continuity in office that would both ensure stability and encourage good public policy. The four-year term for the president was longer than the terms for governors, but obviously much shorter than the terms that monarchs served and shorter even than some of the longer terms in office that had been suggested at the Convention. On the other hand, the president, unlike many state governors, would be allowed to run for reelection as many times as he wished. This would "enable the people, when they see reason to approve of his conduct, to continue him in the station in order to prolong the utility of his talents and virtues, and to secure to the government the advantages of permanency in a wise system of administration" (72:436). Unlimited prospects for reelection would encourage presidents to take the long-term view of public policy and would also encourage honest behavior among those who occupied the office. A limited term in office, in contrast, might tempt presidents to place their own private interests ahead of the public interest against the day when they would be compelled to return to private life.

Before moving ahead with Hamilton's defense of the presidency, it is worth pausing to consider these electoral decisions. What stands out is the Founders' fear of popular election by the people, even by an electorate narrowed by eighteenth-century considerations of race, gender, and property. The people, they were certain, would not choose the best person for the office, but even more important, in order to gain the office, candidates would need to appeal to the people and be tempted to cater to the worst instincts of the population. Although direct election of the president certainly would render him independent of the legislature, it would also create an intimate and ultimately unhealthy relationship between the people and the president. On the one hand the president could exploit the emotions of the population for his own purposes, and on the other he might be overly sensitive to the transitory wishes of an uninformed, self-interested, and ephemeral public opinion. In either event, the Founders' desire for a president of high character who would pursue the public interest would be at risk.

Today, of course, direct election of the president by an electorate much broader than the Founders could ever have imagined is a fact both in the United States and in every other political system classified as presidential. As we shall see, such an arrangement has made a crucial contribution to presidentialism and in a manner that in several respects confirms the fears of those who designed this first republican executive. Even the strongest defenders of popular election of the president would be compelled to admit that appeals to emotion rather than to reason, the employment of the "vicious arts" about which Madison spoke, and a sometimes debilitating attention to public opinion polls as candidates seek election and as presidents seek to govern, are endemic and not necessarily salutary characteristics of modern democratic political systems.

As for presidential tenure, George Washington's decision to step down after two terms in office set an informal term limit for US presidents, violated only once by Franklin Roosevelt, and then permanently enshrined in the 22nd Amendment to the Constitution. Other countries have used term limits (Mexico, for example, restricts the president to one term in office), but many allow an unlimited tenure for the president. Clearly, popular election without term limits, as Hamilton argued, makes for potentially strong presidents.

With the independence of the president from Congress ensured by the newly created electoral system, Hamilton's next task was to reassure those who feared that presidential power would inevitably mutate into kingly power. He did so in the 69th Federalist Paper by offering a point-by-point enumeration of the constitutional limitations on presidential power that in his view made the office substantially weaker than that of the king of England and therefore no threat to liberty. The king had an absolute veto power, but the president's veto could be overridden by the legislature; the king could declare war, but under the Constitution only Congress could do that; the king could dismiss Parliament, but the president could not dismiss Congress; the king served for life, but the president's term was limited, and he could be removed from office before the end of his term for crimes or misdeeds committed against the state; and while the king had the absolute power to make treaties as well as appointments to high office, the president required the advice and consent of the Senate for these actions.

What then would the president contribute? Hamilton's positive argument for presidential power, alluded to in the 9th Federalist Paper, emphasized the need for a strong and energetic government as a means to preserve liberty. In the 70th Federalist Paper, Hamilton made it clear where that energy for government was to come from: "energy in the executive is a leading character in the definition of good government. It is essential to the protection of the community against foreign attacks; it is not less essential to the steady administration of the laws." He concluded that "a feeble executive implies a feeble execution of the government" and a feebly executed government must be "in practice, a bad government" (70:423).

Energy in the executive required in the first instance unity—that is, a singular rather than a collective presidency and the ability of that president to exercise executive power unilaterally. Unity is conducive to energy, Hamilton argued, because "decision, activity, secrecy and dispatch will generally characterize the proceedings of one man in a much more eminent degree than the proceedings of any greater number" (70:424). In defending unity, Hamilton recalled ancient Rome and the problems that ensued there from the sharing of executive power between two Consuls as well as among various lower-level bureaucrats. But in the context of the United States in the late eighteenth century, few were talking about plural executives and more were discussing the possibility of the president governing in consultation with a council, as was the case with the governors of several of the new states. Some of the Founders even viewed the Senate as a de facto privy council for the president, which explains its special role in regard to treaties and the approval of presidential nominees for executive or judicial positions. In any event, Hamilton attacked any collective executive arrangement as undermining both efficiency and responsibility. Such a structure would encourage differences of opinion and public disputes about policy, and while these were both appropriate and welcome in a deliberative body such as a legislature, they would be destructive in the executive branch. And if executive branch decisions were the collective product of a president and a council, who would the country hold responsible for poor decisions—the council or the president? A singular executive meant more efficient and—because responsibility for decisions could be clearly fixed—more accountable decisionmaking.

As to the powers of the president, Hamilton concerned himself with those few issues that had created public disputes: the appointment power, the treaty-making power, and the role of the president as commander in chief. In terms of the latter, some anti-Federalists argued that the president as commander of a standing army would be able to keep his position by force. After the first election, wrote Philadelphiensis, an anti-Federalist, "the people shall not be much troubled with future elections, especially in choosing their king. The standing army will do that business for them."⁹ Hamilton responded to this critique by pointing out that the clause would come into effect only when war was declared by Congress, and that it would amount to the president being in those instances "the first general and admiral of the Confederacy." The only standing army that would exist would be in the form of the state militias, and the president would have control of them only when they were called into the service of the nation as a whole, presumably in consequence of a declaration of war or the need to suppress domestic insurrections (69:417–418). Beyond that practical point, Hamilton argued, the role of commander in chief was an indisputable component of executive power. The direction of war requires "the exercise of power by a single hand," because it "implies the direction of the common strength; and the power of directing and employing the common strength forms a usual and essential part of the definition of executive authority" (74:447).

Hamilton's position was that presidential appointment of administrative officers was far superior to the alternative, which was appointment by the legislature. Presidential appointment would increase the likelihood that the best person would be selected. "The sole and undivided responsibility of one man will naturally beget a livelier sense of duty and a more exact regard to reputation" (76:455). In contrast, appointment by the legislature was likely to involve the same partisan considerations and corruption that the Founders feared if the president himself were to be selected by Congress.

As for the treaty-making power, the Convention had toyed with the idea of placing this power exclusively in the hands of the Senate, a position embraced by those most skeptical of executive power. But Madison argued that the president was a representative of the nation as a whole, while senators were representatives of their individual states, and therefore the president needed to have a role in the making of treaties. The compromise was to join the president and the Senate together in the treaty-making power, with the president having the power to make treaties "by and with the advice and consent of the Senate." Although Hamilton might have preferred an even stronger presidential role, he conceded that it was unwise to vest this power in the hands of the president alone, and confined his discussion of this provision to defending it against those who thought that the House of Representatives also should have a role in the process (75:452–453).

What conclusions, then, can we draw from the constitutional provisions describing the US presidency? First, because those who wrote the Constitution were about to create the first republican executive, they had to overcome the view that executive power was antithetical to republican liberty. At every turn, they needed to reassure skeptics that the presidency would not be a danger to liberty and that the office was so structured that its occupant could never indulge in the abuses associated with the king of England. They consistently emphasized the limited power of the presidency.

These limitations were reinforced by the system of institutional checks that they placed in the Constitution. Even though they knew that George Washington would be the first president, and they had some confidence that the convoluted electoral process that they had designed would produce worthy successors to the first president, they also knew that at some point a less than worthy person might succeed to the office. As Madison famously put it in the 51st Federalist Paper, the men who governed were unlikely to be "angels," and at a later point, writing about the problems of placing the war-making power in the hands of the president, he suggested that future presidents after Washington would not be "such as nature may offer as the prodigy of many centuries" but "such as may be expected in the ordinary successions of magistracy" (Madison 1793). Therefore "auxiliary precautions" needed to be taken. That meant equipping both Congress and the president with the ability to defend their own institutional independence against possible incursions by the other, thus ensuring that "ambition would be made to counteract ambition" (51:322). In war-making, in treaty-making, in ordinary legislation, and in the appointment of government officials, neither the president nor Congress could act unilaterally. Each had the capacity to check the other, thereby ensuring that wise decisions would be made, or, put differently, that unwise decisions would be less likely to be made. This system is more accurately characterized as "separate institutions sharing power" rather than the more familiar "separation of powers" (Neustadt 1980). This is not simply a matter of semantics. Precisely defined executive powers clearly separated from equally well defined legislative powers would create the possibility that either institution would abuse those powers exclusively consigned to it. But by ensuring that powers were shared in virtually every key area of government, the Founders realized Montesquieu's ambition for moderate government aimed at preventing the abuses that would result from concentrating government power in too few hands.

And the beauty of the system was that while it served the purpose of reassuring the population at large that there would be checks on the power of the executive, at the same time it dealt with the concern of many of the Founders who thought that the real danger to the nation was legislative rather than executive abuse of power. One leading scholar of the period concluded that for the Framers, "where once the magistracy [i.e., the executive] had served as the sole source of tyranny, now the legislatures . . . had become the institution to be most feared" (Wood 1969:409). As Madison put it, in legislatures, "measures are too often decided not according to the rules of justice and the rights of the minor party, but by the superior force of an interested and overbearing majority" (10:77).

This last concern of Madison's betrayed the worry of several of the Founders that government action would be taken too hastily, that it would be too responsive to the moods of transitory majorities, that these majorities were likely to be composed mainly of people with more meager resources than those of the property-holding elites, and that these decisions therefore might not be in the long-term public interest, at least as the Founders viewed that concept. But under their constitutional model, in order for government to act, agreement would have to be secured from separate and independent institutions, and such agreements, the Founders believed, would occur only when action was absolutely necessary, clearly in the public interest, and therefore of no threat to the interests of elites such as they.

Some of the Founders did prefer as little government as possible, and for them a system in which policy inertia was a likely outcome was not necessarily a problem. But others recognized that it was possible that too many precautions had been taken against abuse, and that the system could lead to a paralyzed government unable to take necessary action. Hamilton for one feared that they might have gone too far. After completing the exercise of dividing and balancing power, he said, "you must place confidence; you must give power" (Loss 1982:10). He repeated this sentiment in the 26th Federalist Paper: "Confidence must be placed somewhere," he wrote; "it is better to hazard the abuse of that confidence than to embarrass the government and endanger the public safety by impolitic restrictions on legislative authority" (26:168). Although Hamilton's last phrase mentioned legislative authority, it seems clear that the confidence that Hamilton believed needed to be placed "somewhere" ultimately would be placed in the executive, his source of government "energy." And the means for placing that confidence would prove to be the actions of presidents as they filled in the ambiguous gaps that Hamilton and his colleagues had left in Article II. For in the end, it may be that Hamilton was a bit more optimistic about human nature than his colleague Madison was. While Madison lamented the absence of angels to govern men and wrote that "passion never fails to wrest the scepter from reason" (55:342), Hamilton asserted that "there is a portion of virtue and honour among mankind which may be a reasonable foundation of confidence" (76:458).

Hamilton's willingness to place confidence versus Madison's reliance on constitutional structures to prevent abuses set the parameters for the debate over the scope and nature of presidential power that has taken place over the more than two centuries of the Constitution's existence. As the presidency has developed in the United States and in every other country, the questions have always been, first, whether or not the constitutionally inscribed safeguards are sufficient to check or prevent the movement of power and confidence in the direction of the executive branch and, second, whether the restrictions on executive power are too stringent, rendering the government too weak to do what is necessary. Was Hamilton correct that at the end of the day, people wanted to place their confidence in a person who could provide energy, initiative, and leadership, or would they continue to be attracted by Madison's overriding concern that power should not be concentrated in one set of hands? In some respects, this is also a question of Machiavelli's omnipotent Prince versus Montesquieu's moderate government.

Despite the questions and the ambiguities, it is important to remember that what the Founders of the US political system did in Philadelphia in 1787 was to invent the office that is both the subject of this book and the focus of so many political systems. It bears repeating that prior to these decisions, there was in modern history no such thing as an executive who was neither monarchical nor despotic, and who was selected with the participation of his nation's citizens. The arguments for such an office closely track the classical arguments for executives: the need for administration, the need for leadership, and the ability to act in defense of the nation. On the other hand, unlike Machiavelli's Prince, the powers of this executive were to be checked to a significant degree by other independent political institutions. Unlike Locke's executive, the US president had no explicit prerogative powers, although later presidents were to claim that under certain circumstances they did. But unlike Montesquieu's executive, the US president could participate in the legislative process by suggesting measures for the consideration of Congress and through that responsibility could provide policy leadership.

Presidents Around the World

The new US presidency served as a model for the presidential systems that were to be established in Latin America in the nineteenth century and in Africa a century later. In Latin America, those who wrote the post-independence constitutions faced the same challenges as their

North American counterparts—replacing a European monarch and ensuring a government strong enough to provide political order and stability. The leaders of the victorious independence armies saw the need for "a strong executive around which they could unite the varied populations in their new republics" (Kantor 1992:101). The executive was a "device to guide and control the extremist and centrifugal forces characteristic of the region and to forge unifying symbols essential to nationalism in lands rife with separatist tendencies and political factions" (Sondrol 1990:419). Simón Bolivar put it this way: "unity, unity, unity must be our motto in all things. The blood of our citizens is varied; let it be mixed for the sake of unity. Our Constitution has divided the powers of government; let them be bound together to secure freedom" (Sondrol 1990:428). And they would be "bound together" in a president who would "become the sun which, fixed in its orbit, imparted life to the universe" (Gargarella 2010:119).

But as was the case in the United States, the colonial experience had created some skepticism about executive authority. In Venezuela, for example, after the fight for independence had been won, executive power was held by a triumvirate. But Bolivar, in his famous Angostura address to the Venezuelan Parliament, criticized this arrangement in words that echoed Alexander Hamilton's: "Our executive triumvirate lacks, so to speak, unity, continuity, and individual responsibility. It is deprived of prompt action, continuous existence, true uniformity, and direct responsibility. The government that does not possess these things . . . must be deemed a non-entity." He contrasted this arrangement with the US presidency, in which the president "alone exercises all the government functions which the Constitution has delegated to him; thus there is no doubt that this administration must be more uniform, constant, and more truly his own than an administration wherein power is divided among a number of persons, a grouping that is nothing less than a monstrosity" (Bierck 1951:180).

Bolivar coupled his argument for unity in the executive with one for strong executive powers and a clearer delineation between legislative and executive power. Managing the tensions in the ethnically and racially diverse societies that existed in Latin America, Bolivar argued, "will require an infinitely firm hand and great tactfulness." This was a role for a president, "an individual set apart from society charged with checking the impulse of the people toward license. . . . Unless the executive has easy access to all the administrative resources, fixed by a just distribution of powers, he inevitably becomes a nonentity or abuses his authority. By this I mean that the result will be the death of the government, whose heirs are anarchy, usurpation, and tyranny" (Bierck 1951:189). Recommending a constitution for Bolivia, he advocated a presidency that would serve for life as a means for ensuring stability. This also would avoid the necessity of elections, which in his view were likely to be destabilizing events (Davis 1958:259).

In the early days of independence, few Latin American executives resembled the republican model that had been adopted in the United States. Some presidencies were held by military leaders who simply assumed power, others were installed and deposed through military coups, some presidents were appointed by legislatures, and some ruled in an authoritarian manner. Even after more republican presidencies began to emerge later in the nineteenth century, the need remained for a strong president in command of a strong military to ensure stability. In Argentina in the period from 1862 to 1930, constitutional government and the peaceful transition from one presidency to another were constant; nonetheless, every administration was called upon to suppress an armed uprising, and they succeeded in doing so because the presidents were able to depend upon a loyal army to defeat the rebellions (Davis 1958:260). In Chile, the early years of the Republic, according to a student of that period, were characterized by "anarchy and chaos." The Chilean aristocracy, wishing to create and preserve order, established a system based on presidential authority that was "powerful and inclusive" (Tapia-Videla 1977), and the Chilean Constitution of 1833 was the first to create a provision for a presidentially initiated "state of siege" (Gargarella 2010:120).

The nature of the movement from colonialism to independence also militated in favor of a presidency. Latin American countries and African countries in the twentieth century gained their independence from colonial powers through movements typically led by a single figure, sometimes a person with military skill and often charismatic qualities as well. After independence was achieved, these national heroes were natural candidates for the leadership of their new nations, and that leadership position was likely to be the presidency. Just as Washington became the first president of the United States, so too did Bolivar in Venezuela, Nkrumah in Ghana, Senghor in Senegal, Kenyatta in Kenya, Nyerere in Tanzania, Banda in Malawi, and Mugabe in Zimbabwe became the first presidents of their nations. As these newly independent nations struggled for identity and stability, particularly in ethnically or geographically fragmented environments that were often more the product of colonial map makers than demographic or historical affinities, the president was seen as someone who could unify the new nation. He stood as a symbol of national sovereignty and, as the commander of the military, had the resources to maintain domestic order.

Once established, these presidencies persisted, even with the passing of the founding leader; although the transition from the founding president to his successor was sometimes contentious, little or no consideration appears to have been accorded to the adoption of a parliamentary model. As Juan Linz has observed, "the masses of people by themselves prefer a system they know to something unknown and not understood" (1994:47). Parliamentary systems and collective leadership arrangements are intrinsically more difficult for citizens to grasp and understand than presidential systems headed by a single, visible leader with whom citizens can connect at both a political and an emotional level. In the view of some scholars, another explanation for the choices made in the United States and in Latin America was that there was at the time no real parliamentary alternative to presidential systems, because the principle of cabinet government had not fully emerged in Europe until the end of the nineteenth century (Cheibub 2007:151; Cox 1987).

Whatever the originating cause, today the presidential model is dominant in Latin America and Africa, as Table 2.1 indicates. In Africa, some of the postcolonial nations, particularly those that had been under British rule, started out as parliamentary systems, but with only a few exceptions quickly moved to presidential systems and, in a few instances, to semipresidential models (Collier 1978; van de Walle 2003). In Asia, one finds both presidential and parliamentary systems, but more of the former. Europe is still home to the largest number of parliamentary systems, although an increasing number of countries, particularly in Central and Eastern Europe, have adopted semipresidential systems.

Cultural Antecedents to Presidentialism

Some have suggested that there are broader cultural antecedents for the presidential systems that have characterized Latin America and Africa. One scholar depicts social relations in Latin America as "personal, dyadic, hierarchical, and authoritarian," which leads to decisions concerning governmental structures that favor "some form of political monism, including 'strong man' leadership" (Sondrol 1990:421). The roots of this disposition may be found in the tradition of political absolutism and personal government inherited from Spanish colonizers. Although the excesses of such a tradition contributed enormously to the movement for independence in Latin America, the cultural residue of

Table 2.1   Presidential, Semipresidential, and Parliamentary Systems, by Region

	Presidential	Semipresidential	Parliamentary
Africa	Cameroon Côte d'Ivoire Ghana Kenya Malawi Namibia Nigeria South Africa Uganda Zambia Zimbabwe	Algeria Central African Republic Egypt Guinea-Bissau Madagascar Mali Mozambique	Botswana
Asia	Afghanistan Indonesia Iran Pakistan Philippines Singapore South Korea Sri Lanka Taiwan	Lebanon Mongolia	Bangladesh India Iraq Israel Japan Nepal Thailand Turkey
Europe	Cyprus	Armenia Austria Bulgaria Croatia France Georgia Iceland Lithuania Macedonia Poland Portugal Romania Russia Slovakia Slovenia Ukraine	Albania Belgium Czech Republic Denmark Estonia Finland Germany Greece Hungary Ireland Italy Latvia Malta Netherlands Norway Spain Sweden United Kingdom

continues

Table 2.1 continued

	Presidential	Semipresidential	Parliamentary
Latin America	Argentina		
	Bolivia		
	Brazil		
	Chile		
	Colombia		
	Dominican Republic		
	Ecuador		
	El Salvador		
	Guatemala		
	Honduras		
	Mexico		
	Nicaragua		
	Panama		
	Paraguay		
	Peru		
	Uruguay		
	Venezuela		
Pacific and North America	United States		Canada
	Palau		Australia
	Micronesia		New Zealand

Sources: Alan Siaroff (2003) "Comparative Presidencies: The Inadequacy of the Presidential, Semi-Presidential, and Parliamentary Distinction," *European Journal of Political Research* 42:287–312; José Antonio Cheibub (2007) *Presidentialism, Parliamentarism, and Democracy* (Cambridge: Cambridge University Press).

Note: There are judgment calls involved in placing countries in this table, especially when it comes to assigning countries to the semipresidential category.

that tradition remained after the Spaniards had left (Davis 1958:256). In this same vein, Roberto Gargarella identifies a conservative model of constitutionalism that developed in postcolonial Latin America, a model characterized by a political elitism that meant "concentrating authority in one person or group," an arrangement that typically implied "reinforcement of the power of the president" (2010:117).

The caudillo tradition is still another cultural pillar of presidentialism in Latin America. Originally, the caudillos were local "strong men" who organized and armed what we would call today guerrilla forces to fight for independence. Often they were large landowners upon whom peasants depended for sustenance and for land to work. In return, the caudillo received support, loyalty, and a willingness to take up arms on his behalf. Once independence was achieved, central authorities came to view the caudillos as what one scholar calls "the necessary gendarmes" to control the masses, who on a periodic basis would become discontent with various governmental policies (Lynch 1992:234–237). The caudillo, in sum, was a charismatic figure whose "power rested on the personal loyalty of his followers to him and to his destiny" and who ruled in a very personal way (Alexander 1977:3–4).

From this perhaps oversimplified perspective, some have suggested that presidentialism in Latin America may be simply an extension of the caudillo model. In Mexico, according to one scholar, there is a "tendency toward centralization, particularly the accumulation of personal power in the hands of a caudillo, a quasi-military leader. Inevitably, the role of national caudillo is assumed by the president" (Weldon 1997:226). Although these Latin American systems usually have constitutions that seem to restrict executive power along the lines of the US Constitution, such mechanisms are sometimes weak and difficult to enforce, and often fail to constrain presidents who are intent on aggrandizing their power. The cultural norms "not only condone but promote strong, centralist presidential power and the extra-constitutional power position of the Latin American chief executive stemming from his stature as a political boss or general" (Sondrol 1990:428).

More recently, some observers of contemporary Latin American politics have noted the emergence of "electoral caudillos," who, though popularly elected, tend to ignore or circumvent existing constitutional arrangements, practice a politics of personalism, and work to concentrate increased power in their own hands. Preserving popular presidential elections allows them to justify the expansion of their power in democratic terms, as the expression of the will of the people (see Close and Deonandan 2004). The recent presidency in Venezuela and the current presidencies in Ecuador, Bolivia, and Nicaragua may be characterized in these terms.

In Africa, precolonial governmental forms were based primarily on kingdoms and tribes. In the case of the latter, there were many different forms of rule, often involving councils of elders, but also typically involving a chief, or a headman who spoke for the group. Both the kingdom and tribal models, combined with the need to organize militarily against colonial powers, produced a disposition toward presidencies as African nations achieved independence. From a sociological perspective, precolonial African societies were what Max Weber characterized as patrimonial in nature, governed by an individual who ruled by virtue of his personal prestige and power and in which those who were ruled had no rights or privileges other than those granted by the ruler. Power in patrimonial systems is personalized and there is no codified set of laws. Rather, "the patrimonial ruler resists the delimitation of his authority by the stipulation of rules. He may observe traditional or customary limitations, but these are unwritten; indeed, tradition endorses the principled arbitrariness of the ruler." In addition, "all administrative offices under patrimonial rule are a part of the ruler's personal household" (Bendix 1962:425). The ruler provides security for the ruled and selectively distributes favors and material benefits to loyal followers, who are not so much citizens of the polity as they are the ruler's clients.

Several of the founding presidents of independent African nations resembled patrimonial leaders. Discussions of the presidencies of Léopold Senghor in Senegal and Jomo Kenyatta in Kenya emphasize their role as leaders to whom claimants came to settle disputes and to request assistance—often on issues that were more personal than they were political—or to pledge their loyalty. In the case of Senghor, for example, he emphasized access to the presidency for "the numerous supplicants seeking his personal intervention on behalf of their individual or group interests" (Schumacher 1975:71–72). Kenyatta received delegations representing districts and tribes, often accompanied by schoolchildren and performers, whose leaders would express "their sentiments of loyalty and respect" to the president and at the same time "outline various needs and grievances." Kenyatta, in turn, "would thank them . . . exhort them to unity and hard work, and discuss their requests, explaining why some could not be met and undertaking to attend to others" (Leys 1974:246).

Some students of African politics have characterized these postcolonial nations as neopatrimonial societies in which the traditions of patrimonial societies are joined with certain aspects of what Weber refers to as the "rational-legal" model that characterizes the modern nation-state. In rational-legal systems, authority is exercised through written laws and bureaucratic institutions. Most African nations have the formal trappings of rational-legal systems, with written constitutions, statutes, and bureaucracies. But in many of these countries, real political authority more accurately fits the patrimonial model, and the constitutions were "less important as constraints on the abuse of power and acted more as legal instruments that a personal ruler could amend or rewrite to suit his power needs" (Jackson and Rosberg 1982:16; see also Chazan et al. 1992:163–164). Thus, the right to rule was "ascribed to a person rather than an office, despite the official existence of a written constitution." The president undermines the bureaucratic apparatus of the state by utilizing it for "systematic patronage and clientelist practices in order to maintain political order." Presidents centralize and consolidate power, holding all major decisions in their hands. Such presidents are likely "to promote a cult of personality through their domination of the national media, by placing their likenesses on the currency, by seeing to it that their portraits are hung in every public building, and by the broad scale distribution of their speeches and writings" (Bratton and van de Walle 1997:62).

As Léopold Senghor, the first president of Senegal, wrote: "The president personifies the Nation as did the Monarch of former times his people" (Jackson and Rosberg 1982:v). These "big men" presidents exercise absolute power in the sense that they need not deal with other political institutions and actors and tend to rule by decree. In most instances, these presidents are elected and sometimes these elections have been competitive, but more typically, restrictions on the opposition, presidential dominance of the media, along with security arrangements and outright corruption have meant that such elections merely provide a democratic facade for an essentially authoritarian system. And while military coups have fallen out of vogue in Latin America, they are still very much a fact of life in Africa, often resulting in one presidential big man being forcibly replaced by another who is backed by the military.

Semipresidentialism

In Europe, meanwhile, the parliamentary tradition has persisted, although there has been a significant increase in the number of nations that have adopted the semipresidential system, characterized by a popularly elected president who shares power with a prime minister and cabinet who are responsible to Parliament. The great expansion of mixed systems started in the last decade of the twentieth century as constitution makers attempted to provide their political systems with the unifying symbol and the capacity for swift action in the face of crises represented by a nationally elected presidency and the democratic responsiveness represented by a parliamentary arrangement.

In the case of France, Charles de Gaulle had long advocated a strong presidency that would stand above the partisan conflict that characterized the National Assembly and that would be capable of acting in the face of the legislative *immobilism* of both the Third and Fourth Republics. When he was appointed premier in 1958 and charged with developing a new Constitution, that document, not surprisingly, provided for a strong presidency, an institution that reflected in part the Bonapartism that always has appealed to a broad spectrum of the French population (Safran 2009:234). But a purely presidential system would have been seen as contrary to the republican tradition and would have not been acceptable; the mixed system attempted to meld the benefits of a strong president with the republican commitment to parliamentary government.

Political compromises of this sort appear to have played a part in the adoption of other semipresidential systems. In some of the new democracies of Central and Eastern Europe (Lithuania, for example), this model proved to be a way to bridge the gap between conservative elements who favored a strong presidency and more progressive elements who were committed to a parliamentary model (see Krupavicius 2008). In Russia, as that country moved from rule by the Communist Party to a more democratic model, the choice of semipresidentialism also represented a compromise, but also had advantages for the new presidency and its first occupant, Mikhail Gorbachev. It elevated him "above the unpleasant business of managing a vast and inefficient bureaucracy which was left to the prime minister." In this way, the prime minister rather than the president became "the whipping boy for popular discontent." The presidency also was a convenient substitute for the apparatus of the Communist Party as a force standing above the existing formal parliamentary institutions of power. The presidency thus seemed to provide "a new source of legitimacy for a regime with a failing ideology and institutions" (Huskey 1999:16).

Conclusion

The executive is an essential part of any political system, more essential than a legislature or a judiciary given the fact that every state—from the most authoritarian to the most democratic—must have a mechanism for carrying out its policies, for defending itself against aggressors, and for providing leadership for the nation. The challenge facing nations that aspire to democratic standards is how to provide for this essential executive function without running the risk of authoritarianism.

Locke's answer was a legislative power that must predominate, but also an executive with significant prerogatives that he would be expected to exercise for the public good. Montesquieu's answer was an even stronger legislature and a weaker executive, albeit one with significant powers, that would lead to moderate government that would not threaten liberty. Drawing on both Locke and Montesquieu as well as their understanding of the ancients, those who wrote the US Constitution created the first republican executive. Their president would be selected by an Electoral College that would in turn be indirectly selected by the people. That would render him independent of Congress, in which the Founders vested all legislative power, and also increase the likelihood that a person of talent and skill would become president, something that they believed would be unlikely to happen with direct election by the people. The president would have a conditional veto power over the acts of Congress, would act as commander in chief of the nation's armed forces, would play the leading role in negotiating treaties with foreign powers, and would be able, with the consent of the Senate, to nominate those who would constitute his administration. He had the ambiguously worded charge to "take care that the laws be faithfully executed." The president was impeachable by Congress for crimes against the state and he in turn could not dismiss Congress. This constrained presidency, the Founders expected, would soothe the concerns that many citizens retained from colonial times about a powerful executive and its incompatibility with republican liberty. As we will see, however, events that the Founders could not have anticipated eventually rendered their presidency more powerful and less constrained than they had hoped.

The concept of the presidency found favor in the new nations of Latin America, which, like the United States, also had broken away from an abusive monarchy, but still needed to create constitutions that provided for an executive with the power to bring unity and stability to a diverse nation and to suppress insurrections. Historical and cultural norms in Latin America that valued strong leadership by a single person proved to be compatible with political arrangements that called for strong presidencies. Similarly, in Africa, traditional governance patterns that focused on the leadership of a single person led virtually seamlessly to postcolonial systems with strong presidencies, typically with leaders of the independence struggle assuming the office. On both continents, however, presidencies more often than not proved to be less constrained than the US model, to the point that some began to resemble authoritarian regimes.

In Europe, the commitment to parliamentary as opposed to presidential government began to erode as some of those nations came to believe that the leadership provided by the presidency could be of value to their nations. Their answer, particularly in the new democracies of Eastern and Central Europe, turned out to be a mixed system involving shared executive power between an independent president and a cabinet that would be accountable to the legislature. Such arrangements tended to be based less on the US model and more on the Constitution of the Fifth French Republic, where the mixed system had proven to be most successful.

In brief, the task of "taming the prince" proved to be challenging. In the United States, the president is still constrained, compared with his counterparts in other countries, although the institution is much stronger today than its designers had wished. As we will see in the next chapter, the constitutions of other countries generally provided for stronger presidencies than the US model, presidencies with a greater potential to move in the direction of authoritarianism.

Notes

1. All quotations from Aristotle come from Ernest Barker's translation of *The Politics,* published in 1962 by Oxford University Press.
2. This discussion of Greece draws heavily on Christopher Blackwell's *Demos: Classical Athenian Democracy* (2003).
3. The sources on ancient Rome are legion. I have relied here on www.mariamilani.com/ancient_rome.htm.
4. All quotations from Machiavelli's *The Prince* are drawn from the 1908 edition, translated by W. K. Marriott. These quotations are identified by page number alone.
5. All quotations from Locke's *Of Civil Government* come from the 1955 edition, published by Henry Regnery. These quotations are identified by page number alone.
6. All quotations from Montesquieu's *The Spirit of the Laws* come from the 1949 edition, translated by Thomas Nugent. These quotations are identified by page number alone.
7. All quotations from the Federalist Papers are drawn from the 1961 edition, published by the New American Library (see Hamilton, Madison, and Jay 1961). Hereafter, quotations are identified by the number of the paper and the page number on which the quotation is found.
8. There are a number of excellent sources that analyze the decisions surrounding the creation of the US presidency. See, for example, Thach 1923; Ceaser 1979; Robinson 1983; and Cronin 1989.
9. The 74th Anti-Federalist Paper.

3

A Comparative Perspective on Presidential Power

Every presidential system faces the same seemingly contradictory goals that Alexander Hamilton and his colleagues confronted in Philadelphia in 1787—both how to empower the president so that he can deal effectively with the nation's problems, and how to constrain the president to prevent executive authoritarianism. The various attempts to find an appropriate balance between power and constraint are found in the constitutional designs under which all presidential systems operate. Presidentialism is characterized by the gradual erosion of the constitutional provisions aimed at constraining presidents and the enlargement of executive power at the expense of other political institutions and actors. This process is more apparent in some presidential systems than in others; in some countries, constraints on presidential power continue to be relatively robust, while in others these constraints have moved toward the vanishing point as political power has come to be heavily concentrated in the office of the president.

Assessing Presidential Power

Written constitutions typically set out the extent of government power—what government can and cannot do—as well as the boundaries that separate what presidents can do on their own from what other institutions, such as legislatures and courts, can do, and what these constitutionally separate institutions must do together if government is to act. As important as these documents are, they seldom tell the entire story of presidential power. Fred Riggs, a leading scholar of comparative politics, coined the term "formalism" to describe an approach to political power that focused exclusively on the terms of the nation's constitution and failed to consider sufficiently how power was actually exercised and by whom (1967:151–153). Those who studied the Soviet Union, for example, frequently would observe the significant gap between how power was described in that nation's Constitution—a document that seemed to call for, among other things, a powerful legislature—and the highly centralized manner in which the Communist Party actually exercised power.

And as we saw in the discussion of the creation of the US Constitution, many key constitutional terms concerning presidential power are ambiguous and therefore open to interpretation. US constitutional scholars are fond of saying that the Constitution is a living document, which doesn't mean that the words of the Constitution change, but that its provisions can be interpreted differently in light of changing societal and political norms and the nature of the challenges that a nation confronts. So the questions surrounding presidential power in the United States more often deal with how the Constitution has been interpreted by presidents and courts rather than with the explicit words of the document itself.

An approach to understanding presidential power as it is practiced rather than as it is written poses a number of methodological challenges, especially if one wishes to take a comparative perspective. Written constitutions can be easily assembled and their provisions can be parsed, categorized, and compared. But studies of presidential power that go beyond constitutional provisions require the sort of in-depth data that are usually generated by case studies focusing on individual countries. Even within the same country, one can find significant variations among presidential administrations. In the case of the United States, the number of systematic studies of the presidency across all administrations is far outweighed by the number of studies of individual presidents. The best of the latter have been executed by historians and journalists rather than by political scientists and for the most part focus on the skills and character of the president in question, the challenges that he faced, the strategies that he employed to deal with these challenges, and his successes and failures. In countries with less stable political systems, studies of the presidency almost have to be studies of individual presidents. New constitutions and new regimes are usually characterized by significant changes in the formal and informal powers of the president, so generalizations about the exercise of power by presidents operating under different sets of rules would not be of much value.

Understanding the formal and informal nature of presidential power is a separate question from understanding what constitutes the successful exercise of that power, and understanding what constitutes success raises another set of methodological questions. If success for a president means translating his policy preferences into law, one needs to ask how ambitious the president's agenda was. A president with a narrow agenda oriented toward policies that make at most incremental changes to the status quo may accomplish nearly all of his goals, while his counterpart who has a more ambitious agenda that tackles more challenging problems may encounter some failures, but his successes may be extremely important in the long term. Which president can be judged to have exercised power more successfully? There is also the need to distinguish between successful and ethical leadership (see Nye 2008:112). A president who leads his nation toward major changes that ultimately have a deleterious effect on the country or the world at large may be a successful leader in terms of his ability to accomplish goals, but on ethical grounds he may be judged less successful than a president who accomplishes relatively little but who has done no harm to the polity or its people. But these judgments may be easier to make in the long term than in the short term; the assessments that historians arrive at for specific presidents tend to be quite different from those that are offered by contemporary commentators during or immediately after a president's term in office.

Also, different presidents may govern in completely different contexts, even within the same nation. Writing about the US presidency, Stephen Skowronek (1993) argues that a president's ability to succeed depends to a great degree on when he takes office, and that some historical moments are more conducive than others to the major changes that we associate with great presidents. Every president in every country faces a distinct set of environmental factors during his or her term in office. The balance of power in the nation's legislature will vary across presidencies as will the economic and geopolitical challenges that the country faces. In countries with fragile and transitory party structures, context can change dramatically as political parties appear and disappear, as office holders move from one party to another, and as governing coalitions shift. In countries with more stable political party systems, generalizations about context may be somewhat easier to make. Every US president over the past 150 years has been either a Democrat or a Republican, and the congressional majority has been made up of one or the other of these parties over the same period of time. In Brazil, in contrast, over the past fifty years, new political parties have emerged, others have disappeared, and the partisan coalitions that control Congress have changed as well. There have been periods when the military has been an active and even dominant player, such as 1964 through 1985, and other periods, like the present, when they have been on the sidelines (see Mainwaring 1997).

Measuring Presidential Success

These contextual factors are crucial if one seeks to truly measure presidential power. For example, one question that political scientists have focused on is how successful a president has been in gaining approval for his policy priorities. When a president makes a policy proposal, does it become law as he proposed it, or is it altered to a significant degree before it becomes law, or is it rejected in its entirety? This sort of research directs attention to the relationship between the president and the legislative branch of government, because in all presidential systems, the president, at least formally, shares lawmaking power with the legislature.

In the case of the United States, where research of this sort is a virtual cottage industry, explanations of presidential success or failure have focused for the most part on the number of the president's co-partisans in Congress, whether he proposes the policy earlier or later in his administration, and his level of public support.[1] The general consensus has been that the larger the presidential majority in Congress and the earlier that the president makes his policy proposals, the more likely he is to succeed. In a major comparative study, Sebastian Saiegh (2011:89) finds that presidents with single-party majority governments are more likely to have their initiatives passed by their legislatures than presidents whose parties are part of a majority coalition, or presidents whose party is in the minority. But contrary to the findings for the United States, the differences are not substantial, with even minority-party presidents enjoying an average success rate of 62 percent.

In addition to these partisan factors, the formal powers granted to the president under a nation's constitution also constitute an important variable (see Alcántara and García Montero 2008; Jones 1996). Less easily measurable, because it is more subjective, is the degree to which what has been passed by Congress resembles what the president proposes. Sometimes it isn't clear exactly what the president wanted, and even when that is known, it may be difficult to judge how much of what he wanted was approved. Finally, it is important in such studies to differentiate the president's success on relatively minor matters from his success on major policy initiatives. Presumably, succeeding only on the former does not constitute presidential success to the same extent as a record of success on the latter.[2]

Although the approach emphasizing the balance of partisan power and the nature of formal presidential powers allows for data-driven statistical analyses, it does not incorporate other explanations for presidential success or failure. Saiegh (2011) emphasizes the unpredictability of legislative voting behavior as a major factor in explaining executives' failures to gain approval for their proposals. Richard Neustadt (1980), one of the earliest and most influential students of the US presidency, argued that presidential power is primarily the power to persuade, a perspective that leads to a consideration of the personal characteristics of presidents, their leadership styles and skills, and their ability to bargain effectively with members of Congress and with other political actors whose support they require if they are to succeed. These factors, of course, are exceedingly difficult to assess or to quantify and therefore difficult to look at comparatively, either across administrations in one country, or cross-nationally, and because of that are usually not incorporated into systematic comparative models of presidential success. Rather, it is from the in-depth case studies of individual presidents, as told by journalists and historians, and through the memoirs of presidents and those who serve with them, as well as archival documents, that this information emerges.

Finally, it is important to assess the ability of the president to draw upon his connection with the people in order to generate legislative support for his policy agenda. For more than two decades, US political scientists, following the lead of Samuel Kernell (1986), have suggested that presidents' success may depend on their ability to "go public"—to generate public support for their policy proposals by using much the same techniques that they employed in their successful campaigns for office. Although originally conceived as an alternative approach to the Neustadt idea that presidents must bargain with congressional leaders in order to achieve legislative success, it now seems clear that going public can be seen as complementary to the bargaining approach. That is, presidents go public in order to generate support for their policy initiatives, which in turn improves their bargaining position with members of Congress, who, it is argued, will be more responsive to policy initiatives that appear to have the support of the people. The connection that the president has with the people is one of the driving forces of presidentialism and will be more fully discussed in Chapter 6.

Constitutional Powers

In a presidential system, a nation's constitution will specify certain powers that are exclusive to the president and that may not be exercised by other branches of government, particularly the legislature (Shugart and Carey 1992:148–155). These constitutional powers will vary substantially across nations, with some presidents in possession of a more impressive array of powers than others. In order to measure and compare the constitutional power of presidents, one could use a checklist approach that proceeds from a comprehensive list of presidential powers and simply adds up the various powers each president has. The most well known such list was developed by Timothy Frye (1997) and contains twenty-seven presidential powers ranging from the president's ability to dissolve Parliament to his right to convene and participate in cabinet meetings.[3] The problem with such a list is the implied equal weighting of all powers, even though some obviously will be much more significant than others. Such an approach also ignores the gap that often exists between the words of the Constitution and the practices that take place under it.

An alternative approach, developed by Matthew Shugart and John Carey (1992), reduces the list of powers to ten and provides scores from 0 to 4, thus attempting to pick up the nuances of different constitutional systems.[4] Shugart and Carey identify six powers relevant to the role of president in the lawmaking process: his decree authority, his right to introduce legislation for the consideration of Congress, his budgetary power, the rules governing his role in proposing referenda, and two dealing with the nature of his veto power. Three of the remaining four powers refer to the extent of his control of the executive branch of government—specifically his role in the appointment and dismissal of cabinet members and the capacity of the legislature to censure cabinet members. The final power is the ability of the president to dissolve the legislature and to call for new elections. Another way of thinking about these powers is in reactive versus proactive terms. The veto power, for example, is a way for the president to react to legislation that he doesn't support. Proactive powers involve his ability to introduce legislation and propose referenda—in other words, to set the agenda for the legislature and thereby advance his policy proposals. Obviously, presidents with proactive powers are more powerful than those whose powers are solely reactive.

The Veto

Most presidents have the power to veto legislation, although there are exceptions. In Indonesia, if the president refuses to sign a bill within thirty days of its passage, it automatically becomes law (Fish and Kroenig 2009:318), and in Costa Rica, the president is not permitted to veto the national budget (Carey 1997). In some countries, such as Brazil, Colombia, and South Africa, Congress can override a president's veto with a simple majority, which means in essence that the president's veto is just a delaying power, because the congressional majority that passed the original legislation presumably can reassert itself on a veto override. In Shugart and Carey's scoring system, they consider a majority override provision equivalent to the absence of a presidential veto power. But in most countries with presidential systems, the veto is a more potent power, because a successful override requires a supermajority, typically two-thirds of the membership of the legislature, as is the case in the United States. At one time in Ecuador, the presidential veto was virtually absolute, with only budget bills allowed to become law without the president's approval (Shugart and Mainwaring 1997:43).

One major weakness of the veto power, regardless of its finality, is its negative nature. That is, the veto can stop the legislature from acting but cannot necessarily make it do what the president would like it to do. It is not clear, for example, how the veto power could have helped Barack Obama gain congressional approval for his healthcare proposals, or helped George W. Bush gain approval for his successful tax cut proposals or his unsuccessful proposal to restructure the social security system. In fact, a threatened presidential veto may be a more positive power than the actual veto itself. That is, a president, by making a credible threat to veto a piece of legislation, may be able to convince the legislature to amend the legislation in a manner that would make it more acceptable to him, assuming of course that the legislature would rather have some legislation on the topic than no legislation at all. It is difficult to identify veto threats and how seriously they are made or taken, and assessing their impact on legislative decisionmaking is more a task for political journalists than for political scientists, but certainly there is anecdotal evidence from the United States that such threats have worked (Jarvis 2010). And in most Latin American countries, the president has the opportunity to attach "amendatory observations" to those items that he vetoes; these suggestions about how a bill should be changed allow him to turn the negative power of the veto into a proactive agenda-setting power on those items (Tsebelis and Aleman 2005).[5]

In several countries, the other major weakness of the veto power is its all-or-nothing nature. In the United States, even if there is only a single provision of a piece of legislation that the president does not like, he must veto the entire bill to reject that provision. He does not have an item veto—the power to veto specific parts of the legislation while accepting others. In contrast, the president of Chile can veto portions of legislation while accepting other parts, and the president of the Philippines has an item veto for appropriations bills (Croissant 2003:76). In some countries a president's item veto allows him to promulgate the parts of the law to which he does not object, but in other countries the president must send the entire bill back to Congress. In Colombia, when an item-vetoed bill is returned to Congress, the legislature is permitted to consider only the portion of the bill that has been vetoed, so the president does not run the risk of being presented with a new bill with an entirely new set of provisions (Archer and Shugart 1997).

In the United States in 1996, Congress passed legislation providing the president with an item veto that, in the event of a budget deficit, he could apply to specific portions of spending bills or bills providing tax breaks. However, two years later, in 1998, the Supreme Court declared this legislation unconstitutional (*Clinton v. New York*), contending that it violated the constitutionally mandated lawmaking process, which requires that legislation passed by Congress be presented to the president for his signature.[6] Under current US law, the president can propose that certain expenditures be rescinded, with Congress having forty-five days to act. If Congress does not approve the rescissions, the money must be released. This process has never been used successfully, with Congress generally ignoring such presidential requests. In May 2010 the Obama administration proposed a change in the law that would require Congress to vote on such presidential requests within a specific time frame (Calmes 2010), but Congress did not act on the president's proposal.

Signing Statements

To deal with the all-or-nothing deficiency of the veto power, US presidents have made more aggressive use of the written statements, known as signing statements, that for most of US history they have issued upon signing legislation. Typically, such statements have been relatively innocuous documents congratulating the legislators who were responsible for designing a piece of legislation, or noting the legislation's significant impact on a particular public policy problem. Signing statements also have been used by presidents to create a record of their understanding of the law and to signal to the rest of the bureaucracy how he wishes the law to be interpreted and implemented. But more recently, presidents have used these statements to indicate that they do not intend to enforce a portion of the law, in most instances citing constitutional grounds for their position, usually that the legislation in question has infringed on their authority and prerogatives.

Thus, in December 2005, the US Congress included a provision in a supplemental funding bill for the Defense Department that prohibited the use of "cruel, inhuman, or degrading treatment or punishment" against anyone detained by the US government. This section was a response to the reports that torture and other "enhanced" interrogation techniques were being used as part of President George W. Bush's war on terror. When the bill passed Congress, the president signed it, but issued a statement that said, in part, that "the executive branch shall construe Title X in Division A of the Act, relating to detainees, in a manner consistent with the constitutional authority of the President to supervise the unitary executive branch and as Commander in Chief and consistent with the constitutional limitations on the judicial power, which will assist in achieving the shared objective of the Congress and the President, evidenced in Title X, of protecting the American people from further terrorist attacks." What the president was saying, in essence, was that only he, as commander in chief, and not Congress or the judiciary, could decide how the government could deal with those suspected of plotting against the nation.[7]

The volume of President Bush's signing statements is extraordinary in historical perspective. During his administration, he used signing statements to challenge 1,168 provisions of legislation, more than the total number of provisions challenged by Ronald Reagan, George H. W. Bush, and Bill Clinton in their combined twenty years in office. While running for president in 2008, then Senator Obama criticized this use of signing statements and promised that he would not employ them as freely as President Bush had. Once in office, Obama repeated this commitment, saying that "in exercising my responsibility to determine whether a provision of an enrolled bill is unconstitutional, I will act with caution and restraint, based only on interpretations of the Constitution that are well-founded" (Savage 2009).

In his first year as president, Obama issued nine signing statements, much fewer than the twenty-four that Bush produced in his first year. But at least one of Obama's statements provoked serious controversy. Late in 2009, when Congress passed legislation dealing with the International Monetary Fund (IMF), it included provisions that would have required the Obama administration to pressure the World Bank to strengthen environmental and labor standards and would have required the Treasury Department to report to Congress on the activities of the World Bank and the IMF. In his signing statement, President Obama indicated that these provisions of the bill "would interfere with my constitutional authority to conduct foreign relations by directing the Executive to take certain positions in negotiations or discussions with international organizations and foreign governments, or by requiring consultation with the Congress prior to such negotiations or discussions. I will not treat these provisions as limiting my ability to engage in foreign diplomacy or negotiations." In this case, then, the president's signing statement defended his unilateral authority to decide the foreign policy of the United States. The statement triggered a decidedly negative reaction from Congress (both houses of which were controlled at the time by the president's Democratic co-partisans) with the chairs of the relevant committees threatening to cut off IMF and World Bank funding in its entirety if the president ignored congressional wishes. Privately, the Obama administration conveyed to Congress that it intended to follow its wishes in regard to these issues, but that it felt it necessary to issue a formal defense of the president's power in regard to foreign policy (Nather 2009).

The constitutional argument for signing statements turns on the theory of the unitary presidency, which in turn is based on a reading of Article II of the US Constitution. That article begins by vesting the executive power in the president of the United States; it then goes on to instruct the president to "take care that the laws be faithfully executed," charges him with appointing all principal officers of the United States, and empowers him to request in writing the opinions of these officers upon any subject relating to their duties. Supporters of the unitary executive theory take these provisions to mean that the executive power is entirely in the hands of the president, that he has been endowed with hierarchical control of the executive branch, and therefore that he exercises complete control over the executive branch and all who work within it. The only way that Congress can regulate the executive, the theory holds, is by withholding funds, by passing legislation abolishing an agency, or by removing an agency's authority to act in a specific policy area. The latter two actions would require that Congress pass legislation and send it to the president for his signature. Failing such steps, once an agency has been authorized and funded, the president is in charge.

The argument then moves to the view that the intent of the Founders was to allow each of the three branches of the government to interpret and defend its constitutional powers. This view draws inspiration from James Madison's words in the 49th Federalist Paper that "the several departments being perfectly co-ordinate . . . none of them, it is evident, can pretend to an exclusive or superior right of settling the boundaries between their respective powers" (see Kelley and Barilleaux 2006). Aside from constitutional arguments, the theory of the unitary presidency finds additional justification in the idea of accountability. Presidential control of the bureaucracy ensures that an elected official will be accountable for what the executive branch of government does.

This view has been challenged on a number of counts. The first is that the US Constitution envisions the veto as the president's primary instrument for defending his prerogatives. Some of the Founders even believed that the only circumstances that would justify a presidential veto would be his view that an act of Congress was unconstitutional. Although this limited interpretation of the veto power formally lapsed with the presidency of Andrew Jackson, the argument remains that the Constitution does not provide the president with a line-item veto; if he believes that legislation infringes on his powers, he must veto the entire bill. With a signing statement, the president can say, as President Bush did in the Defense Department appropriations bill, or as President Obama did in the IMF bill, that he accepts the money that Congress has provided, but in effect he is vetoing the strings that Congress has placed on the use of these funds. In this sense, critics argue that the signing statement is an item veto by another name.

Second, signing statements also constitute the final word on legislation; a veto can be overridden by Congress, but there is no opportunity for Congress to override a signing statement. The signing statement thus is the equivalent of an absolute veto, because the president asserts that he is not going to enforce the disputed provision of the legislation, but does not return it to Congress so that the legislature will have the opportunity to override his decision. Third, signing statements and the unitary theory of presidential power that justifies them, create the possibility of a constitutional crisis, because, as President Bush asserted, the president can use signing statements to defend his prerogatives not just against Congress but also against the judiciary. The implication is that the president has the final say on the definition of his constitutional prerogatives. The use of signing statements in that manner in effect makes the president the final arbiter of the law and therefore places him potentially above the law. To date, the courts have shown no inclination to challenge the president on this position. As discussed previously, the task of the Enlightenment thinkers was to place the executive under the rule of law. Signing statements seem to do the opposite.

Unilateral Action: Decrees

Although signing statements do not give US presidents the power to make new law, they can allow the president to unilaterally suspend provisions that are on the books. Decree power, on the other hand, gives a president the ability to actually make new laws or suspend existing laws.

In those countries where presidential decree power exists, the nature of the power can vary depending upon the role of the legislature. In Chile, for example, the legislature must authorize the president to issue decrees. In countries such as Brazil and Indonesia, the president does not require advanced authorization, but a decree lapses unless it is approved by the legislature within a specified time frame. In countries such as Peru and Colombia, the decree is in effect unless the legislature votes specifically to nullify it. In countries such as Russia, Cameroon, and the Dominican Republic, presidential decrees cannot be overturned by the legislature, and in Venezuela, Mali, and Tanzania, decree power is supposed to be authorized by the legislature, but such requirements have been regularly ignored by presidents (Carey and Shugart 1998:10–11; Fish and Kroenig 2009).

In regard to the issue areas in which the decree power can be used, in the 1990s, Peruvian presidents had wide discretion because they were able to exercise decree authority "on economic and financial matters, when so required by the national interest." In Brazil, the power is presumably designed for specific situations, but in practice the president has made what one group of scholars refers to as "indiscriminate use of the device" (Alston et al. 2006:18). In Argentina, presidents can issue "necessary and urgency decrees" under "exceptional circumstance" (Fish and Kroenig 2009:37–80). Between 1853 and 1983 in Argentina, only 25 such decrees were issued; between 2003 and 2006, President Nestor Kirchner issued 193 such decrees (Spiller and Tommasi 2008:107–108). What constitutes "exceptional circumstances" is a subject of some dispute. For example, President Cristina Fernández de Kirchner issued a decree in 2008 that increased the Argentinean national budget by $11.6 billion, arguing that the need was urgent and could not wait for the delay that would be involved if the proposal was processed through the legislature (Rose-Ackerman, Desierto, and Volosin 2011:258–259). Even if there are limits on presidential decree power, however, it still gives the president an important public policy advantage, because it enables him to set the agenda and, especially in cases where the decree goes into effect unless the legislature acts, can force the legislature to deal with an issue that it may not wish to tackle.

The availability of the decree power does not guarantee that presidents will use it. In Latin America, where presidential decree power of some sort is relatively common, political scientists have tried to understand the circumstances under which presidents employ that power. Two conflicting schools of thought have emerged. One argues that presidents will use decrees when they are frustrated by their inability to gain congressional support for their proposals. That is, presidents who are unable to move their policies and priorities through a recalcitrant legislature resort to decree authority as a way to break the deadlock and force action (Cox and Morgenstern 2002). An alternative theory is that presidential decrees are more likely to be employed in situations where the president has a supportive legislature that is willing to delegate decisionmaking authority to him, either because it is politically convenient for legislators to avoid responsibility for what may be difficult policy decisions or because a legislative majority shares the president's priorities and wants him to be able to act in an expeditious manner. A detailed study of decrees in Brazil suggests that overall, presidential reliance on decrees generally did increase when congressional support declined, but that for certain individual presidencies, particularly that of Fernando Cardoso in the mid-1990s, decree reliance increased even during a period when the president enjoyed relatively strong support from Congress (Pereira, Power, and Renno 2005).

Toward the end of the twentieth century, as Brazil and Chile moved from military-dominated governing systems to civilian democracies, presidencies were created that were stronger than those that existed during prior democratic periods. In those earlier eras, presidents did not have decree power, but the new constitutions that followed the end of military rule aimed to fortify these presidencies, and one way to do this was to endow them with the power to issue decrees. In Brazil, presidents used this power with relative abandon; in the three-year period between 1985 and 1988, President José Sarney issued 144 decree laws, accounting for roughly 33 percent of the new legislation of the country during that period. His successor, Fernando Collor de Mello, issued 37 decrees in his first sixty days in office (Mainwaring 1997:92, 95; see also Alston et al. 2008:125).

But as Scott Mainwaring (1997) points out, the impact of presidential decree power in Brazil may be somewhat less than the raw numbers suggest. Congress has the power to amend or reject presidential decrees, and when presidents lose popularity, such congressional interventions are more likely to occur, especially given the fact that Brazilian presidents typically operate in an environment in which their political party is a minority in Congress and often an undisciplined minority at that. During the late 1990s, Congress threatened to restrict the president's decree power, something that ultimately occurred with the constitutional amendments of 2002. This suggests some support for the notion that the use of presidential decree power in Brazil to some extent depends upon the sufferance of Congress. Because of party fractionalization and the inevitable drop in public support that most presidents experience after their election, Brazilian presidents ultimately need to negotiate with Congress, their apparently strong constitutional powers notwithstanding. A similar situation exists in Colombia, one in which presidents with a seeming vast array of constitutional powers find it difficult to enact reforms, in large measure because of an exceedingly fractionalized party system (Archer and Shugart 1997).

In Chile, presidents also have made relatively little use of their decree power. Instead, in order to move their policy initiatives through Congress, they have more frequently relied on negotiations with the party coalition that makes up the legislative majority. Given the circumstances of the transition from authoritarianism to democracy as well as the coalitional party structure under which Chilean presidents have operated during the current democratic period, presidents "had more to gain from a combined strategy of cajoling, convincing, and accommodating the opposition than from an imperial imposition of their constitutionally vested authority" (Siavelis 2002:109). It is, of course, also possible that one reason that these negotiation strategies succeeded was that all participants knew that the president had the power to act unilaterally and that this knowledge strengthened the president's bargaining position.

In Venezuela during the 1958–1995 constitutional period, presidents were occasionally given wide-ranging decree authority for a limited time, especially if their parties held majorities in Congress. Such temporary decree authority was typically restricted to certain policy areas, although the restrictions tended to be vaguer for presidents with party majorities in Congress than for presidents who did not enjoy such majorities. But the delegation of decree authority to presidents, majority or minority, usually reflected instances when Congress concluded that action was necessary and concluded as well that the tedious process of congressional deliberation would be unlikely to produce results in a timely manner (Crisp 1997).

Similarly, in Argentina in 1989, in the midst of a period of significant social unrest attributable to hyperinflation, legislators, including members of the opposition, agreed to the Administrative Emergency Act and the Economic Emergency Act, delegating unilateral power to President Carlos Menem to deal with the situation (Mustapic 2002:40). During the 1990s, Argentinean presidents increased their reliance on decree power, issuing an average of 4.4 decrees a month; during the 2001–2003 economic crisis, there were 9.3 decrees a month (Rose-Ackerman, Desierto, and Volosin 2011:258).

Unilateral Action: Executive Orders

Although US presidents do not have formal decree power, executive orders and presidential directives exhibit some of the same characteristics. Executive orders do not make new law; rather they are presidential interpretations of existing law and thus constitute the president's instructions to the bureaucracy about how the law should be implemented. Thus, executive orders are based on the president's power as chief executive to "take care that the laws are faithfully executed" and in that sense their functional equivalents presumably exist in every country. Presidential directives are a bit different; they deal with issues of national security and constitute the president's exercise of discretionary power as delegated to him by Congress as well as by the commander in chief clause of the Constitution.

Presidents can use executive orders entrepreneurially in the sense that they can preempt legislative action by acting first. George W. Bush used an executive order to start his initiative to encourage religious groups to seek federal funds to assist them in dealing with societal problems. President Bill Clinton issued an executive order that barred the federal government from discriminating against workers on the basis of sexual orientation (Macey 2006:2422). When Barack Obama became president in January 2009, one of his first steps was to issue an executive order to close the prison facility at Guantanamo Bay that the United States had been maintaining for the incarceration of suspected enemy combatants. This was a subject of some controversy, and it was not at all clear that there would have been a legislative majority to support it had the president made this proposal to Congress. But it was argued that the unilateral powers that the president enjoyed under the commander in chief clause of the Constitution—the same power that President Bush used when the detention facility was first established—allowed him to act without congressional consultation or consent. On the other hand, Congress was able to respond to this executive order by withholding some of the funds that the president needed in order to implement his plan.

Executive orders can be reversed either by congressional legislation (which presumably the president could veto, thereby protecting his order) or by the decision of a new president. Executive orders, therefore, are not the same as actual legislation, because they can be reversed by a new president's executive order. Obama, early in his presidency, issued orders reversing President Bush's executive orders that had restricted stem cell research and barred aid to international groups that supported abortion rights. Obama also issued an executive order explicitly barring the use of torture in interrogating those suspected of terrorism, reversing a widely suspected but formally disavowed policy of the Bush administration.

As was the case in Brazil in regard to decree power, it isn't clear if US presidents are more or less likely to issue executive orders when they face congressional resistance or when they have supportive congresses. Research has found evidence for both points of view. More executive orders seem to be issued when the president's level of public support is low, but there are also more orders issued when the president's party holds a majority in Congress (Mayer 2002). William Howell's (2003:177) research suggests that presidents are likely to act unilaterally when Congress is gridlocked or when Congress is poised to act in a manner opposed by the president. In the latter case, he may act unilaterally in order to head off congressional action calling for more sweeping changes.

Such studies need to distinguish between significant and trivial executive orders. Many such orders involve rather minor and noncontroversial actions; by one estimate, no more than 15 percent of executive orders are important in the sense that they attract public or congressional notice or make significant changes in public policy (Mayer and Price 2002). Howell (2003:84) has noted an increase in the number of significant executive orders in the post–World War II era, a phenomenon that he believes reflects the growth of presidential power in the last half of the twentieth century. Some of those important executive orders have allowed presidents to stake out positions and to make significant, often dramatic changes in government policy with the stroke of a pen and without congressional approval. Thus, in 1948, President Harry Truman ended segregation in the armed forces with an executive order, and thirteen years later, in 1961, President Kennedy issued an executive order creating the Equal Employment Opportunity Committee and granting it broad enforcement powers.

Unilateral Action: Emergency Powers

Emergency powers are different from decree powers because the former involve the temporary suspension of constitutional provisions at a time when the nation is facing some obvious and clearly defined peril, while the latter constitute a constitutionally authorized policymaking option that is usually exercised in the normal course of administering the law. Emergency powers are in many respects the ultimate challenge to the idea of a limited executive, because they have the potential, depending upon how they are phrased, understood, and applied, to allow the president to ignore the very constitutional provisions that are supposed to limit his power.

To guard against this possibility, some constitutions vest the power to declare a state of emergency with Parliament, while others require that a presidential request for such powers be endorsed by Congress. In Costa Rica the endorsement must be by a two-thirds vote of the legislature, and in Slovakia the requirement is for a three-fifths majority. In Mexico the president can declare a state of emergency, but it must be authorized by Congress if it is in session; if the legislature is not in session, it must be convened without delay. The emergency declaration must be for a limited time and cannot be directed at a specific individual, and certain basic civil rights cannot be suspended (see Martinez 2006:2500).

In Poland, on the other hand, the president is authorized to introduce a state of emergency and need not consult with any other political actors or office holders (Ganev 1997:590). Similarly, Philippine presidents have virtually unchecked emergency powers. In 2006, President Gloria Arroyo, citing national security threats posed by "authoritarians on the extreme left" and "military adventurists of the extreme right," issued an emergency order under which rally permits issued by local Philippine governments were canceled, and the police dispersed assemblies, raided opposition newspapers, and arrested opposition leaders. The president lifted the order after one week, saying that the emergency had passed (Rose-Ackerman, Desierto, and Volosin 2011:267).

In France, Article 16 of the Constitution allows the president to introduce emergency measures to deal with situations "where the institution of the Republic, the independence of the Nation, the integrity of its territory or the fulfillment of its international obligations are under serious and immediate threat, and where the proper functioning of the constitutional public authorities is interrupted." He is required to formally consult (but need not gain the approval of) the premier, the presiding officers of the two houses of Parliament, and the Constitutional Council, and after declaring the emergency he must address the nation and inform it of his actions. However, he cannot use his emergency powers to dissolve the National Assembly. A 2008 amendment to the Constitution provided that the Constitutional Council can respond to a request from parliamentary leaders or sixty members of Parliament to review the exercise of emergency powers to determine if the conditions that provoked the exercise of these powers still apply.

Article 16 has been used only once—shortly after Charles de Gaulle came to power—to deal with the Algerian crisis. More common has been the use of Article 36, which allows the government to declare a state of siege, which means the establishment of martial law and the temporary suspension of certain civil liberties. Unlike the emergency provision, a state of siege can be declared by the cabinet, not by the president, and can last no more that twelve days unless reauthorized by Parliament. In practice, this has meant a joint decision of the president and the cabinet; during periods when the president and the cabinet have been of the same political party, the state of siege is likely to be initiated by the president. This provision was invoked in the autumn of 2005 during three weeks of rioting in more than 250 French towns and cities, primarily involving immigrant populations. At the end of the twelve-day period, the National Assembly voted to extend the emergency for three months.

In the case of the United States, emergency powers do not exist in the Constitution. Rather, they have been created by presidents responding to extraordinary circumstances, especially those associated with war. During the Civil War, Abraham Lincoln declared that he had emergency powers based upon his constitutional authority as commander in chief and his responsibility to see to it that the laws were faithfully executed. Using these emergency powers, he imposed martial law, spent money without the consent of Congress, and issued the Emancipation Proclamation, among other steps. Franklin Roosevelt used emergency powers to declare a bank holiday two days after he was sworn into office, and his executive order to remove Japanese Americans from the West Coast after the attack on Pearl Harbor constituted a similar exercise of such power. George W. Bush's decision to ignore certain provisions of the Foreign Intelligence Surveillance Act (FISA) in order to deal with the threat of terrorism is still another example of a de facto claim of emergency powers.

The term "emergency" implies that time is short because a crisis, perhaps an existential crisis, is at hand, and unless immediate action outside the normal constitutional procedures is taken, serious and adverse consequences for the nation will result. Alexander Hamilton referred to these situations as ones that "would not brook delay" and that would require an energetic executive to act. Presumably, in the face of such a crisis, the constitutional limitations that require legislative consultation or consent might be ignored. The Justice Department, in defending President Bush's actions in regard to FISA, claimed that the president "determined that the speed and agility required to carry out the NSA [National Security Agency] activities successfully could not have been achieved under FISA." That meant that "FISA would impermissibly interfere with the President's most solemn constitutional obligation"—to defend the country—and therefore that applying FISA would in effect be "unconstitutional" (Koh 2006:2356). In other words, almost by definition it may not be possible to limit a US president's assertion of emergency powers (short of impeachment), because he and he alone decides whether or not an emergency exists and what actions need to be taken. Also, because these actions typically involve national security issues, presidents need not (and perhaps cannot) justify them to the public.

Benjamin Kleinerman (2009:8ff.) has suggested that US presidents have erred by declaring that emergency powers are constitutional. First, acts that are contrary to the language of the Constitution are by definition unconstitutional. But more important, Kleinerman argues, when presidents say that such powers are constitutional, it becomes unnecessary for them to defend the necessity of the emergency actions that they have taken. In such a context, presidents will be tempted to conflate the idea of an emergency with their desire to exercise power unimpeded by other political actors. Instead, presidents should frankly admit that they have acted unconstitutionally; such an admission would compel them to explain why such actions were necessary. If the president can convincingly demonstrate necessity, then other political actors, such as legislators, judges, and opinion leaders, are likely to accept the legitimacy (if not the constitutionality) of the president's actions. On the other hand, if the president is unable to make such an argument, that can be taken as an indicator that there is in fact no emergency and that unilateral presidential action is unwarranted.

The problem with this approach is that if there is a general sense that the president has failed to make a convincing argument, it isn't clear what consequences might ensue. In the US context, as we will see, the judiciary has been reluctant to check presidential use of emergency powers and the only power that Congress might have is the seldom used power of impeachment. This also has been the case in the Philippines, where the country's Supreme Court, in a case challenging the president's assertion of emergency powers, concluded that at such times, the Constitution "reasonably demands that we repose a certain amount of faith in the basic integrity and wisdom of the Chief Executive" (Rose-Ackerman, Desierto, and Volosin 2011:268). Because presidents tend to justify their use of emergency powers by invoking apocalyptic scenarios that their actions are designed to avert, there is little likelihood of significant public opposition. In the final analysis, the only real guard against presidential abuse of emergency declarations may be their own sense of self-restraint.

Proposing Legislation

In addition to executive orders, all presidents are permitted to suggest legislation for consideration by the legislature, but in some countries the ability of Congress to amend legislation introduced by the president is limited, and in others only the president can introduce legislation in certain specified policy areas, usually the budget, but sometimes military matters (see Shugart and Mainwaring 1997:48). In several countries, presidents can declare that their policy proposals are urgent; such a declaration requires Congress to act within a specified period of time, and in some instances the failure to act will mean that the proposal becomes law (Carey and Shugart 1998:13). In Ecuador, for example, the president can label a legislative proposal as "economically urgent"; if Congress does not act within thirty days to either approve, modify, or reject the bill, the president can promulgate the bill as an executive decree (Fish and Kroenig 2009:201). Sometimes the ability of the legislature to initiate legislation is restricted in favor of an increased presidential role. In Chile, only the president can initiate bills dealing with the budget, taxes, labor regulations, social security, and the armed forces (Aninat et al. 2008:179). The Colombian and Philippine constitutions restrict Congress's role on budgetary matters (Carey and Shugart 1998:9; Siavelis 2002:16–17; Archer and Shugart 1997; Case 2011:36). US presidents have the constitutional right to suggest legislation for the consideration of Congress, but they have no formal right to actually introduce legislation. In practice, legislation can be written in the White House, but a friendly legislator introduces the bill on behalf of the administration in one of the two chambers. The president has no ability to declare legislation urgent or to set formal time limits for Congress to act.

In several Latin American countries, presidents are permitted to place a referendum on the ballot. This can be either a reactive or a proactive power. If Congress has rejected a presidential initiative, a referendum can give him one more opportunity to enact his policy preferences without gaining the approval of the legislature. Presidents also can use this power proactively by initiating a referendum in order to bypass the legislature entirely. Both sorts of referenda are powerful tools in the hands of a president, but the proactive option is seen as a particularly effective way for a popularly supported president to undermine the legislature, by allowing him to legislate simply by popular consent. In several Latin American countries, both the president and Congress have the right to place a referendum before the people, thereby allowing Congress to check what it may view as arbitrary presidential action (see Breuer 2007).

There are even occasions when nonbinding referenda can be helpful to a president. Although presidentially introduced referenda are not provided for in the Argentinean Constitution, in 1984, President Raúl Alfonsín, faced with congressional opposition to the Beagle Treaty, which he had negotiated with Chile, called for an advisory referendum on the issue. After 82 percent of the voters supported the treaty, the Senate agreed to it, albeit by one vote. Using the referendum in this way can be seen as a version of "going public," in the sense that it allows the president to demonstrate to Congress that there is popular support for his position (Mustapic 2002:41).

Presidential Independence

A second set of constitutional powers of the president affect the degree to which he is independent of the legislature. These include his freedom to decide who to appoint to his cabinet as well as to other administrative positions, whether or not he has the unilateral authority to dismiss his appointees, and whether he can dissolve the legislature. In the United States, most presidential appointees are subject to confirmation by the Senate, but dismissal (with the exception of judges and members of independent regulatory agencies) is a unilateral power of the president. Presidents even have made the argument that they have the authority, citing the unitary theory of the presidency, to dismiss members of independent regulatory agencies, an assertion that has been rejected by the Supreme Court. In Argentina, on the other hand, the Constitution does not require Congress to confirm presidential appointments; the president alone makes the appointments (Rose-Ackerman, Desierto, and Volosin 2011:288). In Russia's mixed presidential system, the president appoints the prime minister, subject to the legislature's approval, but if the legislature rejects the president's nominee three successive times, the legislature is dissolved. The president can dismiss the prime minister at any time, and the heads of several key ministries—defense, foreign affairs, internal affairs, and security—are appointed directly by the president and report to him rather than to the prime minister (Ryabov 2004:92). In France's mixed system, in contrast, the president's nominee for premier must command majority support of Parliament, and the premier appoints the members of the cabinet; however, when the president and the premier are of the same party, the president's role in the process is both significant and decisive.

In some countries the legislature is able to censure the president, and in a few others—France, Russia, Sri Lanka, are examples—the president has the ability to dissolve the legislature and call for new legislative elections. In France, to avoid a situation of a cabinet controlled by one party and a presidency controlled by another, newly elected French presidents have on occasion dissolved Parliament in the hope that new elections would return a Parliament that they would control (see Hayward 1993).

Instruments such as the veto, signing statements, and executive orders, along with decree and emergency powers, and the right to initiate legislation and referenda, constitute the primary elements of presidential policymaking influence. Control over appointments and the right to dissolve Parliament are elements that strengthen the presidency by ensuring its independence from the legislature. These factors are summarized and exemplified in Table 3.1. Arrangements to the left side of the table imply stronger presidential policymaking power and possibly hyperpresidentialism, while those to the right suggest weaker, more constrained presidentialism.

Presidents and Their Parties

As suggested at the outset of this chapter, constitutions do not tell the entire story of presidential power. Though some constitutions provide presidents with a wider array of formal powers than do others, the extent of a president's power and the strategies that he needs to adopt to advance his policy priorities also will depend upon the nature of the country's party system. There are two variables that are important here: whether or not the president's party constitutes a majority of the legislature, and whether or not the legislators who are members of the president's party have strong incentives to support his leadership. The first variable, and to some extent the second, are affected by the system that a country uses to elect its legislators.

There are two broad categories of electoral systems: single-member district arrangements, in which each legislative constituency is represented by only one legislator, and proportional representation systems, in which each constituency is represented by multiple legislators divided among the political parties according to the percentage of the vote that each party receives.[8] Proportional representation systems tend to be associated with a multiparty system, while single-member district systems are characterized by relatively few political parties. Therefore, a single political party is more likely to achieve a legislative majority under a single-member district system than under a proportional representation system. But all proportional representation systems are not the

Table 3.1   Presidential Powers: A Continuum

	More Power ◄————————————————► Less Power			
Veto	Line item *Chile*	Amendatory *Mexico*	Bloc veto *United States*	No veto power *Indonesia*
Veto override		Extraordinary majority *United States*	Simple majority *Brazil*	
Decree power	Presidential decrees are final *Russia*	Congress can nullify *Côte d'Ivoire*	Congress must approve *Colombia*	No decree power *Ghana*
Subject limits of decrees	None *Russia*	Vague *Argentina*		
Emergency powers	Presidential discretion *Poland*	Consultation required *France*	Legislative approval required *Mexico*	None *United States*
Introduction of legislation	Urgency declaration requiring legislative action *Ecuador*	Exclusive presidential power in some areas *Chile*		No formal power *United States*
Referenda	President can initiate *El Salvador*	President or legislature can initiate *Guatemala*	Advisory referenda *Argentina*	None *United States*
Parliamentary dissolution	Yes *Russia*	With restrictions *France*		No *Argentina*
Appointment power	No legislative role *Argentina*	Some appointments require legislative approval *Russia*		Legislative approval required *United States*

same. Systems in which there are a large number of representatives per district and in which a party needs to obtain only a relatively small percentage of the vote in order to gain representation will produce representation for many more political parties than a system with fewer members per district and a higher threshold for achieving representation. In

Brazil, for example, a large number of members per constituency, combined with the absence of a national threshold for representation, virtually guarantees that many parties, some quite small, will be represented in Congress, with no party holding a majority.

Legislative elections under proportional representation tend to be party-oriented, because it is the party's percentage of the vote that determines the distribution of seats. Single-member district systems tend to be more candidate-oriented; compared with proportional systems, more voters are likely to base their decisions on the qualities of the candidate. Because of this, single-member district systems can produce what David Samuels and Matthew Shugart (2003) refer to as separation of purpose between representatives and presidents (see also Shugart and Haggard 2001). Separation of purpose refers to those features of a nation's electoral and party system that create different political and policy incentives for presidents and legislators and therefore make it less likely that legislators will follow the lead of the president, even if they and he are members of the same party. When representatives are elected from local constituencies in a personalized process characterized by voter decisions based less on party affiliation than on perceived candidate qualities, and when congressional elections do not always take place at the same time as presidential elections, "voters are likely to hold executives responsible for national policy issues while at the same time holding legislators responsible for local or regional concerns" (Samuels and Shugart 2003:55). On the other hand, when representatives campaign on party slates, when parties control the nomination process, and when presidential and congressional elections are held simultaneously, separation of purpose will be less apparent, even in single-member district systems.

When those factors that lead to separation of purpose are strong, a president will encounter greater resistance from the legislature, especially when his party does not hold a legislative majority. He will need to engage in intense bargaining or rely on unilateral powers in order to move his policy priorities forward. When there is little in the way of separation of purpose between a president and his co-partisans in the legislature, and especially when his co-partisans control a legislative majority, the president will be likely to gain support for his policy priorities with less intensive bargaining strategies and without reliance on unilateral powers (see Cox and Morgenstern 2002).

Mexico provides an example of how these variables affect presidential power. The Mexican Constitution suggests a comparatively weak president with no decree power, no special budgetary powers, no ability to dismiss the legislature, and no ability to succeed himself in office.

But during most of the twentieth century, the highly disciplined, well-organized Institutional Revolutionary Party (PRI) dominated Mexican politics. The president and a large percentage of the members of Congress were PRI members, and this enabled Mexican presidents to effectively control the nation's policymaking machinery. But in the last decade of the twentieth century, the PRI lost its nearly hegemonic control over Mexican politics; presidents from other parties were elected and there was no majority party in Congress. The power of the presidency decreased, and congressional resistance to presidential initiatives, virtually unknown when the PRI was in control, became commonplace (Casar 2002; Saiegh 2010:59).

In contrast, during the period from 1993 through 2003, South Korea's presidents exercised strict control over their party's internal procedures as well as its financial resources; they also had a great deal of influence over the nomination of candidates to Parliament. Taken together, this meant that presidents could control policy, because "most parliamentarians were dependent on them" (Croissant 2003:81). As we will see, similar arrangements exist in those African nations that are dominated by a single party. Of course, it is also possible that a president who is a member, or even the leader, of a strong and highly disciplined party, may be constrained by the ideological commitments of the party and by the views and interests of other party leaders.

The United States exemplifies the separation of purpose principle. On the one hand, it is well established that the strongest predictor of a president's success in Congress is the number of his co-partisans in both chambers. A president whose party controls majorities in both chambers is more likely to succeed compared to a president who faces situations of divided government when the opposition party controls one or both chambers of the legislature. However, members of the US Congress are elected from single-member districts; although their party affiliations are important factors in their election and reelection campaigns, their success also depends on their personal qualities, and their ability to satisfy local constituents as well as the interest groups that finance their campaigns. In addition, once every four years, legislative elections are held during the middle of a president's term. This perfect recipe for separation of purpose means that even US presidents whose co-partisans constitute a congressional majority may not be able to count on congressional support for their policy priorities.

In France, with the creation of an independently elected president under the Constitution of the Fifth Republic, some worried that one party might control the presidency while another controlled a parliamentary

majority and therefore the premiership. But one unanticipated consequence of establishing the presidency was that the plethora of political
parties that characterized the Fourth Republic was reduced as parties recognized that they would need a broad base of support if one of their own
was to have any chance to win the presidency. One analyst of French politics concludes that now "parties are conceived as presidential machines,
whose primary function is to act as a springboard for presidential candidates and subsequently to act as an organizational resource for the president" (Clift 2005:225). This tendency toward party consolidation also
was encouraged by the decision to replace the Fourth Republic's proportional representation system for electing legislators with a single-member
district system. A later constitutional change that moved parliamentary
elections to the year right after the presidential election reduced significantly the likelihood that the president's party would not control a majority in the National Assembly. All of this has worked to the advantage of
the president's ability to control public policy.

Bargaining

When presidents are limited in their ability to act unilaterally, or when
the structure of the political party and electoral system is not conducive
to presidential control, presidents must rely on what Richard Neustadt
(1980) referred to as the "power to persuade." Neustadt's analysis
focused on the presidency in the US political system—a highly decen-
tralized party system characterized by separation of purpose, with the
president and members of his party often having quite different electoral
and policy agendas. In that context, Neustadt argued that a successful
president had to know how to use his personal and institutional resources
to bargain effectively with those whose support he required in order to
advance his policy priorities. In Neustadt's model, presidential success as
a bargainer depends upon such variables as the president's personality,
his standing among the people, the perceptions of others in the governing
elite regarding his skill and willingness to use the advantages of his
office, and, perhaps most important, a president's understanding of his
power and how his various decisions and bargains affect the prospects
for future successful bargains (see Nye 2008:83).

   Although developed in the context of the US presidency, Neustadt's
approach is applicable to any political system in which presidents cannot count on the support of a unified majority in the legislature, have
limited powers to act unilaterally, and must create a majority coalition if
they are to be able to govern. Doing so requires the skills that Neustadt

enumerated and particularly a president's ability to use the resources in his possession in order to achieve his goals. In most presidential systems, for example, the president has control over a number of governmental appointments, and in political systems with a weak civil service tradition the president may control virtually all government appointments. Presidents can use their ability to distribute patronage appointments as a way to bolster support for their policy agenda among other political leaders. Presidents can use their popular standing with the people to create public pressures on those with whom they are bargaining. And, of course, presidents usually have some influence over the distribution of governmental funds, influence that they can use to reward supporters and punish enemies.

Bargaining will be most difficult and is least likely to succeed in a polarized political party system where the parties are separated by deep ideological differences that they feel prevent them from bargaining with the president or with their colleagues in the legislature (see Jones 2010:35). Bargaining is easier when either there is a group of legislators who care about national policy decisions and are willing to negotiate with the president on the substance of policy, or there are a significant number of legislators who care little about public policy and are more focused on their own political careers or personal well-being. Legislators may have little concern with national policy issues in those environments where they serve relatively short terms in the legislature either because they are formally term-limited, or because there are more attractive opportunities in the public or private sectors. In either case, such legislators may be open to the rewards and incentives that the president can offer.

Bargaining in this sense can be seen as a form of "clientelism," a broad concept that refers to the use by a leader of resources such as positions and money to maintain the loyalty of one's supporters. From this perspective, presidents act as patrons who supply rewards to followers (clients) in return for the latter's willingness to support them. Clientelism can operate in the context of a party system where the spoils of government are utilized to bolster the political position of the ruling party, or they may be just as important, perhaps more so, in countries with weak or fragmented parties and a strong commitment to personal leadership. In such an environment, legislators are not likely to be interested in building a reputation for their party based on policy accomplishments; instead, they may be more interested in building their own personal reputations in their constituencies by bringing home patronage and pork (Shugart 1998). Presidents, in turn, use their control over these resources to build and maintain a personal coterie of supporters.

After his 2006 reelection, President Luiz Inácio Lula da Silva of Brazil confronted a Congress in which his party had greatly reduced numbers, forcing him to enter into coalition arrangements with more traditional centrist parties (Hunter 2008). These coalitions were held together with patronage and pork barrel concessions to those who supported the president and particularly to those who were willing to switch parties. In Brazil, it is typical for about one-third of the members of Parliament to switch parties during a term. Lula was able to entice several deputies to abandon the party under whose label they won election and join one of the parties in his governing coalition by "capitalizing on many politicians' weak attachments to their parties and on the tradition of *governismo*—a pragmatic desire to obtain the clientelistic benefits of being in the government rather than remaining in opposition" (Samuels 2008:162). This has been a typical approach for Brazilian presidents, who often succeed by "coupling deputies' disinterest in broad policy with their desire for pork." Thus pork, as well as other benefits, is for Brazilian presidents "the medium of exchange to members of Congress in return for their votes on critical pieces of legislation" (Ames 1995:342). These coalitions have proved useful to both presidents and parliamentarians. Lula was able to claim credit for achieving national economic goals, while the representatives claimed credit for particularized benefits that they received as their reward for supporting the president (Melo 2008; Alston and Mueller 2005).

Philippine presidents also have succeeded in enticing legislators to abandon the party under whose label they ran for office and join one of the parties in the president's coalition. As is the case in Brazil, this has been accomplished in the Philippines primarily through the distribution of patronage and pork. By exploiting the disposition of representatives toward "strongly prioritizing patronage, therein negating their motivations to impose accountability [on the president] or undertake legislation," President Arroyo, who served from 2004 through 2010, "found the House quite manageable." Indonesian presidents have used similar techniques to create legislative majorities (Case 2011:41). In Colombia, members of Congress also seem to care little about national policymaking; instead, they focus their efforts "on extracting resources to reward supporters with jobs and other private goods. They will tend to involve themselves in policy only when the policy proposal under consideration furthers their primary interest in converting public funds into private payoffs." Members therefore seek to "make deals with the president over support of his programs in exchange for private goods, especially patronage, which can be provided to a Congress member's constituents" (Archer and Shugart 1997:117, 138).

In Africa, where weak or nonexistent party systems and high levels of personal rule persist, "incumbents are able to use the resources within their discretion to assist clients and followers and thereby maintain and perhaps enlarge their political base" (Jackson and Rosberg 1982:42). On that continent, there appears to be "a normative acceptance of clientelism that characteristically extends beyond those who receive immediate benefits from it," as Linda Beck (2008:37) argues; these arrangements produce both access and accountability in the sense that leaders who do not provide particularized benefits are seen as having violated broader societal norms and are held to account by their followers. The degree to which clientelism is embedded in African cultures means that relations between the president and members of Parliament are based almost entirely on particularistic rewards that redound either to the personal benefit of the legislator or to his or her constituency. In Senegal, according to one student of that country's politics, access to state resources seems to be the major motivation for political activity, these resources are largely under the control of the president, and the state is the largest employer in the country. Thus in Senegal, as is the case in Brazil and the Philippines, after presidential elections there is a mass migration of legislators and other political leaders to the president's party; "the heavy concentration of power in the hands of the presidency and the president's personal control over state resources and jobs provides incentives for politicians to join the winning camp" (Gellar 2005:157–158). This, combined with a tacit understanding that national policymaking is the province of the president, means that there is little legislative involvement in the details of the policymaking process (see Bratton and van de Walle 1997:246–248).

Alternatively, when there is a substantial legislative interest in the substance of policy, presidents follow a different strategy. They may appoint people to their cabinet with an eye toward establishing a majority coalition that can solidify support for their policy priorities. These people may be recognized party leaders, or leaders of factions within parties, who can generate support for the president's priorities in Congress. In some Latin American countries, when a member of the legislature is appointed to a cabinet position, he resigns his seat and is replaced by a temporary substitute; however, the cabinet member can reclaim his seat whenever he wishes. The substitute is likely to be selected by the minister or his party, and therefore will be someone who is responsive to the wishes of the cabinet member. It has been reported that occasionally a Brazilian cabinet member will resign his position just as Congress is about to consider an important piece of legislation, resume his legislative position to participate in the debate and vote, and then resign his legislative position and resume his cabinet position, with the substitute once again replacing him in Congress. Through the substitute provision, the cabinet and by extension the president can become participants in the legislative process (Cox and Morgenstern 2002:458–459).

In addition to using cabinet appointments to support their policy priorities, presidents can have a substantial impact on the legislative agenda. By declaring a proposal urgent and indicating that it could go into effect as a decree unless Congress acts within a period of time, the president can move a policy initiative to the top of the legislature's agenda. More informally, presidents can use their domination of the media to highlight the importance of a proposal and to create pressures for the legislature to consider it. And, of course, presidents can engage in direct negotiations with representatives over the substance of their proposals, offering concessions and altering particular provisions in order to produce the necessary majority.

In Chile during the long democratic period prior to the 1973 coup, presidents were often able to work across party lines to produce far-reaching public policy results on issues such as state-sponsored industrial development, the implementation of national welfare and healthcare systems, agrarian reform, and enhanced government control over the copper industry (Valenzuela 1994:200). This also has occurred in the United States, where successful presidents have been those who are willing to negotiate the details of their domestic policy initiatives either to create bipartisan coalitions, or sometimes simply to unify their own party in support of their initiatives. Although US presidents tend to achieve their greatest successes when both houses of Congress contain a majority of members of their own party, important policies have been enacted in situations when one party has controlled the presidency and the other has controlled Congress (Mayhew 1991). For example, President Clinton was able to move significant changes in welfare policy through a Congress controlled by Republicans, and President Reagan was able to restructure the US tax system despite the fact that Democrats were in solid control of the House of Representatives.

Negotiations over policy and the provision of particularistic incentives are not mutually exclusive strategies. In Chile, negotiations and compromises over important national legislation coexisted with earmarks for local projects and laws providing pensions and other dispensations for specific individuals (Valenzuela and Wilde 1979). US Presidents often promise to support the constituency-related projects of certain representatives and senators in return for the latter's support for presidential policy initiatives. Party leaders in Congress, often acting at the behest of the president, have made and delivered on similar commitments. President Obama's healthcare bill contained several such concessions, most notably to the special concerns raised by senators from Nebraska and Louisiana. These concessions and earmarks have been characterized by one scholar as the necessary grease for the legislative machinery to operate (Evans 2004). Beyond these concrete incentives, presidents have more subtle rewards to offer in return for support. Access to the White House, the promise of a sympathetic hearing for representatives from government bureaucrats in charge of distributing funds, and presidential support for representatives' electoral fundraising efforts have been offered to generate support for the president's policy agenda.

Of course, presidential attempts to bargain and to offer particularistic rewards do not always work. US presidents have seen their policy proposals ignored by Congress—as was the case with George W. Bush's 2005 proposal to reform social security and with Barack Obama's cap and trade proposal to deal with global warming—and they always see their proposals emerge in a quite different form than what they had proposed. Similarly, one analysis of Brazilian politics during the 1990s concludes that Brazilian presidents "face constant and crippling difficulties in moving their agendas through the legislature. Many proposals fail to come to a vote. Others cannot get out of committee. Proposals that survive the legislative process emerge disfigured by substantive concessions and weighted down by pork barrel side payments" (Ames 2002:213).

Presidents always can make the decision to eschew bargaining and attempt to accomplish their goals with unilateral actions. In Ecuador in the period from 1979 to 1988, an "extremely loose" multiparty system made it very difficult for presidents to marshal majorities in Parliament and "created incentives for presidents to bypass or ignore the congress altogether in policy-making" (Conaghan 1994:328). Similarly, in the case of Argentina in the 1990s, even presidents whose parties had a majority in Parliament could not rely on support, given the internal fractionalization of the party. In response, presidents came to rely more heavily on their decree powers to move their policies forward and on their item veto powers to purge legislation of provisions that they did not like (Mustapic 2002). As noted earlier, US presidents, frustrated by actual or prospective congressional resistance, have resorted to executive orders to accomplish their policy goals.

A president's ability to act unilaterally can be enhanced by appropriate constitutional provisions, but it also can have a great deal to do with the tradition of civil-military relations in his nation. In all presidential systems, the president is at least formally in charge of the military. However, in many countries, the military is strictly nonpartisan, it has no role in domestic politics, its primary purpose is to advance and defend the interests of the nation against external enemies, and the president is not an active member of the armed forces. The president in such situations cannot use the military to enhance his power domestically, and his term will not be cut short by the extraconstitutional device of a military coup.

This also seems to be the situation today in most of Latin America, although this was not always so. During the last half of the twentieth century, Latin American military leaders regularly intervened in domestic politics, backing one party over the other and threatening and executing military coups; juntas of military leaders governed for significant periods of time in Brazil, Argentina, and Chile, among other countries, and men with military rank often held the title of president. Even during periods of civilian rule, a president who was supported by the military was in a significantly stronger position, because he could explicitly or implicitly threaten his political opponents with extraconstitutional action, thereby ensuring their silence and often their acquiescence. On the other hand, it is also possible that such a military will turn against a president and depose him. In Chile, President Salvador Allende met that fate. His successor, General Augusto Pinochet, governed under significant constraints imposed upon him by other members of the armed forces, who together with Pinochet himself constituted the military junta (Barros 2002).

In Africa, military coups have been a way of life, with presidents regularly deposed and replaced by other ambitious colonels or generals. As the twentieth century came to a close, observers noted "a dramatic retreat of the military from politics," but also that, "even when the armed forces have formally relinquished powers, their hold on state and society, directly or through civilian surrogates is quite extensive" (Agbese 2003:154–155). In this context, most African presidents need to be conscious of the political position of their military, seeking their support to solidify their political position while at the same time understanding that their terms in office could be abruptly terminated by their erstwhile allies.

Conclusion

All presidential systems are characterized by constitutional arrangements that attempt to balance presidential power and prerogatives with restraints that will protect against the possibility of authoritarianism. There are various constitutional formulas for dealing with presidential power, each striking this balance in a somewhat different manner. These documents specify a wide variety of reactive and proactive powers for presidents, and by surveying these constitutional provisions it is possible to develop a sense of which systems endow presidents with greater or lesser degrees of constitutional power. However, it is also important to note that what is written on constitutional paper does not always accurately describe how power in general is exercised in a political system or, more specifically, how much power the president actually has.

There are countries whose Constitution gives the president strong unilateral powers, but whose presidents seldom use those powers. And there are countries, such as the United States, whose Constitution gives the president little in the way of unilateral powers, but whose presidents on occasion have acted unilaterally and extraconstitutionally and thereby established a precedent for their successors. The role of political parties can be crucial. Parties are capable of bridging the gap between the president and members of the legislature, so that when the legislature is dominated by the president's co-partisans, especially if there is a strong tradition of party discipline, his power to act increases, as was the case with the constitutionally weak but in practice quite strong Mexican presidency during the period of PRI domination. But this supposes that the president's party is disciplined and loyal to him, and this is not always the case. In countries whose political systems are characterized by separation of purpose, as in the United States, where the electoral interests of the president and those of the legislators from his party are likely to diverge, the president may not be able to count upon the solid support of a legislative majority, even if his party in fact constitutes the majority in the legislature. In countries such as Brazil, whose electoral system encourages party fractionalization and no party holds anywhere near a majority of the seats in the legislature, presidents also may have difficulty solidifying majorities in support of their policies.

In systems of the latter sort, presidents will need to be able to bargain effectively to produce legislative majorities, and this puts a premium on the political and individual skills of the incumbent. The president also may need to resort to the distribution of incentives such as patronage positions and pork barrel appropriations in order to create and maintain legislative majorities. In some countries, this sort of clientelism is embedded in the political culture and is the primary way in which presidents are able to exercise highly personalized power. In political systems where the military plays an active role, presidents also may be able to generate legislative support for their agendas through the use of coercive tactics.

It is easy to conclude from this discussion that there is no pronounced trend of formal power in the direction of the president. Although many presidents have decree power, and US presidents regularly issue signing statements and executive orders, the exercise of these unilateral powers, especially to effect far-reaching policy changes, tends to be more the exception than the rule. Emergency powers exist, either formally or informally, in a number of political systems, but they too are infrequently used. On the other hand, the fact that the capacity to act unilaterally does exist, either constitutionally or by virtue of precedent, suggests that incumbents can, if they wish, choose to exercise these powers in a manner more consistent with the model of hyperpresidentialism than with that of constrained presidentialism.

Notes

1. See Mezey 1989; Edwards 1989; Bond and Fleisher 1990; Peterson 1990; and Mayhew 1991.

2. See Saiegh 2011:chap. 4 for a summary and refutation of the various critiques of this "box score" approach to measuring executive success with the legislature.

3. See also Metcalf 2000; United Nations Development Programme 2005; and Taghiyev 2006. As well, Steven Fish and Matthew Kroenig (2009) have developed a thirty-two-variable index of parliamentary powers for virtually every country in the world, relying on a reading of constitutional provisions and advice from country experts. Because there is often a zero-sum relationship between legislative and executive power, the inverse of such scores can be interpreted as an index of executive powers—that is, high scores on parliamentary powers could imply low scores on executive powers.

4. The discussion that follows relies heavily on Shugart and Carey 1992.

5. George Tsebelis and Eduardo Aleman (2005) provide a detailed categorization based on various combinations of amendatory, bloc, and item veto options along with the different override provisions.

6. 524 US 417 (1998).

7. These and other presidential signing statements, as well as the presidential executive orders discussed here, are assembled and publicly available at the University of California–Santa Barbara's American Presidency Project, www .presidency.ucsb.edu.

8. Some countries—for example, Germany and New Zealand—combine these systems, with a portion of the legislature elected from single-member districts and the remainder allocated proportionally. Proportional systems also vary in terms of the mechanisms used to allocate seats, thresholds for representation, and constituency size.

4

Presidentialism and the Size of Government

One title that every president has is "chief executive." Quite simply, this means that the president sits atop the executive hierarchy; except for those who work for branches of government designed to be beyond the president's control, such as the legislature or the judiciary, all employees of the national government, both civilian and military, report to him, some directly, and most indirectly, through presidential subordinates. The growth in the size and scope of the executive branch, a phenomenon intimately connected with the expanding role of governments in modern societies, has been a prominent driving force in the rise of presidentialism.

The Growth of Government

At the time that the presidency was created, national governments around the world had relatively narrow missions when compared with the roles that they now play. Those earlier governments were charged with the tasks of defending the nation against foreign adversaries and maintaining regime stability in the face of internal insurrectionary elements. Domestically, the government was responsible for establishing and maintaining an environment in which the economy could function. It created a national currency so that commerce could be conducted, and established systems for enforcing public laws and private contracts. The government collected taxes to pay for roads, service debts, build ships, and pay its sailors and soldiers.

In the United States, the early congresses would meet for only a few months at most each year, and they dealt with a limited agenda of issues. This was because, throughout the eighteenth century and through most of the nineteenth, the national government's role in the lives of its citizens was quite limited. Local governments, which handled issues of education, sanitation, and law enforcement, had the most significant impact on individual citizens. In fact, it was not atypical for members of the US Congress to leave their congressional positions to run for state and local offices, for that was where the political and policy action was. Although national governments may have been somewhat more active in countries with more centralized political systems as opposed to the dispersed power that characterized the US federal system, the role of national government in general, by modern standards, was still minimal.

But beginning in the late nineteenth century and continuing particularly into the early twentieth, the role of government began a steady expansion, first in Europe and then in the United States (see Tanzi and Schuknecht 2000:chap. 1). During this period, the idea of the "positive state" emerged, a state whose government used taxation and spending policies to address the economic and social issues confronting the nation. Thus, public education systems were introduced in France and Prussia early in the nineteenth century, and in the United States a bit later, although in the latter case under the control of local governments. In Europe, the rise of socialist parties during the nineteenth century created pressures on even conservative governments to take steps to protect workers from the vagaries and abuses of the free enterprise system. In Germany under Otto von Bismarck, laws were passed to provide insurance for the unemployed as well as for those who could not work because of illness, and retirement income was made available to those who were too old to work. Similar policies were introduced in England and eventually in other European states. In the United States, the absence of a strong socialist movement meant that such legislation came later, mostly during the Great Depression of the 1930s. But by the mid–twentieth century, the basic idea of the modern welfare state had taken hold in Western Europe and North America, as well as in other parts of the world. Such a state would take ever greater responsibility for the economic security of its citizens, with more extensive public education systems, laws regulating minimum wage and maximum working hours, public housing initiatives, public health facilities and regulations, and various programs to provide a basic level of sustenance for the elderly as well as for many of the disadvantaged members of society.

Governments also began to take a more active role in the economy, funding extensive public works projects, enacting protective tariffs for domestic industries, subsidizing the agricultural sector of their economies, and regulating some of the more problematic and predatory activities of private capital. After World War I, and particularly during the Great Depression, Western governments came to embrace the macroeconomic philosophy associated with John Maynard Keynes, an approach that suggested that government spending and fiscal policies could serve to balance business cycles by restraining periods of economic growth to avoid inflation, and by cushioning and shortening periods of economic downturn. In pursuit of these goals, most nations established or strengthened central or state banks to control monetary policy. They also came to rely upon public works projects and other forms of government spending to maintain employment and assist struggling sectors of the economy while at the same time providing safety net programs to protect individuals during hard economic times. Today, of course, governments do all of this and more. The environment, energy, science and technology, and even the arts and humanities are among the countless policy areas to which the mandate of government programs, initiatives, and regulations now extends.

In Russia and later in China, an even more activist model took hold, one in which government took ownership of, or at least dominated, most industries as well as the agricultural sector of society. These governments developed national planning mechanisms that sought to exercise nearly complete control of the economy. Although few nations followed this model in its entirety, many Western countries took steps to balance or curb the activities of private capital by bringing certain key industries and services under direct government control and strengthening the government's capacity to regulate private economic activity. Even when the government did not seek to exercise control, it involved itself in nurturing new industries by providing research and development incentives through tax structures or direct subsidies, and adopting trade policies meant to encourage exports and therefore economic growth. In sum, all modern governments came to play an active role in their nation's economy, with varying levels of regulation and control of key industries.

Just as important, the twentieth century saw the expansion of one of the original roles of government—the defense of the nation against foreign adversaries. Two world wars, the Cold War, and multiple regional conflicts resulted in the dramatic growth of military establishments the world over. In the United States, the original constitutional plan was for a national military force to be "raised" in order to fight a specific war; once that war was over, presumably most of the military would be disbanded. But after World War II, the United States, along with most major powers, neither disarmed nor completely demobilized their militaries; rather, these countries committed themselves to a standing military establishment for the nation's continued defense, with large numbers of soldiers under arms during times of peace as well as times of war. The organizing, equipping, and arming of these forces required an extensive bureaucratic apparatus and substantial government spending. The Cold War, waged between the Soviet Union and the United States, provoked an arms race as each nation attempted to match the other in weaponry and military prowess. Another part of the Cold War consisted of arming allies or potential allies around the world. The United States armed and trained military establishments in Latin America and other parts of the world as a bulwark against communism, while European nations did the same with many of their former colonies in Africa and Asia. The Soviet Union entered into alliances with Eastern European nations and sent arms to various countries in Africa and Asia as well as to Cuba. Through this process, standing armies, along with expanding military budgets and a growing arms industry that was dependent on government spending, came into being at different times in virtually every nation.

In economically less developed nations, the role of government was in some respects even broader than it was in more industrialized countries. To achieve economic development, government leaders negotiated with donor countries and with international organizations for loans, sought foreign investments from more economically developed nations, worked closely with nongovernmental organizations to assist in providing social services for their citizens, and were the primary source of funds for capital projects such as the building of roads, schools, and hospitals. Those nations that were rich in natural resources negotiated contracts with foreign governments as well as multinational corporations that allowed for the development and extraction of these resources in return for payments that would be made to the government. Some governments nationalized these industries so that they could reap the full benefits of their natural resources. Because private sources of capital tended to be limited, government expenditures as well as international aid became the driving forces of these economies. And, of course, most of these nations quickly came to the decision that they required an armed force to protect against real or imagined threats from foreign powers, more frequently to maintain domestic order, and as a symbol of their nationhood. The large powers, in pursuit of military facilities, allies, and natural resources, were more than willing to provide generous aid to the militaries of these nations, especially when that aid was used to purchase weapons made in the donor nations.

One rough indicator of this expanded role of government is the percentage of gross domestic product (GDP) accounted for by government spending. In the United States, in 1890, that figure, including spending at all levels of government, was approximately 6 percent, with the federal government's share about 2 percent. By 1996 the portion of GDP accounted for by government spending had increased to 32 percent (Tanzi and Schuknecht 2000:6), and by 2008 it had risen to just under 40 percent, with federal government expenditures alone amounting to about 20 percent of GDP. In the United Kingdom, the portion of GDP accounted for by government spending increased from 15 percent in 1900 to 41 percent in 2008. Today, government spending in most European countries is even higher than in the United Kingdom, accounting for more than 50 percent of GDP. In most African and Latin American countries, government spending typically accounts for between 25 and 33 percent of GDP (see Peters 1995:20–21).[1]

The growth in the responsibilities of government had a profound effect on the size and political role of the executive branch. In most representative democracies, the various programs and policies mentioned earlier were deliberated upon and enacted by legislative bodies, but once enacted they still needed to be implemented, or executed. That job by definition fell to the executive branch of government, which meant an extraordinary growth in the size of the bureaucracy. Table 4.1 details the growth in the number of federal government employees per citizen in the United States, from the time that the Constitution was ratified through 2010, with the most striking increase occurring in the first half of the twentieth century. These figures for the United States exclude people on active military duty and people employed by state and local government. If the 1.6 million people on active military duty are included, the federal government has about one employee for every seventy citizens. And in addition, if the 16 million people employed by state and local government are included, there is one government employee for every fifteen citizens. In the United Kingdom, more than 6 million citizens of a total population of 61 million are employed by government at both the national and local levels; in France, over 4 million citizens of a population of 60 million are similarly employed.[2] Table 4.2 documents the growth of total government employment as a percentage of the work force in the United States and seven European nations.

In postcolonial Africa, there was a dramatic increase in the size of the bureaucracy in the decade after independence. As colonial administrators withdrew, the bureaucracy was "Africanized," the military expanded, and government employment became the most lucrative and reliable source of income. In some countries, "a full 80% of government revenues were spent on supporting the civil service." In Tanzania, the number of govern-

Table 4.1   Number of Federal Government Employees per Citizen
in the United States

	US Population (rounded)	Number of Federal Government Employees (rounded)	Number of Federal Government Employees per Citizen
1788	~ 4,000,000	50	1 per 80,000
1900	76,212,000	239,000	1 per 318
1950	151,326,000	1,961,000	1 per 77
2010	308,746,000	2,830,000	1 per 110

Sources: US Office of Personnel Management, Historical Federal Workforce Tables, "Total Government Employment Since 1962," www.opm.gov/feddata/historicaltables/total governmentsince1962.asp; Harold W. Stanley and Richard G. Niemi (2006) *Vital Statistics on American Politics, 2005–2006* (Washington, DC: Congressional Quarterly); US Census, www.census.gov/2010census/data.

Table 4.2   Total Government Employment as Percentage
of the Work Force

	Late Nineteenth Century	1937	1960	1994
Austria	2	8	11	22
Germany	1	4	9	15
Italy	3	5	8	16
Netherlands	4	6	12	13
Sweden	2	5	13	32
Switzerland	2	6	7	14
United Kingdom	5	7	15	15
United States	3	7	15	14

Source: Vito Tanzi and Ludger Schuknecht (2000) *Public Spending in the 20th Century: A Global Perspective* (Cambridge: Cambridge University Press), p. 26.
Note: Due to the scarcity of data in this area, I use older but more comparative data here.

ment posts increased from just under 66,000 in 1966 to more than 295,000 in 1980, and to just over 500,000 in 1991. In Nigeria, the size of the armed forces increased from 11,500 personnel shortly after independence to 231,000 by 1978 (Chazan et al. 1992:55–58; Hammouya 1999). The precise numbers are less important than the simple fact that around the world, government hiring and spending constitutes the single most important component of the economy.

The Work of Government

The work that these people and the government agencies that they staff do as they execute programs and policies is neither simple nor routine. The legislative process that creates government programs seldom yields statutes with specifics that deal with all of the problems and issues implicated by the policy. Legislative institutions lack the expertise as well as the time that would be necessary to produce precise and unambiguous statutes. And as policymaking becomes more complex, it is simply not possible for a legislative body to anticipate every situation that might arise under the law.

For example, a law designed to improve air quality cannot list all possible air pollutants, indicate how much of each pollutant can be safely emitted into the atmosphere, and specify the steps that each industry that emits pollutants must take to restrict emissions to specified levels. Such a task requires expertise—scientists who understand the chemistry, biology, and physics of air pollution, medical people who understand what levels different pollutants would have to reach in order for them to have a harmful effect on humans, industry specialists who understand the technology that needs to be deployed to reduce the level of pollution, and economists who understand the financial impact of air pollution controls on the industries to which these controls are to be applied. Government agencies must draw upon the expertise of all of these people as they develop the regulations that are necessary to implement the legislation that has been passed. If clean air legislation is to be implemented, in other words, people who are capable of doing all of these things need to be employed by the agency responsible for environmental issues, and these experts inevitably will have a great deal of influence on the manner in which the policy is carried out. And, of course, the same principle applies to every government program, from healthcare to space exploration, from foreign aid to farm policy.

The air pollution example illustrates at least three points. First, as government extends its sphere of activity, the size of the bureaucracy must expand, because specialists need to be employed who are knowledgeable about the various aspects and potential effects of the policy that is to be implemented, and because these specialists require support staff, such as clerks, secretaries, and information technology and human resource professionals, to name some obvious examples.

Second, the implementation of public policies involves a substantial degree of discretionary power. Government officials can more aggressively implement some laws than others simply by allocating more personnel and resources to one program than to another. More important, although members of the bureaucracy must operate within the constraints of the law, the general wording of the typical statute provides them with significant latitude as they design implementation regulations. Thus, when the US Congress created the Department of Energy, it charged it with resolving the nation's energy crisis, with the only requirement being that its programs be "equitable" (Meier 1979:48). In making these decisions, government agencies in effect make public policy, every bit as much as the legislature that enacted the original law. An administrative decision under the law that limits or bars the emission of a particular pollutant into the atmosphere, or that requires that a particular technology be employed in order to reduce harmful emissions, has the force of law even if neither the pollutant nor the technology is mentioned in the original statute. Such a decision can result in cleaner air, but in some instances it also can mean the closing of a factory and potentially devastating economic effects on local communities. Two of the most ambitious pieces of legislation that Congress passed during the first two years of the Obama administration dealt with healthcare and the regulation of financial institutions. By one estimate, the two pieces of legislation call for drafting more than 300 separate rules, including the question of what services must be covered by all insurers as part of the "essential health benefits" guaranteed in the Affordable Care Act, and how much a credit card company should be able to charge a shopkeeper for administrative fees (Lichtblau and Pear 2010).

Third, the expanded size and power of the bureaucracy is in large measure a legislative creation. Although the constitutions of countries such as the United States do not provide their presidents with decree power, and in other countries presidential decree power is limited, legislatures in every country have created the functional equivalent of executive decree authority by delegating to the bureaucracy the power to design and issue the rules and regulations that implement legislation. Like decrees, these regulations have the impact of law without their specifics being determined via the legislative process. And as legislative bodies choose to enact ever more complex public policies in ever more expanding policy arenas, their ability to be specific will decrease and therefore the area for bureaucratic discretion and decisionmaking authority will increase. As one scholar has concluded in regard to the United States, but in terms that are applicable to every country in the world, "it is virtually impossible for Congress to act without increasing the power of the executive branch, which must implement new statutes that the legislature produces. The resources and discretion that accompany that task inevitably lead to an increase in the executive branch's power" (Macey 2006:2421).

In France, the delegation of power to the executive and therefore to the bureaucracy is in part a matter of historical habit. During the Third Republic, cabinet ministers tended to serve rather brief terms due to government instability, and thus many did not have time to familiarize themselves with the functions of the ministries that they were supposed to be supervising. This meant that "higher civil servants were often left to their own devices. Parliament implicitly recognized its own weaknesses and its own unwillingness to make detailed administrative decisions by adopting the custom of passing framework laws (*lois cadres*) under which ministers were given vast powers to issue decrees and regulations. These powers in fact devolved upon the civil servants" (Safran 2009:291). The extent of the resulting bureaucratic power is suggested by one 2003 estimate that France is governed by 8,000 laws and 100,000 regulatory decrees that implement these laws (Safran 2003:255). As an example, when in 1986 the French Parliament adopted a bill designed to privatize a number of industries, the law specified which industries could be privatized, but it left to the bureaucracy the details of how quickly the privatization effort should go forward, how the participation of foreigners would be regulated, and how the prices for the industries to be privatized would be determined (Huber 1998:242).

In brief, the growth of the bureaucracy is less a matter of bureaucratic (or presidential) usurpation of legislative power and more a product of an implicit (and often explicit) decision by the legislature that it wishes to act in an expanding list of broader and more complex policy areas and that it lacks the time and expertise to provide anything more than general guidelines about the goals that it wishes to achieve and how it wishes these goals to be achieved. The result, inevitably, is the delegation of its power to decide specific policy details to the bureaucracy and the expansion and empowerment of the executive branch of government with the president at its head.

The Nature of Bureaucratic Power

Because the president is chief executive, he and his policy preferences should influence how bureaucracies exercise their discretionary power. In the words of two presidential scholars, if a US president wishes, he can "review or reverse agency decisions, coordinate agency actions, make changes in agency leadership, or otherwise impose his views on government" (Moe and Wilson 1994:23). During the administration of George W. Bush, environmental legislation was less aggressively enforced than it was during the presidency of Bill Clinton. An analysis of the first year of the administration of Barack Obama found that the number of inspections conducted by the Consumer Products Safety Commission had more than doubled compared with the last year of the Bush administration, while the financial penalties assessed on employers by the Occupational Safety and Health Administration had increased by more than a third. The Environmental Protection Agency "moved quickly to reverse or strengthen Bush administration policies on power plant pollution, lead paint and toxic chemical discharges" (Lipton 2010).

In the United States, the constitutional issue involves the extent to which Congress can delegate its lawmaking power to the executive by passing ambiguous statutes and allowing the relevant agency, and therefore the president, the latitude necessary to interpret them. One classic argument is that lawmaking is a congressional responsibility and therefore any delegation to the bureaucracy is suspect. That argument has had relatively little force since the New Deal period, when the Supreme Court upheld a wide array of legislative delegations of power. In 1984, however, the Court, in *Chevron v. Natural Resources Defense Council,* significantly broadened the autonomy that bureaucrats had in interpreting statutes.[3] In that case, the Environmental Protection Agency had defined some of the terms of the Clean Air Act of 1977 in a way that made the act more favorable to regulated industries. The Court said that two questions were important: whether Congress had, in the precise words of the statute, decided the question, in which case the EPA had to defer to the words of the statute, or, if it hadn't, whether the agency's interpretation was "reasonable." In deciding reasonableness, the Court suggested that it was the intent of Congress to allow the agency to make these judgments on the grounds "that those with great expertise and charged with the responsibility for administering the provision would be in a better position to do so" (Sunstein 2006:2585–2586). There is one area where such reasoning might be problematic—if it could be argued that the executive had interpreted the statute in a manner that might render it constitutionally suspect. When it comes to constitutional issues, Congress must speak clearly, and if questions arise, this is a more appropriate arena for the Court to involve itself.

Based on the *Chevron* decision, the Supreme Court has deferred to executive interpretations of ambiguous statutes and, of course, Congress has not shown any inclination or ability to make its statutes more precise. The judiciary has said in essence that as long as agencies follow their procedures and the decisions that they make do not infringe on constitutional protections, these decisions are presumed to be valid, especially when the statutory language is ambiguous (Macey 2006:2430).

The public policy influence of bureaucracies is not confined to their control of how policies are administered. It extends as well to the initiation and design of the policies themselves prior to or during their consideration by elected officials. When presidents or legislators contemplate new public policies or revisions to existing policies, those in the bureaucracy who are responsible for that policy area are among the people who are consulted, because they are the ones most likely to know what has been working, what has not been working, and how to tackle a new area of concern. Although these policies are formally initiated and ultimately determined by presidents and legislators, members of the bureaucracy are important participants in the deliberation process as the final policy is developed. What bureaucrats propose is seldom approved in its entirety and in some instances ignored, but their proposals and their viewpoints usually do much to shape the contours and define the specifics of what ultimately gets enacted.

This increased influence of the bureaucracy should not be surprising. As German sociologist Max Weber predicted more than a century ago, when societies moved away from traditional systems of domination based upon inherited status and custom, and toward principles of legal domination characterized by a system of rules applied in a nonpersonalized manner, expertise of the sort associated with bureaucracies was certain to become more important. Legal domination, Weber argued, was a defining characteristic of the modern nation-state, and in such states it was necessary to assign specific administrative responsibilities to officials who had the appropriate training and experience. For these people, administration and public service would become a profession, a vocation rather than an avocation, and these people, as career public servants, would not and should not be subject to the electoral process. Because their technical skills and training would become indispensable, and because they would become a permanent part of government, Weber predicted that eventually bureaucrats and bureaucratic institutions would come to eclipse politicians and the institutions associated with representative democracy that were supposed to control the bureaucracy (Bendix 1962:293, 423–430).

The tension that Weber suggested between the politics of representative systems and the need for informed and effective public policy is apparent. Representative government presupposes deliberation and compromise to produce public policy decisions that have the broad support necessary to generate required legislative majorities. But such widely supported policies may not necessarily be up to the task of dealing with the problem that caused leaders to initiate them. However, if good public policy consists of identifying a set of means best calculated to achieve a specific end, then it can be argued that the "politics" of representation must yield to expertise so that these best means can be defined and selected for implementation.

The modern bureaucratic state seeks to transform political and policy issues into technical, professional, and administrative issues. From this point of view, there is little reason to believe, for example, that a legislature can figure out exactly what needs to be done to achieve the goal of clean air, or the goal of sending a rover to Mars, or the goal of providing healthcare for all citizens. These are matters for science and for policy experts. All that one reasonably can ask of representative institutions is that they participate in deciding which goals society should pursue, the general direction that this pursuit should take, and the amount of public funds to be allocated to the undertaking. Such a limited mandate for legislatures, it goes without saying, leaves a very broad scope for bureaucratic decisionmaking.

Finally, it is not just a matter of expertise. A hierarchically organized executive branch is capable of acting more expeditiously than a legislative body that by definition must deal with and seek compromises among a number of people with competing policy preferences. "While Congress has difficulty coordinating its response to rapidly changing events, the executive branch can capitalize on its ability to act quickly and unilaterally to structure agendas, and create new policies before the other branches can organize a response" (Macey 2006:2424).

In addition, there is an interactive relationship between the expansion in the scope of governmental activity that is reflected in the growth of the executive branch, and the expectations that citizens have of their government and by extension of their president. As the government does more, its citizens' expectations of what government can and should do also expand. Citizens come to assume that the state is capable of dealing with virtually every problem that they confront, problems that in earlier times they might have considered insoluble or problems that they would have had to deal with on their own or with the assistance of nongovernmental institutions. But today, if schools are failing, citizens expect the government should be able to do something about that. If farmers are facing economic problems caused by weather or market fluctuations, the state should act to protect them. If people cannot afford medical care, the state should see to it that medical care is available to all. If a natural disaster occurs, the government should have taken steps to protect against its worst effects and it certainly must be able to provide relief after the fact. If people are out of work, the government should take steps to reduce unemployment and support those who are unemployed until new jobs arrive. If citizens are being duped by unscrupulous businesspeople, the government should increase its regulatory activities. And, of course, there is an implicit assumption in these expectations that ways to respond to this agenda of demands always exist, and that in all cases good and successful policies that will achieve broad support can be developed, as long as one has the appropriate mix of expertise and political will. And, most perversely, if these problems persist despite the best efforts of government (and many certainly will), then the government is blamed both for the original condition and for the failure to come up with workable solutions.

The President and the Bureaucratic State

The rise of the bureaucratic state and the expectations that government can and should deal with just about any difficulty have contributed to the prominence, power, and problems of presidents. Because both the civilian and military bureaucracies are part of the executive branch, they are formally under the auspices of the political executives of the state— the president in presidential systems and the prime minister and cabinet in parliamentary systems. Two of the many titles that presidents have are "chief executive" and "commander in chief," underlining their position at the top of both the civilian and military bureaucracies. And because the president's official role is head of government, and because many citizens, albeit simplistically, view "the president" as synonymous with "the government," citizens expect that it will be his responsibility to see to it that the government meets the various challenges that its citizens place before it. In other words, not only does expanding the size of government expand the actual responsibilities and power of the president, it also expands the expectations that citizens have for the president and for the government that he leads, even when there is no mandate and frequently no real ability for the president and the government to respond to these expectations.

Such a set of expectations assumes that presidents have the capacity to exercise complete control of the bureaucracy, an assumption that may not be entirely accurate. Although the president is formally in charge of the bureaucracy, there are limits to what he is able to do. The size and scope of the bureaucracy is a mixed blessing for the president; on the one hand it enhances the size and status of the executive branch, but on the other it inhibits his capacity to exercise control. The very size of the bureaucracy in terms of the number of people, the number of agencies, and its geographic dispersion around the nation and around the world makes it physically and administratively impossible for the president, even with the help of trusted aides, to supervise the entire enterprise. Much, in other words, will go on without the president knowing about it, not because he or his aides are inattentive or incompetent, but because keeping track of it all is literally impossible. Nonetheless, because he is chief executive, he will be held responsible when things go wrong.

In the case of the United States, one vivid example of this occurred in late December 2009. A person boarded an airplane in Amsterdam headed for Detroit and attempted, unsuccessfully, to blow up the plane with explosives secreted in his undergarments. Clearly, various government officials in charge of intelligence and security and at various levels failed to identify the perpetrator, even though there had been prior indications and information provided to some of these officials that this was a dangerous person. It was only a matter of luck that he did not succeed. News commentary after the event blamed the Obama administration for this security lapse and even singled out the president himself, who was on vacation at the time, for not issuing a more forceful response to the event.

A second example occurred in the spring of 2010 when an offshore oil-drilling facility in the Gulf of Mexico blew up, causing a huge outflow of crude oil from the seabed into the Gulf. Repeated attempts by British Petroleum, the company that owned the well, to stop the flow of oil failed. As pollution in the Gulf spread and oil began to move onshore, public discontent rose, and the president became the target for criticism. News reports began to fault Obama for not doing enough to stop the oil leak, although it was not at all apparent what the president or the government that he headed could do that the oil companies could not. More embarrassing for the president was the evidence that emerged that the agency within the Department of Interior that was responsible for ensuring the safety of these facilities, and for ensuring that such blowouts would not do any damage, had been lax in its efforts and had granted waivers on key procedures and equipment that might have prevented the accident (Eilperin 2010). It also became clear that the president knew that there were problems in this agency, the Minerals Management Service (MMS), when he came into office, problems that involved an overly intimate relationship between agency officials and the oil companies. The president had asked the secretary of interior to institute reforms at the MMS, but there had been insufficient follow-through on the request.

In both of these instances, President Obama was held responsible (and assumed responsibility), even though it would be absurd to believe that he would (or should) have been aware of the specific security procedures, security personnel, the day-to-day handling of intelligence data, and the strengths and weaknesses of the procedures in place that were designed to stop the so-called underwear bomber, and also absurd to believe that, having asked the secretary of interior to follow through on the problems at the MMS, he would have checked up on this issue given the relative obscurity of the agency and the fact that no major problems of this sort had occurred in the past. Nonetheless, the president was blamed for both of these instances.

Similarly, economic expansions and downturns, although obviously affected by government policy, are for the most part the product of business cycles that result from the activity of nongovernmental actors whose actions and occasional excesses ultimately determine the state of the economy. Nonetheless, it is a staple of democratic politics that presidents are blamed when the economy is performing poorly, but that they get relatively little credit when the economy is doing well. Bad news, it seems, whether economic, or international, tends to be laid at the door of the president. Both President Obama and President Nicolas Sarkozy faced difficult reelection campaigns in 2012; one reason why both were electorally vulnerable was the weak state of the US and French economies, especially as reflected in high unemployment rates. Although in each case the economic problems were only partially of their making, and both presidents had taken action to deal with these problems, the strong inclination of the public in each country was to place the blame with their president.

As the size of the bureaucracy increases, the size of the national budget also grows. Keeping track of exactly how and to what effect billions and even trillions of dollars are spent in a far-flung bureaucratic structure is a daunting task. In addition, citizens come to be dependent on the various programs on which the government spends money, but at the same time, they worry about the size of the government's budget, are concerned that there is money being wasted either on bad programs or through government corruption, and resist the notion that their taxes need to be raised to support these programs. Discontent over government spending, government deficits, tax rates, or decisions to reduce government expenditures on popular programs may well be directed toward the president by citizens that too often want government services for themselves but also want someone else to pay for them.

The president also is not as free to control the bureaucracy as his title of "chief executive" might suggest. Legislative bodies may restrict the ability of the president to reorganize the bureaucracy, to terminate or merge government agencies, and certainly to create new agencies. And most legislatures retain at least some degree of control over the budgets that keep government agencies running. In many countries, presidential control is also hampered by the fact that most members of the bureaucracy are, as Weber predicted they would be, relatively permanent career civil servants who had already attained their positions prior to the arrival of a president and are likely to remain in their positions long after he leaves office. Presidents in these countries cannot simply remove all of the people with whom they may have policy differences, as the chief executive officer of a private corporation can.

There are several justifications for the protected status of these public servants. The first is that they hold their positions by virtue of their expertise rather than their politics. The argument is that people with the required talents and expertise will not come to work for the government if their careers can be derailed by a change in political leadership. The second justification is that the actions that these officials take should be determined by their expertise and by their sense of what would be best for the nation, rather than by their own or the president's political agenda. If the positions of these officials are at risk, they may decide to discount their expertise and couch their recommendations and decisions in terms designed to please their political superiors. Doing so would be contrary to what the expectations should be for such officials—that is, they should exhibit "neutral competency," which means that they are expected to offer their expert advice to the elected president and his appointees, regardless of their own or that president's policy agenda and goals. If presidents reject their advice or makes decisions that are contrary to their policy agendas and goals, civil servants are expected to adhere to the decisions of their elected superiors.

Although the theory of "neutral competence" has much to recommend it, in practice members of the bureaucracy do have policy preferences that they seek to advance, sometimes explicitly and often implicitly. It would be strange indeed if they did not have such preferences; as experts in the field who have devoted their education and careers to a particular policy area, it would be surprising if they had no preferences for how or whether or to what extent these policies should be developed or modified. These preferences may lead civil servants to resist, modify, or delay the implementation decisions of their superiors. Additionally, the bureaucracy serves as the primary source of information for the president about the state of public policy. If the president wants to modify an existing policy, he must depend heavily upon those who have been responsible for overseeing that policy. And because those in charge of the policy are likely to know more about the area than does the president himself, the president may be vulnerable to manipulation or at least be significantly influenced by the bureaucracy. That is, the president may be at as much of a disadvantage to the bureaucracy in terms of policy expertise as is the legislature.

Advocates of the bureaucratic state argue that this is as it should be. The goal should be good public policy, which means policy based on the best knowledge, rather than policy based on what is politically acceptable. If physicians working for the government determine that cigarette smoking is dangerous for the public health and they advocate public policies designed to reduce, eliminate, or regulate smoking, such policy recommendations should not be trumped by partisan concerns, by lobbyists for tobacco growers, or by questions about the extent of and limits to government intervention. Career civil servants are in place, the argument goes, exactly so that they can provide a nonpartisan direction to government decisions, a direction that does not depend upon the whims and positions of elected officials.

In pursuit of that idea, many nations have seen the proliferation of administrative agencies that are statutorily independent of the president and even the legislature and therefore beyond the control of elected officials. The creation of these agencies is an explicit admission upon the part of elected officials that certain policy decisions need to be removed entirely from the political arena. In the United States, the agency that can have the most timely and telling impact on the state of the economy is the Federal Reserve system, whose governors are appointed by the president for specific terms, subject to Senate confirmation, but who cannot be removed by him or by Congress once in office. The terms of Fed governors also overlap presidential administrations, and so a new president cannot change the membership of the Fed board when he enters office the way that he can change the membership of the cabinet. Central banks in other nations have a similar degree of independence. But for average citizens, the independence, functions, and sometimes the very existence of these bodies are neither apparent nor comprehensible; therefore, the president may find himself in the position of being held responsible for the state of the economy even though an agency over which he exercises no direct control may be part of both the problem and the solution.

Of course, in those societies where a professionalized civil service does not exist or is very weak, presidential control of the bureaucracy is more easily achieved. In much of Latin America, bureaucracies have "functioned as an employment system in the hands of politicians," with infrequent use of "merit criteria for selection, promotion and dismissal of employees" (Zuvanic and Iacoviello 2010:148, 153). Presidents typically use patronage appointments to build their political party or their own political organizations (Geddes 1994:137–138). In Brazil, there are about 18,000 political appointments in the hands of the president (Alston et al. 2008:134), compared with about 4,000 such appointments under the control of the president of the United States (Lewis 2011:76).

In Africa, patronage has been the accepted way to fill many administrative posts, and has been one of the driving forces in the rapid expansion of the public sector as African presidents, like their Latin American counterparts, have sought to reward their allies and solidify their power by distributing government positions (Chazan et al. 1992:179–181). One student of politics in Senegal notes that the administrative apparatus at independence could best be characterized as "patrimonial bureaucrats acting on the political interests and loyalties of the party-state," rather than as civil servants implementing public policy. The bureaucrats in turn reported to high-level functionaries who deferred to President Léopold Senghor, who was head of state, head of government, and secretary-general of the ruling party, on anything other than routine matters (Beck 2008:55).

The Bureaucracy and Presidential Power

The paradoxical impact of the bureaucracy on chief executives is that while its enhanced size, prominence, and influence clearly expand the power and scope of the presidency, these same characteristics can make it difficult for the president to control and bend it to his will. The consequence of this is that while the scope of government as reflected in the size of the bureaucracy contributes to inflated expectations that are directed toward the president, the very same characteristics may restrict the ability of the president to move the bureaucracy in a direction that will meet these expectations. Obviously, the legislature is at an even greater disadvantage as it attempts to control the bureaucracy, which suggests the possibility of the bureaucracy as an independent force in modern political systems, nearly beyond the control of elected politicians. But that is a story for another day. For the president, the point is that the expectation that he can solve problems because he has ostensible control of the bureaucracy (and therefore "the government") almost always exceeds his actual degree of control. As several scholars have pointed out, presidents often find themselves in the position of having to "persuade" the bureaucracy to follow their directions (see Sala 1998).

Presidents, aware of this problem, have regularly sought various means to strengthen their control of the executive branch. In the case of the United States, presidents have made repeated efforts to "politicize" the bureaucracy. During the administration of President George W. Bush, for example, reports emphasizing the perils of global warming written by government scientists were rewritten by nonscientists in the White House to soften the conclusions so that they would better reflect the president's view that the contribution of human activity to global warming as well as the consequences of the phenomenon had been exaggerated. In the Justice Department, the White House worked to influence the decisions of its professional career attorneys about which cases to prosecute, and when some US attorneys resisted such direction, they were removed or threatened with removal from their positions.

A second way in which presidents seek to control the bureaucracy is to ensure that all major agency decisions go through the president's office. In the United States, this process began in 1921 when Congress passed legislation making the president responsible for assembling and submitting an annual budget for the federal government. Previously, each agency had made its own individual budget request directly to Congress; this new process meant that agencies would need prior presidential approval for their budget requests. The same legislation created the Bureau of the Budget, to be housed in the Treasury Department, to help the administration to develop and oversee the budget. Simultaneously, President Warren Harding established the practice of central clearance, requiring agencies to go through the Bureau of the Budget to gain approval of all their legislative proposals, not just budgetary requests, before submitting them to Congress (see Crenson and Ginsberg 2007:21). In 1939, Congress responded to the Brownlow Commission's plea that the president needed help by creating the Executive Office of the President. Among other steps, the legislation moved the Bureau of the Budget to that office, thereby placing the budget process firmly under White House control, and laid the groundwork for a significant expansion of presidential staff, many of whom would have oversight of the bureaucracy as part of their responsibilities.

During the Richard Nixon administration, the bureau was renamed the Office of Management and Budgeting and was given a much broader mandate to help the president to supervise the federal bureaucracy, including the responsibility of reviewing all federal regulations before they went into effect. During the George W. Bush administration, the role of the White House Office of Information and Regulatory Affairs

(OIRA), the unit of the Office of Management and Budgeting charged with supervising the bureaucracy, was strengthened, via executive order, to the point where not only rules issued by agencies, but also the less formal advisory opinions that they developed as guides to citizens and other entities about how the agency intended to implement the law, needed to be cleared through the OIRA. The White House required that one of its political appointees be designated in each agency as the regulatory policy officer through whom all proposed rules and advisory opinions needed to go and with whom the OIRA would work, so that the White House might better control agency rule-making.[4] This strategy is limited, of course, by the probability of long delays in administrative action caused by the inevitable bottleneck that will develop if all decisions, big and small, need to move through a centralized agency that itself may not have the expertise to fully understand the implications of each regulation and advisory opinion. This suggests the larger problem with the strategy—the probability that policy expertise will be traded for political expediency.

To an increasing degree, US presidents and their immediate staff members have become attentive to the political loyalties of those whom they have appointed to bureaucratic agencies—that is, those who are not part of the civil service system and who serve as the president's agents at the upper reaches of federal agencies. The allegiances of the very top officials (cabinet secretaries and agency administrators) always have been scrutinized, but still presidential control was questionable. These appointments often go to leading figures who have policy agendas and political ambitions of their own and who therefore may wish to establish some independence from the president. Agency heads may be people with little knowledge or expertise about the policy domain of the agency, especially when compared with the expertise of those who have made careers in that agency. Such political appointees may be "captured" by those whom they are supposed to supervise, in the sense that they have to rely upon these people for information about the programs and issues that the agency is dealing with. The agency head, as the new person in town, may be unable to change in any substantive way how a complex organization operates, at least in a short period of time, as witnessed by US interior secretary Ken Salazar's failure to change the culture at the Minerals Management Service prior to the BP oil spill in the Gulf of Mexico. Agency personnel, for their part, expect the head of the agency to be an advocate for their mission and budget to the president, while the president expects that person to be his own agent. The conflict often leads to ineffective control by the president.

Finally, bureaucracies often have been able to resist the directives of presidents because they have strong supporters in the legislature. This has been particularly the case in the US Congress, where career bureaucrats have established strong and mutually supportive relationships with long-serving members of key congressional committees and their staff members. These committees authorize agency programs and budgets, and the wishes of these legislators cannot be ignored. To deal with this, US presidents have become much more aggressive in asserting their sole power to control the bureaucracy. They have placed increased emphasis on the theory of the unitary presidency, described in Chapter 3, a theory that argues for the president's absolute power to remove subordinate policymaking officials and to direct the way in which these subordinates exercise discretionary executive power. Presidents argue that they have the power to veto or nullify those officials' exercise of discretionary power, regardless of directions to the contrary from Congress. The core principle of this theory is that when Congress delegates power to a particular agency, it is in fact delegating power to the president to be used at his discretion rather than at the discretion of the agency. Furthermore, once Congress delegates that power, it is in the hands of the president; bureaucrats cannot be required to check back with Congress as they exercise this power. From this perspective, it is the president's understanding of the law that counts rather than the understanding that Congress or the agency itself might have of the law. This view of presidential power provides a complete justification for the George W. Bush administration's decision to rewrite the findings of government scientists on the issue of climate change. The agency and its scientists report to the president, the unitary presidency theory argues, not to Congress and not to the people (Kelley and Barilleaux 2006). The theory of the unitary presidency, along with the greater use of signing statements that follows from that theory, enhances presidential control of the bureaucracy and therefore presidential power, because it is an assertion that the president rather than Congress or the bureaucracy decides whether, to what extent, and how an act of Congress, signed by the president, will be implemented.

Presidents in countries with weak or nonexistent civil service laws find it easier to gain control of the bureaucracy and use that control to both advance their policy priorities and consolidate their power. In Brazil, during its early constitutional period (1946–1964), Presidents Getúlio Vargas and Juscelino Kubitschek used the bureaucracy to implement some of their most ambitious plans. They would get Congress to approve the general outlines of their development plans, and then they would use the bureaucracy, which was in charge of implementing the plans, in order to accomplish their goals (Mainwaring 1997:86–87). In the late twentieth century, as Latin American nations came to embrace the neoliberal economic policies associated with free markets, free trade, balanced budgets, and reduced social services, the movement in this direction was led by so-called technocrats—economic experts, many trained in the United States, who were given extraordinary power by political leaders to implement such changes. In Ecuador during the 1980s, presidents dealt with economic problems via urgent decree, bypassing Congress. But as one student of that country's politics notes, this was not just a way to avoid predictable congressional opposition. "The impulse to make economic policy in this way was also rooted in the technocratic approach of the economic ministers who believed that the solution to the economic crisis involved the discovery and application of technically 'correct' policies. . . . They deeply believed that economics was a science that should lie outside of the realm of politics" (Conaghan 1994:350).

It is not always clear, however, whether presidents rely upon bureaucrats because they believe in their technical expertise, or because bureaucratic power ensures their own power and ability to control policy. Brazilian presidents often use their control of the bureaucracy to distribute resources in a manner designed to reward those legislators who support their policy initiatives. In a number of African countries, so-called administrative-hegemonic regimes emerged in which the executive, the bureaucracy, and the "coercive apparatus" of the state are the key institutions; "main policy decisions are centralized around the leader [i.e., the president] and his close advisors. Specific technical and professional decision-making is carried out in the bureaucracy" (see Chazan et al. 1992:137–140). In Nigeria, the idea of "permanent secretaries" inherited from the British, along with the political neutrality that goes with it, was discarded in the 1979 and 1989 constitutions in favor of "director generals" who would be appointed by the government. The "principal norm" of the new system was administrative loyalty to the government of the day and therefore to the president (Olowu 1996).

In Senegal after independence, the centralized bureaucratic structure left by the French was Africanized and the governing party, under the leadership of President Léopold Senghor, "evolved steadily into the party of the bureaucrats with the expansion of the state. Senghor's technocratic vision of the state and his commitment to Jacobin centralizing traditions nurtured the emergence of a new class of technocrats and civil servants. . . . By the mid-1970s, civil servants controlled most of the ministries and had become major forces within the ruling party." The president exercised complete control of the bureaucracy. "Ministers wanted to be sure that the president approved of what they were doing before they would act, even on the simplest matter" (Gellar 2005:47, 53). This, of course, created significant governing inefficiencies, the inevitable result of an overly centralized approach. In the 1990s in Senegal, under President Abdou Diouf, there was a movement toward decentralization and the empowerment of local governing bodies. Although improvements occurred, the power of central administrators and therefore the president was essentially undiminished, because the state maintained a strong supervisory role, with the power to approve (or disapprove) local budgets, contracts entered into by local authorities, and changes in local tax rates, among other policies (Gellar 2005:57–58).

Legislative vs. Bureaucratic Power

Not every problem before a society is amenable to a governmental solution. Almost inevitably, presidents will fail to meet popular expectations, and this can spell trouble, either in the form of a loss of public and political support or, in some countries, in the possibility of civil disturbance. Interestingly, it is seldom the bureaucracy that bears the brunt of this popular disenchantment, even though the term "bureaucrat" is often a term of opprobrium. In most societies, citizens tend to blame their elected leaders for poor public policies or for policies that do not deal effectively with their concerns, and this is particularly the case for the president who, as we have observed, is viewed by large numbers of citizens as the equivalent of the government.

The tendency to hold presidents responsible for policy failures does not mean that citizens think of the legislature as blameless. In the case of legislatures, the indictment is usually directed more at the institution itself than at its individual members, whereas in the case of the president the indictment is directed at him personally rather than at the institution of the presidency. In the United States, Congress is typically held in very low esteem, while its individual members are generally viewed more positively, as witnessed by their very high reelection rates. But judgments about Congress as an institution are rather harsh and come from both sides of the US political spectrum. On the left, Congress is charged with being too conservative, too responsive to those with financial power, and therefore resistant to proposals to help more economically disadvantaged members of society. On the right, Congress is charged with being too responsive to public opinion, too willing to support extravagant public spending, and unwilling to make difficult choices that might jeopardize its members' chances for reelection. And from both the left and the right, Congress is charged with being a refuge for corrupt politicians who are single-mindedly focused on their own political ambitions and financial advancement and in possession of neither the talent nor the expertise nor the will to make good public policy.

Similar findings appeared in a study of public opinion in twenty-five countries in Europe. Majorities in twenty-three of these nations declared that they had "no confidence at all" or "not very much" confidence in Parliament. These data, from 1999 to 2000, showed the lowest level of confidence in Parliament in the newer democracies of Eastern and Central Europe (only 19 percent of the Russian respondents indicated high levels of confidence in the Russian Parliament), but the figures were not much more encouraging in Greece, Ireland, Italy, Britain, and Germany, where only about a third of the respondents indicated high levels of confidence in Parliament (Dogan 2005).

This critique is not confined to US and European legislatures. There is public opinion evidence from Latin America that those citizens who regard state performance as substandard or who believe that crime and corruption are prevalent also express low confidence in parties and legislatures (Mainwaring 2006:22). Looking at public opinion data from eighteen Latin American countries, Sebastian Saiegh (2010:69) concludes that in most countries, the general public does not have a high degree of confidence in the legislature. There may be good reason for such perceptions. Some political scientists have argued that legislatures, because they tended to represent more conservative and parochial interests, were likely to resist change (Packenham 1970; Huntington 1968; see also Mezey 2009). A recent empirical analysis concludes that presidents "have usually been in the forefront of far-reaching policy reforms, particularly when those reforms imposed costs on powerful constituencies" (Gerring and Thacker 2004:312).

Certainly, many Latin American legislators have resisted economic reforms designed to fight inflation and balance national budgets. Because their political careers can depend upon the support of those who benefit from government spending, representatives have resisted calls for fiscal austerity. Proposals to reform pension systems, to reduce government expenditures, or to revise other public policies supported by well-organized interests have been opposed by representatives who are fearful of the electoral consequences of such decisions. Distributive policies that provide pork barrel spending in the constituencies of the representatives and that serve the interests of local elites have been protected by representatives who are more interested in maintaining their hold on office or otherwise advancing their careers than in dealing with the nation's fiscal challenges. And legislators and their supporters often benefit from a system that populates the bureaucracy with patronage rather than professional appointees.

This dynamic was quite apparent as several Latin American nations embraced the neoliberal model of economic reform. In Brazil, for example, between 1985 and 1994, congressional opposition prevented residents from implementing a number of measures designed to stabilize the economy in the face of triple-digit inflationary pressures. Most economists had agreed that earlier legislation that resulted in the indexing of wages and pensions to the cost of living was a major contributor to this problem. However, proposals to end the practice were resisted in Congress, both by representatives beholden to trade unions and even by more conservative politicians who, though rhetorical supporters of such steps, were loath to act for fear of electoral repercussions. Congress also resisted executive attempts to reduce public sector employment, increase taxes, and collect debts owed to the government by private businesses, as well as initiatives aimed at reforming the social security system (Mainwaring 1997). In 1995, President Fernando Cardoso vetoed a move by Congress to increase the minimum wage by 40 percent, a step with significant and adverse budgetary implications given the statutory linkage between the minimum wage and social security payments (Kingstone 1999:202).

In Chile, the 1973 military coup had as one of its goals "a new constitutional order characterized by a far more powerful president [and] a weakened parliament" that would create a new society wherein "market forces and an open, export-oriented economy would unleash entrepreneurial skills, and boost production and economic growth" (Valenzuela 1994:166). The Brazilian military coup of 1964 was justified in almost identical terms by those who led it (Hagopian 1996:1–2). Judgments about the merits and morality of the Chilean coup aside, clearly the military junta that came to power successfully implemented the neoliberal reform agenda, a task that might well have been more difficult if the traditionally strong Chilean Congress still had been functioning. When representative democracy returned to Chile, various constitutional amendments restored many of the prerogatives of Congress, but the budgetary powers that had been exercised by Congress in the period prior to the coup were moved to the president. This constituted tacit recognition that macroeconomic policies of the sort instituted under the Augusto Pinochet regime needed to be maintained by the technocrats in the bureaucracy, and that they would be put in jeopardy if the powers that Congress possessed prior to the coup were restored. This concern seems supported by cross-national studies that show that the likelihood of budget deficits increases as legislative authority over the budget increases, because legislators seek to accommodate as many particularized requests as possible. This tendency, the authors of the study suggest, can be combated by enhancing the executive's power in budget-making or by introducing electoral reforms that reduce the incentive to pursue funding for local projects (Hallenberg and Marier 2004; see also Persson and Tabellini 2003; Cheibub 2006).

In addition to resisting what might be called politically conservative (i.e., neoliberal) policy initiatives, legislative institutions can be equally resistant to more progressive policy proposals. Most representatives are drawn from that portion of society that benefits from the status quo, or they hold their office through the support of such elites. Because those who already possess money, property, and power have inordinate influence in representative institutions, legislators are unlikely to support changes that might threaten their own or their patrons' interests. Reform proposals that call for a more equitable distribution of land, or proposals that would benefit workers at the expense of those who employ them, or proposals to reduce the power of large private enterprises, are likely to be resisted by legislative institutions.

All of this suggests that those who wish to see significant change in society, whether they come from the left or the right, have an interest in supporting an increase in the power of the presidency and the bureaucracy and a decrease in the power of legislative institutions.[5] One scholar reports that support for a strong presidency in France has come from both the right and the left. The right hoped that "a charismatic authority figure would help maintain the existing economic order and temper a Parliament in which the underprivileged classes were represented." The left "expected such a figure to counterbalance a Parliament that was regarded as the preserve of the privileged classes" (Safran 2009:234–235).

The recent election of a number of populist Latin American presidents who have been advocates of progressive economic reforms has made it clear that a disposition toward executive power is the sole preserve of neither the right nor the left. In Argentina, Brazil, and Chile, progressive presidents who campaigned on platforms calling for significant changes have had to modify and moderate their agendas in the face of congressional resistance (Hochstetler 2008). But in the cases of Bolivia and Ecuador, reformist presidents decided to bypass Parliament entirely, using referenda to force through constitutional revisions that enhanced presidential powers and created legislatures more likely to support their initiatives. They also resorted to decree authority to implement land reform in the case of Bolivia and to broaden and accelerate state control of natural resource extraction in the case of Ecuador.

Implications of the Bureaucratic State

The rise of the bureaucratic state and with it presidential power is justified by its supporters in terms of the policymaking deficiencies of legislative institutions. As far back as the nineteenth century, scholars and commentators predicted this "decline of the legislature" in the face of the need for a more rational approach to public policy (see Bryce 1971). John Stuart Mill, the great advocate of representative government, wrote that the proper role of the legislature was to "watch and control" the government, rather than to design public policy, a task for which he thought legislatures were "radically unfit." He recommended that government policies be designed by panels of experts, presumably under the auspices of the executive, and then submitted to the legislature for either their approval or disapproval.

Popular perceptions of civilian bureaucrats are mixed. Although some associate them with government waste, red tape, and delay, others think of them as public policy experts and in many countries they are viewed as fairer and less likely to be corrupt than politicians (see Peters 1995:chap. 2). Because they do not run for reelection, their decisions are seen, perhaps naively, as devoid of political influence. Although their actions seldom receive universal endorsement, civilian bureaucrats are thought to be, particularly by elites, in the best position to make tough, even unpopular decisions for the public good. In Latin America during the last two decades of the twentieth century, bureaucrats were the ones who led the neoliberal reforms that aimed to reduce government expenditures, especially those designed to help the poor and disadvantaged, and to free private enterprise from government regulation. In systems influenced by Marxist philosophies, bureaucrats designed five-year economic plans, led the nationalization of key industries, and imposed state control over a variety of economic activities.

The larger point here is that modern societies have come to subscribe to the notion that there are technological solutions or fixes for virtually every problem that they confront. It is assumed that the failings of human behavior and often the vagaries of nature itself can be compensated for or rectified by science and technology. Politics is seen as a hindrance to this process. On economic issues, political resistance dooms proposals for higher taxes and lower government expenditures, although both may be necessary to avoid economic disaster; technocrats, or experts, outside of politics can make the necessary decisions to restore financial sanity that politicians simply won't make. On environmental issues, political resistance to steps that will change the lifestyles of average people as well as the manner in which many industries conduct their business will prevent essential action to forestall ecological disaster. Politicians should get out of the way and allow scientists to develop and implement the solutions. All of this constitutes a case for bureaucratic control.

However, this calculus changes to the extent that the bureaucracy is seen as an institution associated with patronage and corruption. When presidents populate the bureaucracy with political cronies rather than policy experts, and use the institution and the policies that it administers primarily to solidify or advance their own political base, government officials are unlikely to command widespread respect, and the policies emanating from the bureaucracy are unlikely to produce significant gains for the nation. In Latin America, many programs designed as part of economic development plans "end up transformed into particularistic benefits as they are implemented by a partisan bureaucracy," with supporters of the president and the governing party benefiting to the detriment of those for whose benefit the program was originally designed (Geddes 1994:136). In much of Africa, in the view of one scholar, the state has "become a material object hijacked for personal, class, or group interests" (Kalu 2009:133). "Corrupt practices have permeated the civil service" and "structures intended as institutional vehicles of development, by their inefficiency, became obstacles to effective growth" (Chazan et al. 1992:57).

The rise of the bureaucratic state and the resulting movement of policymaking authority toward the executive raise some traditional and still crucial questions or dilemmas for political systems, especially those that claim a commitment to representative democracy. Assume for a moment that bureaucratic decisionmaking under the hierarchical control of the president is more efficient and better able to develop timely, rational, and effective policies that deal with important challenges before the nation than is decisionmaking in a large, collegial body such as a legislature. The question then is whether the resulting efficiency and effectiveness are worth the cost of dispensing with, or significantly marginalizing, the role of elected officials. Without unduly loading the question, is a policy developed with relative dispatch and with its major components designed by experts preferable to one that takes a much longer time to develop because of the need to hear more voices and to consult more broadly, and about which experts have less to say? The irreducible point is that democratic systems almost by definition privilege collegiality, consultation, and debate over hierarchy, efficiency, and expertise. Such a commitment presumes that a policy that is the product of broad consultation is intrinsically better than a policy that has not been shaped in this manner. But can this presumption withstand the challenges of a fast-moving world with myriad problems calling for high-level expertise, and in which some policy options are objectively better than others?

But bureaucrats, after all, are not elected and not directly accountable to the voters. Ceding significant policymaking power to them therefore does violence to a fundamental principle of representative democracy. The fact that they are ostensibly under the control of an elected president preserves to some extent the idea of popular control, but even then, and even given expansive interpretations of presidential power (e.g., the theory of the unitary executive), the scope of bureaucratic activities, the technicality of so much of bureaucrats' work, and their relative permanence as compared with the transient nature of presidents and their appointees raise questions about the extent to which bureaucrats actually are controlled by elected officials. And as we have seen, even if the president is able to exercise control, this may come at the expense of bureaucratic expertise.

Mill's argument was that control should rest with the legislature and indeed every legislative body has a mandate of some sort to oversee the bureaucracy and the rest of the executive branch. But in many countries, even those with very strong legislatures such as the United States, most representatives are not particularly interested in the mundane work associated with effective policy oversight. The general view is that members of the legislature engage in oversight when they are attempting to get a bureaucrat to respond to the needs of their constituents or to elites within the constituency, or when there are highly publicized failures or instances of corruption in the bureaucracy.

One analysis suggests that representatives approach this task from a "fire alarm" perspective rather than a "cop on the beat" perspective (McCubbins and Schwartz 1984). That is, legislators will engage in oversight only when a crisis develops and a political fire needs to be extinguished. Such efforts usually engender positive press coverage for the representative as she publicly calls officials and private citizens to account for their misfeasance. During 2011 in the United States, Congress engaged in broadly publicized hearings on the financial crisis that hit the country in 2008 and 2009 as well as hearings on the failures that led to the British

Petroleum oil disaster in the Gulf of Mexico in the spring of 2010. Former and current government officials as well as leaders of the financial institutions that were most intimately involved were interrogated in regard to the financial crisis, and oil company executives, those companies in charge of drilling rigs, and personnel from the Department of Interior were questioned in regard to the environmental crisis in the Gulf of Mexico. There is little record, however, of earlier oversight efforts that might have encouraged bureaucrats to take steps that could have prevented these crises.

In brief, there is scant evidence that legislators are prepared to engage in the sort of consistent oversight that can prevent disasters or solve small problems before they become big problems, because that work tends to be less glamorous and entail fewer political benefits. In the United States, Congress has attempted to deal with the problem of overly broad delegations of power to the executive with various procedures that are built into the law that in essence require the executive to check with the legislature before moving ahead with an implementing regulation. The most formal of these processes is called the legislative veto (see Fisher 1997:141–157). In essence, that device tells the relevant agency that they have broad discretion as they seek to implement the legislation, but that they must submit certain decisions to Congress (sometimes to one chamber, sometimes to a particular committee) before putting them in force. If the relevant legislative body votes to object, the executive cannot go forward; if, however, there is no objection, the regulation can proceed. The development of these mechanisms constituted an attempt to square the inevitability of legislative delegation of decisionmaking authority to the bureaucracy with the felt need of the legislature to prevent abuses of that authority.

Presidents, of course, resisted the legislative veto, arguing that it infringed on their power as chief executive. Unfortunately for the designers of the legislative veto, the US Supreme Court agreed with the presidential position, declaring this mechanism unconstitutional in the landmark case of *INS v. Chadha,* decided in 1983.[6] The Court's view was that the job of the legislature was to legislate and the job of the executive was to execute and that once the legislature had completed the legislation and the president had signed it into law, the executive branch was free to carry it out as it wished. As far as the Court was concerned, if Congress was concerned with how a law was being administered, the remedies at its disposal were either to pass legislation that provided the bureaucracy with precise instructions on how the statute should be implemented, thus reducing the discretion of the bureaucracy, or to rectify what it felt to be inappropriate uses of bureaucratic power by revising the law.

Although *Chadha* rendered legislative vetoes officially unconstitutional, Louis Fisher (1997:152–159), a leading scholar of congressional procedure, finds that they continue to be enacted and, despite formal presidential insistence, typically registered in a signing statement, that they will be ignored, they continue to be used and respected on an informal level. Bureaucrats and the presidents to whom they report realize the importance of maintaining good relations with powerful members of Congress who control their budgets and have the ability to pass legislation restricting or eliminating the jurisdiction of government agencies. In addition, the executive does not necessarily wish to invite Congress to be more specific in the legislation it passes; presidents and bureaucrats appreciate the discretion that statutory vagueness provides them. This mutual interest means that administrators will check with key members and their staffs on an informal basis as they develop implementing regulations, that they will be responsive to questions or concerns that come from the legislature, and that they likely will avoid proceeding if these consultations suggest that what they plan to do has substantially departed from the intentions or wishes of those who wrote the legislation. Because all of this happens informally, it is difficult to verify how frequently these consultations take place. The fairest conclusion is probably one that suggests that while the legislature has ensured itself the potential for limiting the bureaucracy, the sheer size and complexity of the task means that a significant amount of bureaucratic discretion remains and that legislative intervention is at best episodic.

Where does all of this leave presidents, the ostensible chief executives of these sprawling bureaucratic enterprises? Clearly, they are in a better position to control the bureaucracy than is the legislature, because those who directly supervise the bureaucracy serve at the pleasure of the president. As two scholars of the US presidency note, presidents, through the skillful use of their power to appoint the leaders of various agencies, can exert significant control over the actions of those agencies (Fine and Waterman 2008). Of course, as we have noted, the size of the bureaucracy in terms of the number of people and agencies involved, as well as the political constraints imposed by partisan and congressional forces on whom the president can appoint, will mean that this strategy is unlikely to succeed across the full span of the bureaucracy. Perhaps the fairest conclusion is that presidents, if they wish, can control parts of the bureaucracy most of the time, but will be unable to control all of the bureaucracy all of the time. On the other hand, in those hyperpresidentialized systems with weaker traditions of bureaucratic neutrality, and in smaller countries with less sprawling bureaucracies, presidents may well have an easier time exercising control.

However, if there is a presidential advantage, either real or perceived, in exercising control of the bureaucracy, it also comes with presidential responsibility. When things go wrong in the bureaucracy, when incidents of misfeasance or malfeasance arise, or even when the bureaucracy makes an honest attempt to deal with an issue but fails to resolve it, the president, as chief executive, is saddled by the public and the legislature with the responsibility. The buck, as President Harry Truman advised, does stop at the president's desk. However, that seems to be a relatively small price to pay for the extraordinary amount of power that a presidentially controlled bureaucracy gives to the president to determine and influence the course of public policy.

The concern in this connection is that the power of the bureaucracy, effectively unchecked by the legislature yet under the ostensible control of the president, overly empowers the president. Writing about the US presidency, but in terms that could apply to other presidencies as well, one scholar concludes that by "creating new organization, expanding the scope and powers of existing institutions, and unilaterally altering crucial administrative procedures, presidents have been remarkably successful in gaining control of the government's institutional apparatus, outmaneuvering Congress and only rarely being blocked by the courts" (Mayer 2002:109). For example, in June 2012, President Obama, frustrated by Congress's failure to enact the "Dream Act" that would have given legal status to undocumented young people who came to the United States as children, instructed the Immigration and Customs Enforcement (ICE) agency to suspend the detention and deporting of most of these people and to set up a process for allowing them to work in the country legally. The president's decision was condemned by his opponents as an example of arbitrary executive action that ignored the policy expertise of bureaucrats as well as the prerogatives of Congress in order to help him to secure the Latino vote in the upcoming presidential election. All of that may be true, but for our purposes the episode underlines the connection between the bureaucratic state and the aggrandizement of presidential power.

Conclusion

Modern governments have extended their reach to virtually every corner of their societies. Through regulations, monetary, fiscal, and trade policies, and the sheer size of their budgets, they impact every area of their nation's economy. They deal with policy areas as diverse as education, energy, agriculture, the arts, the environment, space exploration, and healthcare, as well as the more traditional areas of national defense and the construction of roads. This expansive and growing agenda is in part the product of the expansion of knowledge that took place in the twentieth century. There was no need for a space agency before scientists and engineers understood how rockets could be sent to outer space. When no one understood the causes or the consequences of environmental degradation, nothing much could or would have been done about it. But as experts came to know more, solutions presented themselves that eventually took the form of public policies to address the issue.

The expansion of government is also in part the product of a modern sensibility that government has a responsibility to provide protection and support to its most vulnerable citizens, whether they are defined by age, medical condition, or economic status. And it was a product of a view that free market systems, left to their own devices, could produce results that were contrary to the public interest. Businesses needed to be regulated to protect their employees as well as those who consumed their products, banks needed to be regulated to protect their depositors, and large corporations needed to be regulated to protect against monopolistic practices.

The result of the expansion of governmental agendas—an expansion that took place in every economically developed nation and even in most less developed nations—was the growth in the size and prominence of the bureaucracy. As public policy areas multiplied and became more complex, legislative bodies lacked the time and the expertise to develop statutes that contained precise instructions on how to accomplish the goals embodied in the laws that they passed. That task was turned over to bureaucrats, who were empowered to implement these policies; this assignment carried with it a great deal of discretionary power, as bureaucrats made the specific decisions that turned the general terms in which most legislation was phrased into the specific regulations and procedures under which those affected by the law would have to live. These same bureaucrats also became central players as new policies were developed or existing policies were revised. All of this was justified by the assumption that bureaucrats were experts who would have the time and the talent to make these policy decisions, and the result of their efforts would be good policy in the public interest. Legislators, in contrast, generally were not experts on public policy, and their decisions were likely to be influenced by political and electoral concerns rather than by the public interest or by the specialized knowledge that was appropriate to that policy area.

In all political systems, the expansion and empowerment of the bureaucracy has resulted in the strengthening of the executive branch of government. In presidential systems, the president as chief executive formally presided over the bureaucratic hierarchy and from that position could presumably influence or determine the decisions that bureaucrats made. Discretionary power for the bureaucracy became in essence discretionary power for the president, power akin to the decree power possessed by many presidents. Ironically, it was legislatures—presumably adversaries of the president in the sense that when the president's power increased, the legislature's power usually decreased—that played the key role in the aggrandizing of the bureaucracy as they created more public policies that required more people with more discretionary power to implement them. In some countries, presidents and bureaucrats worked closely together to marginalize representative institutions and to implement major new policies. It has even been argued that such a presidential-bureaucratic alliance is the only way to generate significant changes, either progressive or conservative, in the policy status quo—changes that representative institutions are seemingly genetically programmed to resist.

The other result of the empowerment of the executive branch was the further inflation of the expectations that the public had of the government and the president. As governments began to do more, people came to expect that every new problem was or should be vulnerable to governmental solution, and these expectations came to focus most sharply on the president. This was not always good news for the president. As the bureaucracy became both more expansive and more expensive, the capacity of the president to supervise everything that was happening became more problematic. In addition, in many countries the bureaucracy was dominated by career public servants whose tenure in office was guaranteed by civil service laws and who typically possessed greater expertise in the policy areas within their responsibility than did the president and his staff. Although the growth of the bureaucracy meant more power to the president in comparison to the legislature, the president's new and in some ways more difficult challenge was to control the bureaucracy and harness its efforts to the task of implementing his agenda. Of course, presidents may be able to exercise more control if they are able to staff the bureaucracy with patronage appointees who are beholden to them, as is the case in many Latin American and African countries, but the price of that strategy is likely to be a diminishing role for policy expertise. Other attempts to centralize all bureaucratic decisions in the president's office also may sacrifice expertise and create policymaking bottlenecks as well. But whether or not presidents are able to exercise control, they still are forced to accept responsibility for the actions, inactions, and failures of those over whom their authority sometimes may be more apparent than real.

The real question is whether the bureaucratic state is in the end susceptible to complete political control, either by the president or by the legislature. The latter largely has given up on that task, responding only to the "fire alarms" set off by disaster or highly publicized failures. Presidents continue to work aggressively at the task, but as they do so, they need to be able to resolve the tension between expertise and political control. And finally, if presidents actually are successful in gaining control of the bureaucracy, the possibility that presidentialism will deteriorate into authoritarianism must be considered.

Notes

1. Data are drawn from www.stats.govt.nz/NR/rdonlyres/EF423908-04F5 -4778-9897-149B90D7D9A0D/0/GovernmentSpendingandReceipts.pdf; www.usgovernmentspending.com/us_20th_century_chart.html; http://blog .jparsons.net/2009/03/us-government-spending-as-percentage-of.html; and www.ukpublicspending.co.uk/uk_20th_century_chart.html.

2. For the United States, Stanley and Niemi 2006:265–266; for the United Kingdom, www.statistics.gov.uk/cci/nugget.asp?id=407; and for France, Safran 2009:291–292. Even these figures underestimate the economic impact of the government. In the United States, if one considers not just government employees but also those employed by federal contractors, as well as those whose salaries are paid by grants from the federal government, the true size of the federal government in 2005 may have been as high as 14.6 million employees, or one out of every fifteen citizens over the age of twenty who draw their paychecks directly or indirectly from the federal government (Light 2006).

3. 467 US 837 (1984).

4. Executive Order 12866, January 2007. The Obama administration retained Order 12866 with minor adjustments embodied in Executive Order 13563, issued in January 2011.

5. Sebastian Saiegh (2010:75) offers a more nuanced analysis, suggesting that legislators in Brazil and Chile have the capacity to be constructive participants in the policymaking process, while in other countries legislatures operate more as "blunt veto players" employing gate-keeping and delaying strategies.

6. 462 US 919 (1983).

5

Presidentialism and Globalism

The arguments in support of strong executive power always have been most compelling in regard to international policy decisions. Issues of war and peace, the negotiation and establishment of alliances and treaties, a nation's foreign policy posture, and the many other dimensions of a nation's relationship with other countries around the world have been policy domains that presidents and other executives have dominated.

Throughout history, consuls, princes, kings, and presidents have claimed and exercised extraordinary power at times when their nations were faced with war. Locke, even as he made the case for the primacy of legislative power, posited a federative power that would place the nation's foreign policy and control of its military in the hands of the king. It was in the context of this federative power that Locke developed the notion of executive prerogatives; in other matters falling under the purview of the executive, he had to act within the law (see Kleinerman 2009:2). As one contemporary commentator has put it, "war acts on executive power as an accelerant, causing it to burn hotter, brighter, and swifter" (Yoo 2009:vii). Presidents and those who have supported dominant presidential power in this arena have offered several justifications for that position.

The Arguments for Presidential Control

First, in a nation's relations with other countries, there is a greater premium on secrecy and the confidentiality of information than there is in domestic policy. If existing or potential enemies become privy to the military or diplomatic plans of a nation, the success of those plans will be jeopardized. These decisions rely heavily on information generated by a nation's diplomatic and intelligence services, which report to the president. This information must be closely guarded and carefully distilled so that apparent facts can be verified and the identity of confidential sources protected. Leaders also expect that the discussions that they have with their counterparts in other nations will be treated with discretion. If such interchanges are to be productive, differing points of view need to be expressed frankly and fully, and this cannot happen in public arenas, where the potential for domestic and international embarrassment as well as diplomatic and political repercussions is high. That is why these discussions typically take place in private, and why their results are reported to larger audiences only in carefully phrased joint statements that often conceal as much as they reveal. If secrecy is important, presidents and their military and diplomatic advisers are in a better position to maintain confidentiality, it is argued, than are the members of more open and accessible institutions such as legislatures.

Second, the president is likely to have more information about international matters than most legislators will possess. In addition to its intelligence agencies, the nation's ambassadors to other countries report to the executive branch, and the Department of State (or Ministry of Foreign Affairs) houses experts on the conduct of diplomacy and on the politics and plans of foreign nations. It is the president and his ministers or cabinet members who confer with other heads of states and governments about their intentions and needs. These various information sources all come together at the presidency, putting that office in a unique position to construct the "big picture"—to combine military, diplomatic, and intelligence data with the nation's various political, economic, and strategic interests in order to produce a coherent whole that can provide the basis for informed decisions. Most legislators will not have that same ability, and given the nature of this information, much of it cannot be openly and completely shared with a legislative body. In contrast, when it comes to domestic politics, there is little information that cannot be shared with legislators. And in those policy areas, the information legislators have may well be as much and even better than a president will have.

Third, the ability to act quickly is vital, especially when war is imminent—when a nation has been attacked, or is about to be attacked, or is about to launch an attack of its own. Legislatures, whatever their virtues might be, are not known for their ability to act quickly. In fact, legislatures are not supposed to act quickly; they are deliberative bodies designed to be arenas in which competing viewpoints can be aired and fully discussed, and such a process by definition takes time. These strengths and defining characteristics of legislative bodies are incompatible with rapid decisionmaking. Dispatch as well as secrecy are at a premium in military and diplomatic affairs, and both are more likely to be maximized to the extent that decisionmaking power is vested in fewer rather than in many hands.

Fourth, a nation's armed forces cannot be directed by a collective body that will of necessity speak with many voices. The military is organized in a hierarchical rather than a collegial manner. Votes are seldom taken in military establishments, and orders that come from superiors are not normally subject to debate. When decisions about military tactics and strategy are taken, especially during an ongoing conflict, it is expected that these decisions will be implemented without question. In this sense, the executive branch is structurally compatible with the military; it too is organized in a hierarchical manner and the president, as chief executive, is free to make decisions that he expects will be obeyed. Similarly, in the area of foreign policy, hierarchic control is also advantageous; an ambassador to a foreign country cannot wait for a collective body such as a legislature to develop instructions on how she should proceed in negotiations with her counterparts. Such instructions need to come from the chief executive or his designee.

Fifth, executive control provides accountability. That is, when the president makes decisions, there is little question about who is responsible for those decisions and who needs to account to the nation for the policy, particularly if it fails. It is easier to hold an individual accountable than it is to hold a collective institution such as a legislature accountable. And because accountability is an essential element of democratic theory—citizens cannot exercise control over decisionmakers if they do not know who is responsible for decisions—strong presidential power can be seen as compatible with democracy. In the US context, wars always have been connected to the presidents under whom they were waged—Franklin Roosevelt and World War II, Lyndon Johnson and Vietnam, George W. Bush and Iraq—and it has been these presidents, rather than congresses with whom they have governed, who have been held to account for the successes or failures of these military encounters.

Finally, in matters that involve foreign powers, some argue that visible dissent weakens the nation's position when dealing with other nations, erodes the public's confidence in its leaders, and allows adversaries to take into account and exploit internal differences. While conflict over domestic policy and priorities is expected and even welcome in an open and democratic society, in external affairs it is important for the nation to speak with one voice. For their part, other nations expect to be dealing with one person who can speak for the country, commit it to a course of action, and deploy its military, diplomatic, and financial resources in support of those actions. Because the president is the only nationally elected political leader, he is the only office holder who can make a legitimate and plausible claim to speak for the entire nation. Legislators are elected from smaller constituencies and although many, even most, believe that they have the needs of the entire nation in mind when they address foreign and defense issues, their views may well be filtered through a local or partisan prism, especially if these issues have domestic ramifications.

Public Attitudes

Citizens are more likely to support stronger executive power on international matters than on domestic issues. When it comes to questions of national safety and security, they are inclined to turn to the president and the military officials who advise him. In most nations, the military is generally well thought of. In the United States, it evokes higher levels of trust from the public than do any of the three formal branches of the government. In 2011, 78 percent of a national sample reported a great deal or quite a lot of confidence in the military. In comparison, confidence in the president was at 35 percent, in the Supreme Court at 37 percent, and in Congress at 12 percent.[1] In Latin America, a survey of seventeen nations found that in all but two of these countries, more than 50 percent of the respondents indicated that they trusted the armed forces (Montalvo 2009). Despite the strong public commitment to democracy in these countries, there is some evidence that because the military is associated with order and public safety, public support for military coups or other sorts of domestic intervention by the military increases as fear of crime and internal unrest rises (Perez 2009). That is probably why those who have led military coups frequently cite disorder as a reason for their intervention. When President Ferdinand Marcos closed the Philippine Congress in 1972 with the support of the nation's military, he "claimed that there existed a serious threat to national security," pointing "to the collapse of law and order in the country, the rise of warlord armies, and the threat that the government was going to be overthrown by various insurgency groups" (Casper 1995:44). Similar terms have been used by military leaders in Latin America and Africa to justify the steps that they have taken to depose sitting governments.

In Africa, attitudes toward the military seem to vary by country and time period. For example, according to data collected between 1999 and

2001, 94 percent of the respondents in Tanzania, 80 percent of the respondents in Mali, and 64 percent of the respondents in Ghana indicated that they trusted the military (Logan 2008). In Nigeria, a 2003 survey found that 55 percent of the respondents expressed some degree of trust for the military, though only 17 percent said that they trusted the armed forces "a lot," and just 3 percent said that they trusted them "a very great deal." But this trust clearly does not translate into support for military rule; in 2001, as Nigeria transitioned from military to civilian government, 81 percent of the respondents in one survey rejected the idea of a military regime, and 72 percent said that they supported the newly elected civilian president, Olusegun Obasanjo. However, by 2003, as dissatisfaction with economic conditions increased along with security concerns, Obasanjo's approval rating had dropped to 39 percent, and the percentage of respondents who rejected military rule had dropped to 69 percent (Lewis and Alemika 2005). Nonetheless, support for military rule across Africa is relatively low; data for 2005–2006 indicate that majorities in seventeen out of eighteen African nations reject the idea.[2]

Because military activity against external enemies evokes the deepest symbols of national identity and patriotism—symbols with which presidents as heads of state are also identified—dissent from the direction that the nation has chosen to take in the international arena, particularly in terms of military actions, is more likely to be viewed as inappropriate or even unpatriotic, as compared with dissent on purely domestic matters. The old expression in the United States is that "politics stops at the water's edge." Although there is some evidence that Congress can constrain the president on military action when it is controlled by the opposition party (Howell and Pevehouse 2007), normally, when presidents decide to engage in military action, their public support tends to increase, and Congress tends to go along. Pleas to "support our troops" become synonymous with pleas for support for the policy decisions and policymakers that placed them in harm's way. But when a war drags on with no end or victory in sight, public support for both the war and the president who championed it tends to deteriorate, and legislative opposition is likely to become more vocal.

The Transformation of the US Presidency

It has been in the area of foreign and military policy that US presidents have been most successful in advancing their powers beyond the explicit limitations set by the language of the Constitution. For instance, the

Constitution states that the president shall make treaties "by and with the advice and consent of the Senate," implying a founding aspiration for a joint responsibility in foreign policy rather than for unilateral authority in the hands of the president. In the first year of his presidency, George Washington actually did solicit the advice of the Senate on a treaty that he wished to negotiate with Native Americans in Georgia. However, the discussions with the Senate proved unproductive, and many senators seemed to believe that it was inappropriate for Washington to be consulting with them on this issue. Washington viewed the whole episode as a waste of time, and from then on, he and those who followed him negotiated treaties with the advice and participation of their advisers, cabinet members, and members of the civilian and military bureaucracy. At most, a few senators would be informally consulted, but the role of the Senate as a whole was reduced to one of consenting (or not) to the final document. Such consent, of course, has never been guaranteed. On many occasions, the US Senate has rejected—or failed to act on—important treaties that presidents have asked it to approve, including the Treaty of Versailles, which ended World War I and established the League of Nations, as well as the Kyoto Protocol, designed to deal with climate change.

Today, however, US presidents have, to an increasing degree, circumvented the constitutionally mandated treaty process by negotiating executive agreements with other nations. Sometimes these documents have been submitted to Congress for majority approval (rather than the two-thirds approval required for treaties), and sometimes presidents have ignored Congress entirely. By one count, as of 2000, more than 16,000 executive agreements had been entered into, compared with approximately 1,700 treaties (Stanley and Niemi 2006:339). Although most executive agreements deal with relatively minor matters, there are many that constitute substantial commitments by the president on behalf of the nation. At the end of World War II, US membership in the International Trade Organization resulted from an executive agreement that was not submitted to Congress; the North American Free Trade Agreement also was an executive agreement that President Bill Clinton submitted to Congress for its majority approval (see Crenson and Ginsberg 2007:254–255).

Although the marginalization of the Senate's role in regard to international agreements has enhanced presidential foreign policy making power, a more significant precedent for the expansion of presidential power occurred in Washington's second term in office. With a war being waged in Europe between England and France, Washington, faced with pressure to support the British against the French revolutionaries, as well as countervailing pressure to reciprocate the support that France provided to the colonies during the American Revolution, made the unilateral decision to issue a Proclamation of Neutrality. Although there was no explicit constitutional authority for the president to issue such a proclamation, Washington viewed it as an "inherent power" of the president—a power that, although not stated specifically in the Constitution, came with the office. The substance of Washington's decision is less important here than its implications for presidential power. Although there was no reason why Congress could not have participated in this crucial foreign policy decision, there was nothing in the Constitution that prevented Washington from acting on his own. In doing so, Washington firmly established the principle that presidents would be in charge of deciding the foreign policy of the United States. More generally, Washington's decision made clear that the vagueness in the Constitution's grant of executive power to the president would be an invitation to presidents to interpret the document in the broadest terms.

Placing limits on the power of the president in his role as commander in chief proved to be even more challenging. The narrow reading of that power, offered by Alexander Hamilton in the Federalist Papers, held that the president would be in charge of the military once the nation was engaged in war, with the power to decide to go to war along with the power to raise and support the military firmly lodged with Congress. But in December 1791, President Washington ordered the army to take offensive action against Native Americans in the Northwest Territories and, under certain circumstances, to attack British positions that were in alliance with these tribes. Washington neither consulted with Congress on these decisions nor asked for its approval. He did ask Congress to increase in the size of the army and to provide the extra funds to support the escalated war, a request that Congress, after much debate, ultimately approved. In the view of one scholar, this incident established a precedent for future decisions about war: the president, in his role as commander in chief, could initiate hostilities, and the only way that Congress could stop him, if it wished to do so, was through its constitutional power to control both the funding and the size of the military (Yoo 2009:78–80). In other words, the proactive power of Congress to declare war was in effect a dead letter, replaced by the solely reactive power to refuse to fund the undertaking.

This may have been a reasonable approach when there were a relatively small number of men under arms during times of peace and the president, if he wished to go to war, would of necessity have had to ask Congress to raise and support a larger military force to fight a war under his command. But what if there were an armed force in existence during peace time, as there was by the mid–nineteenth century, and as there would be on a much grander scale by the middle of the twentieth century? Could the president use his power as commander in chief to deploy those troops in a manner that would make war inevitable, and if he did, would Congress really be able to refuse funding once the nation's troops were engaged in battle?

That question was answered in 1846 when President James Polk, using his power as commander in chief, moved US troops to the country's southern border at a time of great tension between the United States and Mexico. To no one's surprise, shortly after they arrived, they were attacked by elements of the Mexican military. Polk ordered the troops to respond, which meant that the nation was in fact at war with Mexico even if war had not been formally declared by Congress. The Mexican-American War bitterly divided Congress and the nation between supporters and opponents of the conflict, but the fact that the war was already taking place and the blood of US soldiers had been shed left opponents in Congress with few alternatives but to provide the funds and the manpower that the conflict required. After the war, however, Congress passed a resolution censuring Polk for a war "unnecessarily and unconstitutionally begun by the President of the United States" (Crenson and Ginsberg 2007:17).

The point to note is that although the Constitution suggested that the president's power as commander in chief would come into effect only after Congress declared war, Polk's action demonstrated conclusively that the president, by moving troops to an area where hostilities were very likely to take place, could in effect start a war that, once begun, Congress would have no option but to finance. Thus, one century later, President Dwight Eisenhower sent a small number of troops to advise the South Vietnamese army, at the time embroiled in a civil war with North Vietnam, a commitment that his successor, President John Kennedy, continued and expanded. It was only a matter of time until these "advisers" would be drawn into the conflict. When in 1964 two US warships operating in international waters off the coast of Vietnam were allegedly attacked by North Vietnam (there is significant doubt about the circumstances of the "attack"), Congress responded with the Gulf of Tonkin resolution, essentially authorizing President Lyndon Johnson to engage in full-scale military combat while avoiding an actual declaration of war. The result, nonetheless, was a war that raged for more than a decade, involving at its peak more than 250,000 US troops in the field, costing, in the end, nearly 50,000 US lives and many times that number of injuries, creating huge divisions among the citizens, and influencing discussions of US foreign policy for decades to come. The merits and demerits of the Vietnam War, however, are not important here; for our purposes, the point is that the war began and continued because of unilateral decisions taken by four US presidents—Eisenhower, Kennedy, Johnson, and Nixon—in their role as commander in chief, to commit troops to a part of the world where they were likely to be drawn into conflict, and to keep them there until the president decided that their mission was accomplished. For its part, Congress was left with no viable alternative other than to provide the president and his successors and the troops that they commanded with what they said that they needed to succeed. This was especially the case given the president's control over all of the essential information and the resulting inability of Congress to challenge the Johnson administration's version of what happened in the Gulf of Tonkin, or later, the state of the ongoing war effort.

Similarly, in 2003, Congress had only President George W. Bush's narrative of the intelligence information that suggested that Iraq had developed "weapons of mass destruction," that Saddam Hussein was connected with the September 11, 2001, attacks, and that Iraq had attempted to buy uranium from Niger. Based on that version of the "facts," Congress agreed to support a war with Iraq, although President Bush had made it clear that he would have gone to war even if Congress had not agreed. By the time that it became apparent that the president's intelligence information was faulty, the United States was already at war, just as it was in Vietnam by the time that the Pentagon Papers suggested that President Johnson's account of what happened in the Gulf of Tonkin was not entirely accurate and that the war was not going as well as the nation had been led to believe. Once at war, decisions about its strategy, its tactics, and about how or whether to bring it to an end were entirely in the hands of the president, with the only constitutional option available to Congress being the politically untenable one of cutting off funds to soldiers in the field.

The possibility that the president's power as commander in chief to move and deploy troops would expand to the capacity to actually make war was foreseen by many. One of the members of Congress most strongly opposed to Polk's actions in regard to the Mexican-American War was Abraham Lincoln, who was a representative from Illinois at the time. Lincoln's view was that Polk's strategy essentially gave the president the unilateral power to declare war, something that he viewed as dangerous. "Allow the President to invade a neighboring nation whenever he shall deem it necessary to repel an invasion, and you allow him to make war at his pleasure," Lincoln said in a letter to one of Polk's supporters. The president would become the sole judge of the interests of the nation and the dangers that the country faced. Lincoln went on to note that the decision of the Founders to place the war-making power in the hands of Congress "was dictated by the following reasons: Kings had always been involving and impoverishing their people in war, pretending generally, if not always that the good of the people was the object. This our [constitutional] convention understood to be the most oppressive of all kingly oppressions, and they resolved to so frame the Constitution that no one man should hold the power of bringing this oppression upon us."[3]

Ironically, once Lincoln became president some twelve years later, he dramatically expanded the war-making power of the presidency as he sought to deal with the crisis of Southern secession. Enunciating the idea of emergency power discussed earlier, Lincoln, among other things, spent money, raised the size of the military, declared martial law, imposed a military blockade on Southern ports, and issued the Emancipation Proclamation, all without the prior approval from Congress that the Constitution required. Lincoln justified his actions by citing the emergency that the nation was confronting and arguing not that he was exercising his constitutional power but rather that because of the crisis, it was necessary for him to transcend both the law and the Constitution. "Measures otherwise unconstitutional," he said, "might become lawful by becoming indispensable to the preservation of the Constitution thru the preservation of the Union."[4] In regard to the blockade, even though it was taken at a time when Congress had not yet declared war, the Supreme Court, in the *Prize Cases,* agreed that Lincoln's decision was constitutional, and Congress never seriously challenged his expenditure of funds without congressional authorization.[5]

Lincoln's argument for emergency powers in the context of the Civil War—the most serious challenge to its survival that the United States had or would face in its history—is compelling. Few today would dispute the moral correctness of issuing the Emancipation Proclamation, although legal purists would point out that this action had no basis given the Constitution's acknowledgment of slavery and the lack of any explicit presidential power to issue such a proclamation. But Lincoln justified the proclamation as a war measure, pointing out that it applied only to those who were being held in servitude in states that were in revolt against the Union and that it was a wartime necessity, because slaves were being impressed into the Confederate armies.

This rationale suggested the possibility that a whole range of presidential actions of dubious constitutionality could be justified in terms of national security under the expanding definition of the president's commander in chief power. Lincoln's actions thus established a precedent that his successors would use, and not always in exactly the same context as Lincoln did and not with as convincing an argument as Lincoln marshaled. Most notably, at the outbreak of World War II, President Franklin Roosevelt issued an executive order for the removal of all US citizens of Japanese descent from the West Coast and their incarceration in inland detention camps for the duration of the war with Japan. Although a clear violation of multiple provisions of the Bill of Rights, the Supreme Court, in the case of *Korematsu v. United States,* upheld the president's actions, citing his power to protect the nation in times of "emergency and peril."[6] Thirty years later, Richard Nixon attempted, this time unsuccessfully, to connect his actions during the Watergate affair to national security concerns. After he had been driven from office, he made the statement that any violations of the law that he or his aides may have committed were not in fact illegal if the president ordered them—an extreme but not implausible extension of the Lincoln and Roosevelt precedents. In the wake of the terrorist attacks on the United States in September 2001, President George W. Bush also engaged in a range of surveillance and detention activities of dubious constitutionality, claiming that they were necessary to protect the security of the nation and justified under his power as commander in chief. His office of legal counsel in the Justice Department argued that even criminal prohibitions against torture do "not apply to the President's detention and interrogation of enemy combatants pursuant to his Commander in Chief authority" (Koh 2006:2357). In addition to these steps, Bush ordered an attack on Afghanistan that toppled the Taliban regime and issued an executive order creating a new cabinet position, the secretary of homeland security, who was given the power to coordinate the efforts of federal, state, and local agencies as well as private entities to fight terrorism (Macey 2006:2428). And in 2011, President Barack Obama, without consulting Congress, made the unilateral decision to commit US air power to an effort by the North Atlantic Treaty Organization (NATO) to protect Libyan civilians from being massacred by forces loyal to Colonel Muammar Qaddafi. However, the operation's goals shifted to an air war in support of the rebel effort to remove Qaddafi from power, an undertaking with limited support from the American people and with dubious chances of being approved by Congress had the president sought its approval.

The point then is that the president's commander in chief power, as interpreted by Lincoln, Roosevelt, Nixon, George W. Bush, and Obama, allows him to be the sole judge of the extent of that power. Hamilton's assurances in the 74th Federalist Paper that the commander in chief clause was simply an expedient to ensure hierarchical control over the military after the people, through their representatives in Congress, had decided to engage another nation in hostilities, has in essence become null and void, and the possibility that such a power could extend to domestic issues—a concern of several of those who debated the merits of the new Constitution at the end of the eighteenth century—has become quite real in the early years of the twenty-first century.

Constraining the President's International Role

Attempts to constrain this presidential power through the courts or through congressional action have not been particularly successful. During the twentieth century, the idea that the president had certain prerogatives in the area of foreign and defense policy that he did not possess on purely domestic issues became settled law from the perspective of the judiciary. In the Supreme Court case of *United States v. Curtiss-Wright Export Corp.*, decided in 1936, the Court indicated that while a decision by Congress to delegate broad discretionary powers to the president in domestic matters might be constitutionally suspect, such a delegation in international matters was acceptable. The president, the Court said, was "the sole organ of the federal government in the field of international relations."[7] The next year, in the case of *United States v. Belmont,* the Court used the same argument that it made in *Curtiss Wright* to uphold the constitutionality of an executive agreement negotiated by the president that was not submitted to Congress.[8] Eight years later, in the *Korematsu* case, the Court upheld Roosevelt's executive order removing Japanese Americans from the West Coast.

But in 1952, in the case of *Youngstown Sheet and Tube v. Sawyer,* the Court seemed ready to place at least some limits on the president's power as commander in chief.[9] President Harry Truman made the decision to end a steel workers' strike by seizing the steel mills, arguing that his actions were justified by the fact that he was commander in chief, the country was at war in Korea, and the continued production of steel was a wartime necessity. The Court rejected Truman's position and in an important concurring opinion, Justice Robert Jackson developed a test to judge whether a president's actions overstepped the Constitution. Jackson argued that the president was on the strongest ground when he acted in pursuit of explicit congressional authorization. Absent such an authorization, the president must rely on his own independent powers, or on powers shared with Congress. In those instances, the president's decisions are more vulnerable to challenge, although he is on somewhat stronger ground if Congress has not acted. Finally, if the president takes steps that are incompatible with the expressed or implied will of Congress, such actions are the most problematic and must be most carefully scrutinized. In *Youngstown*, the Court decided that the seizure of the steel mills fell into that third category.

Despite Justice Jackson's categories, congressional efforts to curtail presidential war and foreign policy powers have generally been fruitless. In 1973, Congress passed the War Powers Resolution over President Nixon's veto. The aim of the resolution, designed in the aftermath of the Vietnam War, was to provide Congress with a more effective way to end US involvement in hostilities while implicitly conceding to the president the right to engage US troops in hostile action without congressional consent. The resolution encouraged but did not require the president to consult with Congress before dispatching troops, and it required him to gain congressional consent within a sixty-day period in order to keep the troops engaged. If such consent was not forthcoming, the president would be required to withdraw troops. Although the act constituted informal recognition of a unilateral presidential power to start a war, no president of either party has recognized the constitutionality of the War Powers Resolution, with all arguing that it was an infringement on the president's constitutional authority as commander in chief, particularly the section that would compel the president to withdraw troops in the absence of a congressional authorization to keep them in the field. Although President George H. W. Bush consulted Congress before launching the Gulf War in 1990, President Clinton consulted before intervening in Bosnia, and President George W. Bush consulted before going to war in Iraq, each president made it clear that they were prepared and legally able to proceed even if Congress did not agree.

The men who wrote the US Constitution were fearful of placing the power to start wars in the hands of the president. James Madison, writing as a critic of George Washington's decision on the Proclamation of Neutrality, said this: "In no part of the constitution is more wisdom to be found, than in the clause which confides the question of war or peace to the legislature, and not to the executive department." He argued that "the trust and the temptation would be too great for any one man" and that "war is in fact the true nurse of executive aggrandizement." He concluded with the following:

In war, a physical force is to be created; and it is the executive will, which is to direct it. In war, the public treasures are to be unlocked; and it is the executive hand which is to dispense them. In war, the honours and emoluments of office are to be multiplied; and it is the executive patronage under which they are to be enjoyed. It is in war, finally, that laurels are to be gathered; and it is the executive brow they are to encircle. The strongest passions and most dangerous weaknesses of the human breast: ambition, avarice, vanity, the honourable or venial love of fame, are all in conspiracy against the desire and duty of peace. Hence it has grown into an axiom that the executive is the department of power most distinguished by its propensity to war: hence it is the practice of all states, in proportion as they are free, to disarm this propensity of its influence. (Madison 1793)

But as the office has developed, there have been relatively few restrictions placed on the president in regard to his conduct of the nation's foreign and military affairs, either by the courts or by Congress. For example, the Supreme Court has refused to deal with cases questioning the legality of conflicts that have been fought without congressional declarations of war, and they have never considered the questions raised by the fact that even though the War Powers Resolution is on the statute books, presidents have made the unilateral decision to ignore the law. The Court, in this respect, has perhaps been conscious of its role as the "least dangerous" branch of government (to use Hamilton's phrase from the 78th Federalist Paper), with "no influence over either the sword or the purse; no direction either of the strength or of the wealth of society" (78:465). Courts, especially in times of conflict, have recognized their inability to enforce their decisions and are inclined to support presidential actions that test the limits of their constitutional power or alternatively assert that Congress, by virtue of its power of the purse and its impeachment authority, has sufficient resources to check the president.

On the other hand, in a series of cases decided in the first decade of the twenty-first century, the Supreme Court did place a series of restrictions on presidential powers in regard to the treatment and rights of individuals detained at the US base at Guantanamo Bay, Cuba, as part of the war on terror. The Court decided, contrary to the position of the George W. Bush administration, that detainees did have the right to challenge their incarceration in federal court, that trying detainees before military tribunals violated the Uniform Code of Military Justice as well as the Geneva Conventions, and that Congress could not strip the federal courts of their power to hear habeas corpus petitions from detainees. Writing for a plurality of the Court in the 2004 case of *Hamdi v. Rumsfeld*, Justice Sandra Day O'Connor, referring back to the *Youngstown* case, stated that "we have long since made clear that a state of war is not a blank check for the President when it comes to the rights of the Nation's citizens."[10]

Two years later, in the 2006 case of *Hamdan v. Rumsfeld* the Court decided that the president needed explicit congressional authorization before deciding that an enemy combatant could be tried before a special military tribunal.[11] And in the 2008 case of *Boumediene v. Bush,* which dealt with use of military commissions to try enemy combatants and the government's argument that such defendants should not have access to the federal courts, the Supreme Court made it clear that the government's powers in regard to war were not unlimited and that the Court would continue to maintain the appropriate constitutional boundaries, especially when it came to the rights of individuals.[12]

Despite the occasional reversals, the leading role of the US president in determining foreign and military policy is now beyond dispute. In terms of foreign policy, presidents since Washington have assumed that these were issues for them to determine. Barack Obama's late 2009 decisions to increase the US troop commitments to Afghanistan and expand the nation's counterterrorism efforts inside Pakistan were made unilaterally. As he forged ahead with these and other foreign and defense policy decisions—withdrawal from Iraq, seeking sanctions against the Iranian government, dealing with the Israeli-Palestinian conflict, intervening in the Libyan civil war, expanding the use of drones against suspected terrorists—he did so as presidents before him had done—working with his civilian and military advisers, checking with influential members of Congress on an informal basis, but ultimately making the decisions on his own.

A Comparative Perspective

Executive domination of international and military matters is found in every political system in the world and has been one of the driving forces of presidentialism. Today, virtually every nation has a standing armed force, even if it is at peace and war is unlikely, and the control of those forces is for the most part in the hands of the executives. The French presidency shares some similarities with the US arrangement in the sense that the French Constitution also requires that a declaration of war must be authorized by Parliament. Although it gives the president of the Republic the power to negotiate and ratify treaties (Article 52), it also identifies specific categories of treaties that should be ratified or approved only by an act of Parliament (Article 53). Despite this, many significant foreign policy decisions have been made solely by the president, including granting independence to Algeria, blocking British entry into the Common Market, withdrawing France from NATO's unified military command, and holding referenda on the Treaties and Constitution of the European Union (Safran 2009:201–202). The French Parliament also has the power to determine "the general organization of the military," but these provisions notwithstanding, during the last three decades of the twentieth century, French presidents deployed troops to Zaire, Chad, Lebanon, and the former Yugoslavia without debate or authorization by the National Assembly. When President François Mitterrand sought parliamentary approval for French participation in the Gulf War, he did so through a vote of no confidence, meaning that if the legislature said no, the government would resign, significantly reducing the likelihood of a negative decision (Martinez 2006:2492). And early in 2013, President Hollande made the unilateral decision to send troops to Mali to stop the advance of extremist forces on that country's capital and other major towns and cities.

In most countries, including the United States, departments or ministries of war have been renamed departments of defense—a semantic change justifying a large standing military establishment even in times of peace by implying a constant need for the nation to be prepared to defend itself against real or imagined enemies. And in many countries, such armed forces are dedicated not just to dealing with external threats but also to the control of internal insurrection or discontent. In the latter role, they often have been used to bolster the power of incumbent presidents against their domestic opponents, although they also have been instruments for the removal and replacement of presidents, as occurred in several Latin American and African nations during the last half of the twentieth century.

The maintenance of a nation's military is an expensive proposition. Soldiers need to be recruited, paid, housed, and fed. The military requires equipment—guns, planes, missiles, tanks, and ships—all of which cost a great deal of money. In the United States, military expenditures constitute about 20 percent of the federal budget, or about 4 percent of the country's gross domestic product. One study of Africa in the 1980s concluded that "the proportion of African funds going to equip and pay the military has been steadily rising, reaching for example over 40 percent in Ethiopia, and 25 and 20 percent respectively in drought ravaged Mauritania and Mali" (Whitaker 1988:43). In Latin America, the percentages vary, with Chile and Ecuador spending just over 20 percent of the federal budget on military expenditures, and most other Latin American countries spending around 10 percent.[13] Such expenditures tend to fluctuate from year to year, sometimes rising because of arms races or actual hostilities between nations causing countries to increase their military commitments. Increases also can be driven by a desire to back a more assertive foreign policy, on the assumption that a country with significant military might should be able to drive a tougher bargain with its adversaries compared to a country with a smaller military commitment.

Even without an arms race, having a large, well-equipped, and modernized military is viewed, particularly by smaller nations, as an important symbol of nationhood. Many countries around the world that have trouble finding sufficient funds to feed and educate their children always seem to have sufficient funds to support their armed forces. Those countries that produce armaments also have a vested interest in expanding their own military arsenals as well as those of other nations. In the United States, the mutually beneficial relationship between those who make the military hardware, the armed forces who use that hardware, and the members of Congress who appropriate the money to buy that hardware and in whose districts that hardware is built is well known. Arms-producing countries contribute to the expansion of weaponry in poorer nations by providing military aid on favorable terms as a way to maintain their own domestic arms industries and to create friendly relations with governments that may be helpful to their own security or economic interests. It is estimated that three-quarters of the global arms trade involves exports to developing countries, and one study showed that sixteen African countries spent more on arms than they received in foreign aid (Ayittey 1991:459).

Presidents and the Military

In every nation, all of these resources in men and materiel are under the auspices of executive leaders. In stable countries with a strong commitment to civilian government, these resources are primarily instruments of presidential power in the international arena. In less stable nations, they also can become instruments for maintaining executive power, as presidents intimidate and in some countries terrorize their domestic opponents. Whatever the case, the military might available to the president, and to be used as his virtual discretion, is a major contributor to presidentialism.

The intimate ties between presidents and their military establishments have been a traditional source of concern to those who view presidentialism as a potential danger. In the United States, when the Constitution was ratified, some critics of the document worried that making the president commander in chief of the nation's armed forces would tempt him to deploy them against his domestic opponents and in the end use these forces to keep himself in office beyond his allotted term, thereby creating a virtual monarchy. For those with that view, the constitutional provision barring a person from serving simultaneously as a military officer and as president did not seem sufficient. Writing under the pseudonym of Cato, an opponent of the new Constitution referred to the presidency as "the generalissimo of the nation" with "command and control of the army, navy and militia. . . . Will not the exercise of these powers therefore tend either to the establishment of a vile and arbitrary aristocracy or monarchy?" Another opponent, Philadelphiensis, put it more simply: "Who can deny but the president general will be a king to all intents and purposes, and one of the most dangerous kind too—a king elected to command a standing army."[14]

A military dictatorship did not come to pass in the United States; George Washington's rejection of the suggestion from some quarters that he do exactly that was an important precedent that led to the strong commitment to civilian rule. Nonetheless, several US presidents and presidential candidates have been drawn from the ranks of military heroes. From Washington to Obama, of the forty-three men who have held the office of president of the United States, twenty-five served in the military during wartime, and another six served in the military but saw no action. Although a president must resign from the armed forces before he can take office, presidents such as Washington, Jackson, Harrison, Grant, Theodore Roosevelt, and Eisenhower made their names and reputations as military men. And although John Kennedy did not have a military career, his exploits as a naval officer during World War II provided an early and important boost to his political fortunes.[15]

In part, this is attributable to the way in which the public views military service. As noted earlier, in the United States, citizens hold most political institutions in relatively low repute, but tend to think well of the nation's military. The military is depicted, not inaccurately, as the protector of the nation, with its members selflessly risking their lives for the safety of their fellow citizens and the security of the country. The military is also at least publicly nonpartisan, and so those who lead it can make the credible claim that they stand above the partisan conflicts of the day and therefore for the good of the nation. One student of professional military organizations puts it this way: "Identification of the military with national pride and honor creates a sort of political aloofness on their part, based on the conviction that politics is beneath military honor. They stand for consensus; politics implies competition, rivalry, and conflict between interest groups. They symbolize the intent of the whole nation; politics seeks the interests of particular groups within the nation" (Khuri 1982:14).

Wars, as Madison noted, create heroes, and such nonpartisan heroism, combined with the claim that one stands for national unity as opposed to divisiveness, can be an effective platform from which to launch a quest for the presidency, as US military generals such as Washington, Jackson, Grant, and Eisenhower did. Indeed, Eisenhower's political views were so vague before his presidential candidacy that he was wooed by both Democrats and Republicans. And because citizens see the preservation of national security as a crucial part of the president's job description, it is argued that service in the military provides a person with special expertise in this aspect of the position.

In Europe, military men have as a rule not found their way into high government positions, primarily because of the strength of the political parties and the parliamentary system, both of which privilege those who have come up through the political ranks to the position of head of government. It has been suggested as well that two world wars in Europe worked to discredit military institutions, particularly in Italy and Germany (Cheibub 2007:154). It is also the case that since the end of the colonial period, most European nations have not been involved in shooting wars to any great extent. The only European country where a military person has led during a period of democracy has been France—the one Western European country with a strong presidency—where Charles de Gaulle became the first president of the Fifth Republic. This occurred, however, in relatively close proximity to the end of World War II, when de Gaulle established his credentials as a national hero, and also in the midst of a crisis involving the French colonies in North Africa and a possible mutiny by elements of the army. Notably, none of de Gaulle's successors to the French presidency have been drawn from the military. Beyond de Gaulle, the only other instances of military leadership in Europe have been in authoritarian systems such as Spain's under General Francisco Franco, or Greece's during the brief period in the 1970s when it was under a military dictatorship.

Outside North America and Europe, the ascension of military leaders to presidencies is more common. These countries generally have weaker political parties and have not as firmly institutionalized the principles of civilian rule. In Asia, presidential systems such as Pakistan's and Indonesia's have had a long history of military presidents, while in the Philippines and Sri Lanka, civilian presidents have been heavily influenced by the military. In Latin America and Africa, military people have been more prominent as government leaders, and in many of these countries the military has taken an active role in both installing and removing presidents. Often, presidents have themselves been military officers, or recently retired officers, and even when they have been civilians, at times they have used the military internally to intimidate their opponents. At the same time, they have worked to maintain strong ties with military leaders in order to prolong their own tenure in office— ties that typically take the form of presidential support for large military budgets and inflated salaries for soldiers and their officers.

In Latin America for much of the twentieth century, "the military arrogated to itself the power of deciding when constitutional rights had been violated and when the time had arrived to enforce the law." Latin American armed forces were "highly political groups" that were intimately involved in policymaking on a wide range of issues, but particularly on those issues relating to their organization, such as budget, manpower decisions, and equipment purchases (Lieuwen 1962:150–152). They justified their interventions in politics in terms of their self-defined role as protector of the nation's constitution and preserver of law and order. Sometimes they acted at the behest of an opposition group of politicians, and almost always they acted to protect their own institutional interests (see Casper 1995:32). Subscribing to what political scientists called the national security doctrine, Latin American military leaders focused on the threat to the nation posed by insurgent, left-wing guerrilla movements and their elected allies. The armed forces, in the view of their leaders, "had the obligation of ensuring the national defense through the only means available, the complete control of society and government until such time as this threat could be eliminated" (Farcau 1996:18).

Late in the twentieth century, the political scientist Guillermo O'Donnell (1978, 1988) identified an alternative to the national security model—a regime that was dominated by a combination of military and civilian bureaucrats, clustered around a president who was sometimes a military person himself or was supported by the military. Compared with the national security model, what he calls the "bureaucratic authoritarian model" emphasized what is required to modernize a nation economically and to implement the neoliberal economic agenda. The combining of military and civilian bureaucrats in this approach makes some intuitive sense, because there is something of a natural affinity between these two bureaucratic institutions. Decisionmaking in both institutions takes place in a hierarchical environment rather than through the collegial process that characterizes legislatures and cabinets. Leadership positions in both of these organizations are presumably awarded on the basis of merit rather than the electoral criteria that characterize democratic arrangements. Both the military and the bureaucracy tend to view democratic political processes as slow, inefficient, and largely incapable of reaching the technically best policy solutions. They share "an almost innate rejection of party politics and the belief in technical and apolitical solutions for the country's problems." Both view themselves as exponents of modernization and tend to think of elective offices as dominated by the forces of tradition and inertia. In Chile, the military saw democracy "as an auspicious arena for corruption, demagogy, and anarchy, and eventually communism. On their part, engineers and, later, professional economists, have often questioned the ability of democracy to impose and to maintain the application of rational developmental policies despite their potentially high electoral costs" (Silva 2001:90). In Brazil, the 1964 military coup sought "to reorganize the state in such a way as to increase administrative efficiency and capacity for autonomous action" by concentrating power in the federal executive and depoliticizing the policymaking process "by transferring major policy decisions to a technobureaucracy" (Hagopian 1996:2). Similarly, many African nations saw close partnerships between the military and the bureaucracy. In Ghana, according to one observer, "the civil service became the military's most important ally" (Tordoff 1984:137).

Among the characteristics of the bureaucratic authoritarian state, according to O'Donnell, is an "organization in which specialists in coercion have decisive weight" with the goal of excluding the "popular sector, which is subjected to strict controls designed to eliminate its earlier presence in the political arena." This sort of state "endeavors to 'depoliticize' the handling of social issues, which are entrusted to those who deal with them according to the supposedly neutral and objective criteria of technical rationality." The regime closes "the democratic channels of access to the government." Instead, access is limited to "the armed forces, large enterprises, and certain segments of the state's civil bureaucracy" (1988:31–32).

The bureaucratic authoritarian model is compatible with the notion of presidentialism in the sense that both the military and the civilian bureaucracy are part of the executive branch of government and therefore under the auspices of the president. Less clear is whether power in such systems is held individually by the president, as the presidentialism model suggests, or is held more collectively by a military junta of which the president is either a part or perhaps a puppet. Thus, in Nicaragua, President Anastasio Somoza García was the one in charge, as President Hugo Chávez was in Venezuela, but in Argentina in the 1980s, about which O'Donnell was writing, the armed forces as a whole were in charge, as was the military in Brazil and Chile during the period when they dominated the politics of these countries.

But as most have observed, the current situation in Latin America is quite a bit different, with the virtual disappearance of direct military rule and even military coups. Between 1930 and 1980, the thirty-seven countries that made up Latin America experienced 277 changes in government, of which 104 took place via military coup. From 1980 to 1990, 7 of 37 changes took place via coup. Since 1990, there have been coups only in Peru, Haiti, and Honduras (Valenzuela 2004:5). Rather, a more institutionalized role for the military has developed in the context of traditional representative government. As noted earlier, public support for the military in Latin America also appears to be relatively high. An analysis of these data suggests that past military excesses are not as important in explaining country-by-country variation in trust in the military as are measures of economic growth and prosperity (Montalvo 2009). Although there are country-specific explanations for this transition, particularly emphasizing factionalism within the armed forces (see Farcau 1996), one of the prevailing explanations that may apply more generally is that with the disappearance or at least the weakening of the Marxist alternative, the new focus on the neoliberal economic approach places a premium on good relations with international lending agencies. Such organizations tend to be committed to democratic practices and frown on military intervention (see Cammack 2001:187). Whatever the explanation, the military role has receded across Latin America, although it has not disappeared entirely. In Peru, for example, the military was instrumental in keeping President Alberto Fujimori in power after his election victory, and supported him when he disbanded Congress. In Chile, the military seems to have foresworn extraconstitutional interventions while at the same time maintaining an institutionally guaranteed role in government decisionmaking (see Agüero 2001; Barros 2002).

However, during the first decade of the twenty-first century, in Paraguay, Chile, Argentina, Bolivia, Ecuador, Venezuela, and Nicaragua, leftist presidents—traditionally anathema to the military establishments of those countries—have taken power through democratic elections, with no apparent threat of military action to thwart the election results. The military has even assisted several of these presidents as they have sought to carry out some of their more controversial reforms. What isn't clear, of course, is whether the shift away from military intervention is a temporary response to a changed international environment or constitutes a more permanent change in the civil-military relationship. When President Manuel Zelaya of Honduras was removed by military coup in June 2009, these actions were roundly condemned throughout the region and led to the suspension of Honduras from the Organization of American States. This reaction to an extraconstitutional intervention against a leftist—or at least populist—president suggests a strengthened commitment to respecting the outcomes of elections, especially if one compares this to how such events were viewed three decades previously.

It is possible that strong presidents may be a key factor in keeping the military on the sidelines. In the earlier period, the political stalemate and delays in dealing with pressing issues that resulted when a legislature or a highly fractionalized party system prevented governments from acting seemed to invite—or at least provided the justification for—military interventions in a number of Latin American nations. If presidents have the power to break deadlocks and to act, such stalemates will be less likely to occur. It is also possible that the democratic legitimacy that attaches to popularly elected presidents may strengthen their ability to control the military. Put differently, presidents who are installed by the military may be more easily dispensed with by the military, because they will lack the support of civilian constituencies.

The current African experience in regard to the role of the military has been somewhat different from Latin America's. In many, perhaps most, African countries, the soldiers have not confined themselves to their barracks; instead, they have been active participants in government as well as prime movers in deposing and installing new governments. In Africa, the movements toward independence from colonial powers were by and large led by civilians. Therefore, at the time of independence, there was no organized military and no military tradition based on "past glories, real or imagined." But by the end of the 1970s, this had changed; with the help of developed nations, these new nations rapidly created armed forces, sometimes to maintain domestic order and in some instances to protect against foreign adversaries. But unlike in Latin America, these new African military establishments were not highly professionalized and obviously did not have a tradition of service to the state. In short order, these organizations became increasingly politicized, with many African presidents drawn from the ranks of soldiers or former soldiers (Jackson and Rosberg 1982:35–36). In September 1980, Benin, Burundi, Congo, Equatorial Guinea, Ethiopia, Liberia, Mauritania, Niger, Rwanda, Somalia, Sudan, Togo, Upper Volta, and Zaire all had presidents who simultaneously held military rank (Jackson and Rosberg 1982:288–304). By 2008, the list was much smaller, including Chad, Equatorial Guinea, Guinea, Sudan, and Uganda, although the military continued to be an active player in a number of countries with civilian presidents.[16]

In the context of such a politicized military, it may not matter if the president is a military person or a civilian. In Africa, presidents drawn from the military "tend to perform much like civilian leaders. . . . [T]hey often operate personalist or patrimonial regimes, they can be as corrupt or inept as civilian rulers, they are as likely to turn to dictatorial methods, and their claims to the contrary notwithstanding, they do not necessarily manage the state more efficiently or productively" (Le Vine 2004:280). Because the political institutions associated with democracy, such as political parties and legislatures, tend to be relatively weak, and because power tends to be exercised in a highly personalistic manner by military and civilian leaders alike, there are few institutional constraints or norms that can discourage ambitious individuals from using or attempting to use force or other extraconstitutional means to achieve power. Thus, the rule of any president—whether of civilian or military background—may be contingent on the sufferance of the military. One student of francophone African nations observes that "civilian rulers in Africa have had good reason to be wary of their militaries, and it is always a problem to find the right mix of rewards, incentives, and controls that will keep them content-ed and loyal." The traditional rewards have been large budgets, inflated ranks—lots of officers—and various informal payoffs and perquisites (Le Vine 2004:202).

Presidents with military backgrounds face the same threat of a coup from their disgruntled colleagues as civilian leaders do. Writing in 1986, one analyst concluded that "almost one half of black Africa's states are governed, in one form or another, by their armies," and that in several other countries, "although the military does not rule at the center, there is an overlap and symbiotic relationship between the senior ranks of the armed forces and the top officials of the hegemonic vanguard party" (Baynham 2001:5). Between 1956 and 2001, there were 80 successful military coups in the 48 independent sub-Saharan African states, 108 failed coup attempts, and 139 reported coup attempts (McGowan 2003).On the other hand, military coups appear to have become somewhat less fre-quent in Africa in recent years, for some of the same reasons that they have disappeared in Latin America—the need to maintain good relations with the major players in the globalized economy and the problems that military intervention create for such a relationship. But unlike in Latin America, coups continue to occur in Africa, and many of the continent's civilian democracies continue to operate under the strong influence of military leaders. There are relatively fewer examples in Africa of the military tak-ing the strictly neutral approach to civilian government—one thinks of Tanzania and South Africa—than has been the case in several Latin

American nations. To the extent that primordial or clientelistic ties characterize the armed forces of African nations, the allegiance of soldiers will tend to be toward particular leaders rather than to the professionalized military establishment. In Latin America, the longer tradition of a professionalized military encourages a loyalty to that institution rather than to a political leader, and so while military coups may once again occur in Latin America, they are more likely to occur because the institutional interests of the military are threatened rather than because of personal ties between soldiers and incumbent or insurgent politicians.

Of course, the challenge presented by presidential power, fortified with either the active or tacit support of the military, is how that power can be constrained so that it does not become arbitrary or authoritarian, while at the same time being sufficient to allow the government to act. As mentioned earlier, one way to achieve this balance is through a strengthened political party system that can provide a president with the legislative majority that he needs to act, thus avoiding the stalemates that often provide an excuse for military interventions, while simultaneously providing an institutional structure that can restrain executive unilateralism (see Fitch 1998:180–181). Unfortunately, the modern era has seen a continuous weakening of political parties and the emergence in several countries of either highly fractionalized party systems that cannot provide a dependable majority, or political parties that are little more than personal election vehicles for presidents and therefore either cannot constrain him, or in effect dissolve after the election and therefore can neither help him to govern nor restrain him from overreaching. As will be discussed more fully in the next chapter, it is precisely this decline of political parties that has contributed to the growth of presidentialism, concentrating citizen attention on the individual president rather than on his party affiliation. Absent a strong political party system, presidents, in order to lead, may be forced to deal with the military, using it to help them gain compliance and maintain order in return for their commitment to respect and support the military's financial and institutional demands.

Domestic Issues and International Issues

In addition to military matters, an increasing number of issues that in the past might have been considered purely domestic are now on the international agenda. In a globalized world, national economies are interconnected as never before. Issues of trade, monetary policy, immigration, and climate control, to identify just four examples, cannot be dealt with by one nation acting alone, but rather must be handled with bilateral or multilateral agreements or understandings among nations. For many countries, negotiations with bodies such as the International Monetary Fund (IMF) and the World Bank have significant consequences for domestic politics, and are handled exclusively by the executive branch. In the period from 2010 through 2012, all heads of government in Europe and to a lesser extent in other parts of the world were in discussions about the threat to the euro posed by the possible debt defaults of a number of countries. The reason is that in a globalized and interconnected economy, it is rare than an economic crisis will affect only one nation. As the number of domestic policy issues with no international ramifications contracts and the number with an international dimension expands, the authority and prominence of the president increases. The number of international agreements that any nation is party to is so large that even if a legislature had the power to review and approve them all, it would have neither the time nor the expertise to do that well. Legislative bodies cannot negotiate trade agreements with foreign countries or loan arrangements with the World Bank; they cannot value and revalue their national currencies; and they alone cannot solve environmental challenges. Dealing with these global issues is a responsibility that falls primarily to the executive branch and significantly broadens the scope of presidential responsibilities and therefore presidential power.

In the United States, President Obama took the lead in working with other nations on the issue of climate change. In December 2009, he flew to Copenhagen and there played an instrumental role in salvaging an interim agreement when the international conference failed to reach something more substantial. In regard to economic matters, he and his advisers were in continuous negotiations with other Western powers on developing a coordinated strategy to stimulate their economies in the face of the global recession that he faced in the beginning of his administration. And in regard to the relationship between the United States and China, the primary issues have been economic (the undervaluing of the Chinese currency, US-China trade, and Chinese ownership of a substantial portion of the accumulated US debt) or have been linked to economic concerns (Chinese reluctance to support US sanctions against Iran, connected with China's interest in maintaining fuel supplies and other economic activities in Iran). How or whether these issues are resolved will have as important an impact on the lives of ordinary Americans as it will on the international role of the United States. The point is that the line between domestic and international issues has become less distinct and, because of that, the role of the president in these issues has expanded.

Similar presidential dominance of these issues is seen in other nations. In Brazil, for example, the president is given nearly unilateral power over currency exchange rates and tariffs (Mainwaring 1997:100). New presidents in Bolivia and Ecuador have reoriented their nations' foreign policies, distancing themselves from the United States and strengthening ties with Cuba and Venezuela. Each has adopted policies on natural resource extraction that have had a significant impact on relations not just with the United States but also with other nations in Latin America. For many countries in Africa and Latin America, their interactions with organizations such as the World Bank and the IMF are of crucial importance, and this further empowers the technocrats in the executive branch who are best able to communicate with the international bureaucrats who run these agencies, and who understand what needs to be done to gain their support.

The increasingly permeable boundary between international and domestic policy is also illustrated by the issue of terrorism. In this case, an international issue—the threat of violence against a country and its citizens instigated and organized by individuals outside the country—becomes a domestic issue in the sense that a nation may need to institute policies designed to protect against terrorism that will restrict the actions of its own citizens. So just as the growing international dimension to domestic issues expands the power of the presidency, the domestic implications of issues that are generally thought of as international and therefore presumptively under the auspices of the president will expand the power of the president domestically. If the claim of the president of the United States is that his responsibility to protect the nation using his power as commander in chief cannot be questioned, it is difficult to find an argument to restrict that power when it is designed to protect the nation against domestic insurrections—as Lincoln did during the Civil War, or as Roosevelt did at the outbreak of World War II, or arguably as Presidents Bush and Obama have done in regard to the terrorism threat. Indeed, the result of the gradual erasing of the boundaries between international and domestic issues must be enhanced presidential power.

Of course, there will be instances in which bringing the results of the executive's work to fruition will involve the national legislature. Certainly, in the case of the United States, any attempt to deal with climate change will require the agreement of Congress. And while presidents negotiate trade treaties, at least in the United States most of these need to be approved by Congress. President Clinton expended a great deal of his political capital early in his presidency to get a reluctant Congress to agree to the North American Free Trade Agreement, and several other free trade agreements between Latin American nations and the United States remain in limbo, having been agreed to by presidents but either rejected or shelved by Congress. But despite the capacity of Congress to thwart presidential policy priorities on these matters, the initiative remains very much in the hands of the executive, and Congress is restricted for the most part to saying either yes or no. This is an important reversal of the original notion of Congress being the place where policy originates and the president's role restricted to saying either yes, by signing legislation, or no, by exercising his veto. And once again, this reversal, having taken place over a number of years, is an indicator of the movement of the United States in the direction of presidentialism.

Conclusion

The metaphor of a shrinking world is by now a cliché; nonetheless, it has been real enough to have had a dramatic impact on the way nations conduct themselves and on the power of their chief executives. If, as the poet said, no man is an island, then today no nation is an island, at least from a policy perspective. The fate of every country, it seems, is connected with that of many other countries. To the extent that there are international dimensions to public policy, the influence of executive leaders grows, not simply because this has been a traditional arena for executive prerogatives, but also because there are strong arguments to be made for that tradition. And as the number of policy areas with a significant international dimension expands and the number of purely domestic policy areas contracts, the power and prominence of the president will increase and the ability of other political institutions to constrain presidential power will decrease.

For some, the most disturbing aspect of all of this is the generally undisputed power of the president over a nation's armed forces. In nearly every nation, the president can order the military into action, with the prospect of significant loss of life and national honor. Because there seems to be no governmental decision with a greater potential for national catastrophe than the decision to go to war, it would seem that this would be the archetypical policy area where power should be shared by many rather than concentrated in the hands of a single person. Yet the prevailing arrangements, buttressed by arguments of hierarchy, secrecy, national unity, and dispatch, in fact place this power precisely and to a large extent exclusively in the hands of a president, despite what a nation's constitution might say.

The military also consumes in every nation a disproportionate share of governmental budgets. In many nations, the military also plays an important role in suppressing domestic insurrections, maintaining order, and sometimes deciding which civilian leaders will be allowed to rule and what policies they will pursue. Such a role allows civilian rulers in the office of the president to expand their control over a wide range of public policy areas, drawing on the explicit backing of the military to discourage or intimidate political opponents. In doing so, they often find common cause with civilian bureaucrats with whom they share a disdain for politicians, especially legislators, as well as a commitment to hierarchy and to the existence and pursuit of technologically correct public policy solutions as opposed to what they view as the compromised and ineffective policies that are likely to emerge from representative institutions. As presidential systems move toward the authoritarian end of the presidentialism continuum, they utilize both the civilian and the military bureaucracies over which they preside to strengthen their control over public policy, and they come to depend even more on the military to encourage obedience. As they do so, they may run the risk that they themselves will become beholden to the military. In order to stave off the possibility that they will be removed by disgruntled military leaders, they will avoid policy decisions with which these leaders may disagree and do nothing that threatens the resources and institutional autonomy that the military establishment values so highly.

In sum, the task of restraining the presidential prince becomes much more challenging as the prominence of international issues on the nation's agenda increases. The power of the president is further enhanced to the extent that he is in control, or has the backing, of a well-financed and well-equipped military establishment. In countries with highly professionalized militaries that are committed to political neutrality and civilian rule, the threat is that presidents will use their authority over the military to engage the nation in foolish or unnecessary conflicts and thus create an atmosphere in which they can extend and enhance their control over domestic politics. This can occur even under constrained presidentialism, because the constraints available to other political institutions in regard to foreign and defense policy are relatively weak. In countries with more politicized militaries, executive alliances with the military, or control over it, present additional threats to civil liberties and the possibility of hyperpresidentialism.

Notes

1. Gallup Poll, June 2011, www.gallup.com/poll/148163/Americans -Confident-Military-Least-Congress.aspx.
2. "The Status of Democracy, 2005–2006: Findings from Afrobarometer Round 3 for 18 Countries," Afrobarometer Briefing Paper no. 40, November 2006, www.afrobarometer.org.
3. Letter from Lincoln to his law partner William Herndon, February 15, 1848, in Lincoln 1953, vol. 1:452.
4. Letter from Lincoln to Albert Hodges, April 4, 1864, in Lincoln 1953, vol. 7: 282.
5. 67 US 635 (1863).
6. 323 US 214 (1944).
7. 299 US 304 (1936).
8. 301 US 324 (1937).
9. 343 US 579 (1952).
10. 542 US 29 (2004).
11. 548 US 557 (2006).
12. 553 US 723 (2008).
13. "Military Statistics: Expenditure: % of Central Government Expenditure (Most Recent) by Country," www.nationmaster.com/graph/mil_exp_of_cen_gov _exp-military-expenditure-of-central-government.
14. Cato writes in the 67th Anti-Federalist Paper, and Philadelphiensis writes in the 74th Anti-Federalist Paper.
15. "Presidential Military Experience," www.heptune.com/preslist.html #Military.
16. "Presidents, African Heads of State and Governments," www .japanafricanet.com/directory/presidents/index.html.

6

Presidentialism and the People

Presidencies are about power, administration, and leadership. In terms of power, as we have seen in Chapters 3 and 5, the issue is the president's capacity to both influence and determine public policy, a capability that depends upon constitutional provisions, political factors such as the structure of the party system and the role of the military, and whether or not the issue at hand has an international dimension. In terms of administration, as we have seen in Chapter 4, the focus is on the president's responsibility to execute or carry out the law, a responsibility that also includes significant discretionary power for the president and the bureaucrats who report to him. In terms of leadership, the focus is on the ability of the president to set a course for a nation and its people that his fellow citizens at both the mass and elite levels are prepared to follow. This complex, crucial, and increasingly intimate relationship between presidents and the public is a key driver of presidentialism.

Types of Leadership

What makes a person's claim to leadership legitimate in the eyes of those who are expected to follow him? Why in other words is someone accepted as a leader by others? People may follow a leader simply because they fear the consequences of noncompliance. A tyrant may lead and his subjects may follow, not because they have willingly consented to his right to rule, but because, as Machiavelli advised, they fear the consequences of a refusal to follow. This type of leadership differs from leadership based on the implicit or explicit consent of followers. In those instances, although fear of the consequences of disobeying may be one of the reasons why some people follow such a leader, most follow because they accept his leadership role. When people willingly accept a leader's right to lead, we refer to such leadership as legitimate.

At one time, the legitimacy of leadership claims was religiously based. Many monarchs claimed that their right to rule was divinely authorized, and the shared religious faith of the population led the people to accept the monarch's right to lead. In the modern world, papal leadership of the Catholic Church is legitimized in similarly divine terms, as is the rule of the ayatollahs in Iran. Closely associated with legitimacy claims based on divine right are claims based on tradition. In some societies, the right to lead belongs by tradition to an elder, or to the head of a family who, particularly over an extended time period, have provided the leaders for the polity in question. This claim of legitimacy is based on custom and history; the leader always has been the head of this particular family, or the eldest member of the community. Such a leader exercises authority by virtue of his status, and his leadership is legitimate because it is in accord with long-standing custom.

Another basis for the legitimacy of leadership is charisma. A person can assume a leadership role because he is able to make a convincing claim that he embodies special characteristics that create a bond between himself and his putative followers. Rather than the custom-based legitimacy of traditional leadership, the charismatic leader, according to Max Weber, "possesses charisma by virtue of magical powers, revelations, heroism, or other extraordinary gifts" (Bendix 1962:294). Today, the term "charisma" has acquired a somewhat broader meaning. Modern commentators have discussed charisma in terms of an "ability to articulate a compelling vision of a bright future," and others have discussed a capacity to inspire followers "to perform above and beyond the call of duty by appealing to their emotions and enduring motives" (Emrich et al. 2001:527). In general, a charismatic leader is one whose connection with his followers is based more on his personality, his rhetorical skills, and his ability to arouse the passions of his followers than on his qualifications to lead or on his ability to address specific policy questions. Weber argued that such leaders are especially well-suited to deal with societal needs that are out of the ordinary, because of the "extraordinary gifts" of body and mind that their followers believe that they possess. In such instances, masses of people virtually "surrender themselves to heroic leaders" (Bendix 1962:300).

In modern societies, leadership came to be legitimized in both constitutional and democratic terms. What Weber called "legal domination" was depersonalized leadership relying upon a set of laws that governed the behavior of all members of society, including those who were responsible for making the law. Systems of legal domination are characterized by accepted procedures for leadership selection and by permanent, collective governing structures such as bureaucracies and legislative bodies. If a leader has come to office through a constitutionally mandated set of procedures, the fact that these procedures have been followed is sufficient to legitimize his role as leader. If the constitutional procedures require that leaders be selected by a popular vote, then leadership is legitimized by democratic criteria. Such a person is entitled to lead because the people have selected him or her as their leader or because they have acquiesced to the procedures by which that person was selected.

Although analytically distinct, in the real world these different bases of legitimacy often coexist. For example, Charles de Gaulle came to the presidency of France by virtue of his special, charismatic connection with the people of France, derived from his role as wartime leader of the Free French. His ascension also was legitimized by a popular vote that supported both his assumption of power and the new Constitution, which he played a leading role in designing and under which he would govern. Charisma also has played a role in the selection of presidents through regular constitutional processes. Barack Obama, by virtue of his rhetorical skills, his race, and his compelling personal narrative, was thought by many to have established a charismatic relationship with his followers that helped propel him to the presidency. Finally, tradition continues to play a role in leadership selection, even in democratic political systems, where the children of leaders sometimes are able to rise quite quickly to leadership positions based as much on their family name as on their political talents.

As we seek to understand presidentialism, the key distinction among Weber's three ideal types of leadership—traditional, charismatic, and legal—appears to be between the personalized leadership associated with both the traditional and charismatic forms, and the depersonalized leadership associated with legal domination. Although modern nation-states are almost by definition characterized by legal domination, elements of personalized leadership, particularly in the role of the presidency, are also present and often in tension with the practices associated with legal domination. As suggested earlier, a primary task of modern constitutionalism (or, for our purposes here, legal domination) has been to place limits on executive power. Modern presidential systems operate in the context of such written constitutions, but the personalized leadership associated with the office of the president can challenge the limitations imposed by such documents. Presidential claims to emergency powers assume that under certain circumstances the president can decide on his own to violate the law or even the constitution if he believes that the good of the nation requires it. Such a position, widely albeit implicitly accepted in most presidential systems, and not without its merits, is incompatible on its face with the rule of law (rather than men), which is the essential component of theories of legal domination.

Leadership and Political Culture

The Weberian approach suggests that political structures and forms of political leadership are at least in part culturally based and that how a society legitimizes its leaders may have something to do with modernity. In those societies where forms of traditional domination are still apparent and where legal forms have not become well entrenched, presidentialism and the personal leadership that it implies may be more culturally congruent with the nation's political culture than is the more depersonalized, more institutionalized leadership associated with legal domination.

In most of precolonial sub-Saharan Africa, for example, villages were presided over by a chief who, though constrained by norms and institutions that emphasized some degree of consultation, was nonetheless "the political, social, judicial and religious head of the people. As such, he had wide ranging powers" (Ayittey 1991:94). During the colonial period, European powers established a system of administrative chiefs who, acting under the direction and control of the colonial power, ruled in a somewhat less consultative and more authoritarian manner than was the case in precolonial times (Mamdani 1996:43–61; Agbese 2009:101).

This tradition of rule by the chief did not disappear with the end of colonialism. In most newly independent African nations, chiefs and their councils continued to be an important governing force at the local level, and with the departure of the colonial power most returned to a more consultative mode of decisionmaking. More than four decades after independence, there is some evidence that African citizens still hold a generally favorable view of such leaders. In a series of questions asked in a survey conducted in fifteen sub-Saharan African states in 2002–2003, respondents were asked if, as alternatives to democracy, they would prefer rule by traditional leaders, a one-party state, military rule, or a presidential dictatorship. Majorities in every country preferred democracy to all four alternatives, but only 54 percent rejected rule by traditional leaders compared to the 77 percent who rejected presidential dictatorship. Respondents reported more frequent contact with traditional rulers than with any government officials, and were more likely to go to chiefs or elders to resolve conflicts. In seven countries in southern Africa, traditional leaders and presidents were thought of more highly in terms of being interested in people's problems, trustworthiness, and being free of corruption than were legislators and local government officials (Logan 2008).

These data may simply reflect the greater access that citizens have to their local leaders as compared with their more distant central government officials. But in one survey, respondents in twelve sub-Saharan nations were asked about their level of trust in various political institutions. The presidency was found to be the most trusted institution and, although the differences were not huge, in all but two countries citizens expressed higher levels of trust in the president than in members of Parliament (Armah-Attoh, Gyimah-Boadi, and Chikwana 2007). In South Africa, the job approval rating of the president between 1995 and 2006—a period that included the presidencies of both Nelson Mandela and Thabo Mbeki—was consistently higher than the job approval rating of other political leaders and institutions.[1]

This suggests that tradition and culture can produce a certain level of comfort with the singular leader, whether a president or a traditional chief. That may help us to understand the rapid disappearance of parliamentary systems in postcolonial Africa (see Fatton 1990) and their replacement by presidential systems in which presidents rapidly acquired a great deal of power. Despite the public rejection of the concept of one-man rule and strong support for the idea that presidents must obey the law and the courts, one observer of African presidencies notes that in many of these nations, regardless of their constitutional arrangements, "power is intensely personalized around the figure of the president. . . . He is literally above the law, controls in many cases a large proportion of state finance with little accountability, and delegates remarkably little of his authority on important matters" (van de Walle 2003:310).[2] Sometimes the president achieves a sort of "political divinity" as he "is portrayed as embodying the idea, dignity, and even the sacredness of the state" (Jackson and Rosberg 1982:23). In other words, the president and the state come to be virtually indistinguishable. This was especially the case for the founding set of African presidents, many of whom had led their people to independence and served for extended periods of time once independence was achieved. Sometimes, these leaders attained a combination of paternal, political, and religious status in the minds of their people. One president of Equatorial Guinea had the title of "the Unique Miracle." Kwame Nkrumah, the first president of Ghana, was called among other things "the

Redeemer" and "the Messiah." In Kenya, Jomo Kenyatta preferred to be called *Mzee,* or "the Elder." Other presidents were described with more familiar sobriquets—"the Father of the Country," "the Man of the People," "the Great Helmsman" (shared with Mao Tse-tung), and "the Father of Independence and Pioneer of African Unity" (Le Vine 2004:326; Chazan et al. 1992:164).

Naturally, such appellations did not make it easy for dissenters or political opponents to voice their opinions, and many of these political systems eventually evolved in the direction of hyperpresidentialism. In Africa, "leaders of this sort chose to dominate rather than compromise, to dictate rather than to reconcile" (Chazan et al. 1992:162). In the case of South Korea, to take an example from another continent, one observer notes that cults of personality surrounding the president "have thwarted democratization attempts over the decades, despite various constitutional structures that attempted to limit the executive's power. . . . The Korean concept of *daekwon,* or ultimate power, denotes the power of the highest office in the South Korean political system: the presidential power or the presidency" (Martinez 2006:2507). The Korean term for the incumbent president is *daetongryong,* a term that generates special awe in Korean culture.

And in newly democratized Russia, President Boris Yeltsin, in the view of some observers, adopted a patriarchal style, viewing himself as "head of the household, as a leader who demanded total loyalty to himself and his commands." He viewed his election as president as "validation for his right to interpret the will of the people." He thought of himself as "a people's tsar, benevolent and caring, though strict when necessary" and did not believe that he had to explain himself to anyone (Breslauer 2001:73, 76). Yeltsin's successor, Vladimir Putin, did not adopt the same style, but consolidated power in the hands of the president to an even greater degree than had Yeltsin. Public opinion data suggest that a significant number of Russians support such a system of personalized singular leadership, described by some as "an elective monarchy that discourages any public accountability to the electorate by the powerful head of state." In one survey, more citizens saw the presidency as the primary engine for societal change compared to any other political institution or actor, with the Duma being mentioned by less than 2 percent of the respondents, compared to larger percentages who mentioned academics, teachers, and the intelligentsia. This disposition toward executive control may be traceable in part to a long history, even from pre-Soviet times, when "locally elected government centered on a single authoritarian elder" who was essentially free to govern as he saw fit and bore no obligation to those who elected him to office (Petukhov and Ryabov 2004:280, 289).

In Latin America, the caudillo tradition emphasized a strong leader tied to a group of followers by a reciprocal set of commitments. In the view of many scholars, this tradition provided the cultural and historical underpinnings for the strong presidencies that have been typical of that region. Such arrangements do not appear to be at odds with public opinion. A 2008 America Barometer survey of twenty-two Latin American nations and the United States showed that presidential job approval was higher than congressional job approval in twenty-one instances (Rodríguez Raga and Seligson 2008). In one 1992 survey of Chilean voters, 55 percent of the respondents thought that the president was doing his job well, while only 22 percent said the same thing about their congressional representative. More tellingly, 60 percent of the respondents said that they were not exactly sure what their deputy was doing, while only 20 percent said the same thing about the president. Three-quarters of the respondents thought that deputies only worried about the people at election time, and more than 85 percent thought that there was not enough contact between deputies and the people (Siavelis 1997:332–333).

These findings are similar to the African data cited earlier and suggest that presidents in general are more trusted by, visible to, and approved of by the people than are members of the legislature. However, because principles of legal domination have had a significantly longer period of time to penetrate Latin American political culture than they have in Africa, few Latin American presidents came to be as indistinguishable from their states as did their African counterparts. The distinction between Africa and Latin America can be understood from the perspective of what political scientists call institutionalization. In some ways comparable to Weber's concept of legal domination, institutionalization refers to the creation of permanent structures and practices in a society as contrasted with the shifting and transitory characteristics of systems in which leadership is highly personalized. When political allegiances to particular leaders are stronger than allegiances to the nation's political institutions, the capacity of these institutions to constrain the behavior of such leaders is questionable. In an environment where the level of institutionalization is relatively low, the mandates and limitations of the various governmental institutions are likely to be ambiguous, permeable, and transitory; this allows the ambitious leader to draw more responsibilities into his orbit, responsibilities that otherwise might be discharged by other actors or institutions. If, for example, judicial institutions have not been well established and their legitimacy has not been broadly accepted, presidents can take it upon themselves to interpret a nation's laws and its constitution and essentially to become judges of the legitimacy of their own actions. Or if political parties appear and disappear on a regular basis, or if they consist of nothing more than a small cadre of politicians who have no roots in the society, they can do little to constrain or restrict the actions of political leaders, even leaders who are ostensibly their co-partisans.

In Senegal, for example, most deputies "have little attachment to the National Assembly as an institution" so the body remains weak, "with poor attendance and little will and capacity to check the powers of the president or to initiate legislation on its own." Similarly, judges are "reluctant to make controversial decisions that contradict the will of the president and [are] tempted to take bribes because of low salaries and lack of transparency in judicial processes." Senegalese political parties are composed of personal followers of particular leaders and are the instrument for these leaders to negotiate benefits with the president (Gellar 2005:158–160).

In nations with stronger, more institutionalized traditions of constitutionalism and legal domination, individual leaders are subject to greater constraints than they are in less institutionalized systems. But even in those nations, presidentialism and the politics of personalism that goes with it can erode established boundaries among institutions. Especially in troubled, difficult, or dangerous times, the potential for personalized presidential leadership, whether based on tradition or charisma or both, may jeopardize existing constitutional restrictions on presidential power. In the United States at the outbreak of the Civil War, more than seventy years after the Constitution had been ratified, Abraham Lincoln took a number of steps that he frankly admitted were unconstitutional but in his view were necessary if the Union was to be preserved. A hundred years later, French politicians under the Fourth Republic, faced with the Algerian crisis and a potential revolt of the military, had reached a political stalemate on what if anything could or should be done. At that point, the nation turned to Charles de Gaulle, and acceded to his demands for a new Constitution that would establish a strong presidency to replace its parliamentary system. And forty years later, after the September 11 attacks on the United States in 2001, powers seemingly beyond constitutional limitations flowed to President George W. Bush, sometimes with the approval of Congress and sometimes by his own unilateral actions, but in any case without any significant public or congressional resistance.

Escape from Freedom

The reason that a nation and its people accept the leadership of presidents or would-be presidents even if their actions or proposals appear to test constitutional limits is in part a matter of political psychology. Central to the discussion are the ambivalent views that many citizens of modern states hold concerning the concept of freedom and the role of strong government leaders. Freedom, at least as an abstract idea, is a nearly universal desire. Certainly, wars and revolutions have been fought in the name of individual liberty, and political leaders of various ideological stripes pledge their commitment to individual freedom and often justify their actions in those terms. Throughout history, one of the primary threats to freedom has been strong one-person rule, and constitutions were developed both to prevent arbitrary rule and to protect liberty. It may sound odd therefore to suggest that this ostensible commitment to freedom can be, to any degree, ambiguous.

This ambiguity can be traced in part to the ambiguous nature of the concept of freedom itself. When pressed about the meaning of freedom, most individuals, after saying predictable things about the right to do anything that they want to do, would acknowledge that certain limits on what they and others can do are necessary and desirable. These limits might be justified by concerns for public health and safety (freedom does not mean the right to assault someone else), for national security (freedom does not mean the right to engage in treasonous acts), or for the larger collective good (freedom does not mean the right to refuse to pay taxes). Others will say that their economic status prevents them from exercising a full measure of freedom (for example, quitting one's job and heading to the nearest beach), and those of a more anthropological bent might acknowledge that the mores and culture of the society—for example, religious beliefs or social institutions such as marriage and family—place even greater constraints on their freedom than government does. In sum, there are tensions between the concept of freedom in its purest and unlimited form and the values associated with public order, a society's economic and cultural stability, and the collective well-being of all members of society.

The point is that public order, stability, predictability, and security are as important to individuals as freedom is, even though these values may not be as frequently or as publicly articulated by them or by their political leaders. As Locke suggested, it was the quest for these values that drove people to abandon the completely free, but dangerously unstable and unpredictable, state of nature for the relative safety and order offered by civil society. But what happens when members of a civil society come to believe that the arrangements that they have established are not providing them with a sufficient degree of personal security, or that the degree of freedom that is prevalent in the society has created unacceptable levels of insecurity and unpredictability? In other words, what happens when the freedom that people enjoy creates a new set of fears?

Psychologist Erich Fromm (1941) grappled with this question as he tried to explain the rise of fascism in democratic Europe in the mid-1930s. He argued that the level of individual freedom that characterized modern democratic societies created a sense of individual isolation that resulted in deep anxieties. In the more traditional and highly structured societies of the Middle Ages, people had relatively little in the way of freedom, but the same rigid social structure that restricted their freedom also provided them with a sense of security; everyone knew precisely their place in the order of things, a place that was, for many, not very pleasant and essentially immutable, but nonetheless predictable and therefore in a perverse way comforting.

But as states moved toward modernity, the traditional communal and familial structures that restricted one's freedom weakened, social structures became more fluid, cultural norms began to shift, and one's place and role in society became less well defined. One of the consequences of this enhanced level of personal freedom was increased levels of anxiety; people were freer, but their social, cultural, and economic security were, at least subjectively, more uncertain. To reduce the anxiety that this uncertainty provoked, individuals sought alternative means to provide structure to their lives, with many retreating to organized religion to provide the same assurances and sense of solidarity that traditional connections had provided in an earlier period. Others sought refuge in the cultural norms and personal relationships that defined their tightly knit local communities.

Such alternatives, however, became less effective as society became more complex, as technology led to faster and more unpredictable changes, as residential mobility and suburban culture eroded community values and institutions, as the forces of modernity undermined organized religion, and as a shrinking world meant that forces well beyond one's control or even the control of one's government could make an individual's life markedly better or worse. These changes rendered the social and cultural norms of contemporary mass society so fragile that the freedom it offered created frightening uncertainties for individuals and produced as a result high levels of individual anxiety. As one scholar put it, "Alienation, anomie, despair of being able to chart one's own course in a complex, cold, and bewildering world have become characteristic of a large part of the population of advanced countries" (Edelman 1985:76).

In such a context, Fromm argued, some may seek to deal with anxiety by identifying with, and even submerging themselves within, a mass movement of some sort that provides them with that missing sense of solidarity with others who are like them. Fromm believed that the Nazi movement, with its emphasis on Aryan superiority, its clear identification of enemies and outsiders, and its appeal to national and racial pride, provided Germans with a sense of reassurance, order, and connection with others who were like them, an especially attractive commodity at a time of national humiliation and deepening economic crisis.

Alternatively (or simultaneously), citizens may seek reassurance and order by connecting with a leader. As individuals come to believe that they live in a world that they can neither understand nor influence, a desire to attach oneself "to reassuring abstract symbols rather than to one's own efforts becomes chronic. And what symbol can be more reassuring than the incumbent of a high position who knows what to do and is willing to act, especially when others are bewildered and alone?" (Edelman 1985:76). Individuals thus choose to "escape from freedom" by turning to a more authoritarian "man on horseback" who promises to provide purpose, stability, protection, and, most importantly, reassurance. People are more likely to turn to such a leader when they feel threatened—by a sudden loss of economic status, by civil disorder or criminal activity, or by a menace from a foreign power. Such leaders need not necessarily deliver solutions for the problems that the nation faces. Rather, individuals are prepared to accept and support a leader who is able to "dramatize his competence," and to "appear to be in command" (Edelman 1985:77–78).

Rhetoric and Symbols

In order to dramatize their competence and arouse popular support, such leaders use their rhetorical skills to appeal to the passions more so than the reason of their prospective followers, and in doing so they manipulate public opinion to their own advantage. In brief, they use the tools of demagoguery that, as noted in Chapter 2, those who created the US presidency warned against. In their appeals to the public, they identify themselves with popular and patriotic symbols; they name and vilify those whom they have declared to be the enemies of the people, either foreign or domestic, and they pledge to defend the nation against such forces. As candidates for office, they often fan the fears of the public by exaggerating both the problems that the nation confronts—because they know that it is the fear itself that evokes unquestioning support from their followers—and their capacity to solve those problems. Thus they promise order and safety to replace chaos and danger, pride in place of humiliation, superiority in place of inferiority, leadership in place of inertia, strength in place of weakness, hope in place of despair, and a return to the mores of an idealized past in place of the cultural chaos of contemporary society. To the extent that there are policy positions attached to such appeals, they are phrased in the most general terms so as to command broad support: Who could possibly disagree with a leader who promises to achieve national security and economic stability, to preserve or restore traditional, patriotic values, who offers change from an unacceptable status quo, and holds out the hope of either a better future or a return to a romanticized past?

Such leaders employ language and rhetoric rife with symbols calculated to persuade citizens to follow them. They work to establish "strong emotional and affective bonds" between themselves and prospective followers (Emrich et al. 2001:528). They attach themselves to important events in their nation's history; they refer to past glories, condemn past humiliations, and promise future greatness (see Edelman 1985:6). Because of their role as head of state, all presidents are well situated to employ such a rhetorical approach. The current president of the United States is the successor to the country's national heroes and martyrs—George Washington, Thomas Jefferson, Abraham Lincoln, Franklin Roosevelt, John Kennedy. When the president appears in public, bands play, flags wave, and people rise and applaud. He is addressed by his formal title (Mr. President) rather than by name, he is saluted by members of the nation's military, and every word that he utters is reported and preserved. When presidents speak, quite apart from what they are saying, they speak as the leader of the nation, embodying and standing for its history, its military might, and the unity and aspirations of its people. They speak from behind a rostrum with the presidential seal affixed to it and behind them one typically sees the US flag—another powerful symbol of the nation. Consciously or not, they manipulate these symbols that are so intrinsic to their office in order to evoke support for themselves and for their policy objectives.

Such leaders need not actually possess extraordinary talents or skills or have viable plans for the future of their countries. Because they traffic in symbols rather than in actions, it is difficult and perhaps unnecessary to determine in an objective sense the feasibility of any actions that they propose to take, or the success or failure of what they do once in power; rather their success or failure is calculated in terms of their ability to serve the psychic needs of the individual citizen—to convincingly and consistently articulate and deploy words and symbols that provide comfort and reassurance, and the appearance if not necessarily the reality of action (see Edelman 1985:77).

Not all aspiring leaders follow an approach to leadership that is dominated by rhetoric and symbols. Many eschew the apocalyptic phraseology and millennial promises that characterize the most demagogic leaders, and most are able to articulate substantive and achievable policy goals. But all who aspire to elective office, and all who desire to retain their office and expand their influence, will be tempted to utilize this language and to adopt it as part of their effort to gain popular support. In other words, it will be an important component of the rhetorical repertoire of every president and presidential candidate and in some cases it will be the sum total of their appeal to the people. After all, every nation is vulnerable to crisis or catastrophe and all are part of a world that is increasingly globalized, exceedingly complex, and seemingly changing on a daily basis. Citizens of every nation, no matter how strong their institutions, no matter how committed they are to the rule of law rather than to the rule of man, are vulnerable to the sort of fear and anxiety that charismatic and demagogic leaders can exploit. Examples come from every corner of the world and in various political and historical contexts.

Thus one analysis refers to the founding presidents of postcolonial African nations as "prophetic leaders" who, in the crucible of the fight for independence, saw themselves as "engaged in a fundamental political struggle for freedom and independence and against racial subjection and colonialism." These ambitions were conveyed to the population as a means to generate popular support, and for their people these leaders became visionaries. Kwame Nkrumah, the first president of newly independent Ghana, displayed in the words of two students of the era, "considerable organizational and manipulative skills" as well as "an awareness of the appetites and interests that move men in newly liberated and rapidly changing societies." And "to millions of people living both inside and outside the continent of Africa, Kwame Nkrumah is Africa and Africa is Kwame Nkrumah" (Jackson and Rosberg 1982:200–201).

In the case of France, Charles de Gaulle assumed a similar role. He was the national hero of the French forces in exile during World War II, but after liberation he withdrew from politics when the designers of the new Constitution for the Fourth Republic refused to create a strong presidency. When in the spring of 1958 the country faced political paralysis and a military revolt, it turned to de Gaulle. René Coty, the incumbent head of state, referred to him as "the most illustrious of Frenchmen who, in the darkest years of our history, was our leader in the struggle for freedom and who, having united the nation around him, rejected dictatorship in order to establish the Republic" (de Gaulle 1971:27). After assuming the newly created presidency of the Fifth Republic, de Gaulle made it clear that "the indivisible authority of the State is entrusted completely to the President by the people who elected him." For de Gaulle, says one scholar, the president was "the only political representative of the nation fully and unequivocally responsible for its destiny" (Mahoney 1996:118). De Gaulle, who at an earlier point had written that "France cannot be France without greatness," saw the presidency as a way to restore such greatness (Mahoney 1996:16). In a radio address to the people in 1962, he depicted the presidency as the "guide of France," the office "in charge of the destiny of France and the Republic," and "the inspirer and orienter of national actions" (Safran 2009:200). At a later point, he would recount the day of his ascension to the presidency by saying: "I believed it was my duty to be her [France's] head in order to save her from civil war, to spare her from financial and monetary bankruptcy and to build with her institutions meeting the requirements of the times and the modern world" (Mahoney 1996:67). These sentiments are reflected in the Constitution of the Fifth Republic, which describes the president as "the protector of National Independence, of territorial integrity," and charges him with the responsibility of ensuring that "the Constitution is respected" and for "ensuring the continuity of the state" (Suleiman 1994:143).

In Venezuela, President Hugo Chávez framed his 2006 reelection race as a choice between the nations becoming "a truly strong and free country, independent and prosperous," or instead "a country reduced once more to slavery and darkness" (Hawkins 2010:55). Earlier, in the period immediately following military rule, presidents such as Carlos Menem in Argentina and Alberto Fujimori in Peru came to power in near crisis conditions characterized by hyperinflation, virtual economic meltdown, and sociopolitical chaos. The fact that each, in the words of one scholar, "had the courage to attack the crisis head on . . . demonstrated and reinforced his charisma and boosted his support," and in general each succeeded, "thus guaranteeing the predictability that people need for planning their daily lives. This success, in turn, led to an outpouring of popular support which strengthened the position of the neopopulist leaders" (Weyland 2003:1107). Put differently, strong leaders like de Gaulle, Menem, Fujimori, and Chávez enabled citizens, at least in the short term, to reduce the anxiety that shadowed their lives during difficult periods of social, economic, and political upheaval. The same calculus explains the often positive public reactions to military coups engineered by generals who justify their actions by claiming that their goals are to restore order and provide stability. Once again, people may be willing in such an environment to sacrifice democratic niceties and turn toward the "man on horseback."

Mass Media

Today, appeals by singular leaders, charismatic or traditional, demagogic or not, are facilitated by modern forms of mass communication. At one time, a leader could speak only to those who were assembled to hear him. If he wished to speak to an entire population, he needed to do so by undertaking time-consuming travel among population centers or through the printed word. Although printed documents certainly have the capacity to stir people's emotions—one thinks of Tom Paine's *Common Sense* or Karl Marx and Friedrich Engels' *Communist Manifesto*—the spoken as opposed to the written voice has the greater potential to move mass publics and to bind followers to aspiring leaders.

With the invention of electronic forms of communication in the twentieth century and their rapid dissemination to much of the population, leaders gained more direct access to their people. President Franklin Roosevelt, in the midst of the Great Depression, was able, through a series of radio addresses that were heard across the United States, to reassure a frightened citizenry that action was being taken, that things would get better, and perhaps most importantly that someone was in charge. Things, of course, did not get better right away, but Roosevelt's rhetorical skills were credited with holding the nation together through a difficult and trying time until, ultimately, conditions actually did improve.

At the same time, in Germany, Adolf Hitler was able to use the radio as well as mass rallies to convince an entire population that they were a master race besieged from within and without by racial and religious inferiors, and that if they followed him, they and their country would be returned to its former glory. And a few years later, Charles de Gaulle, in exile in England, used the radio to encourage resistance to the Nazi occupiers. In his memoirs, he noted that "whatever I had been able to say and disseminate by this means had certainly contributed towards strengthening national unity against the enemy" (de Gaulle 1971:288). In Argentina, Juan Perón and his wife, Eva, used the radio on a regular basis to rally personal support for himself and his leadership.

In postcolonial Africa, the electronic media tended to be state-controlled. This enabled the first president of Cameroon, Ahmadou

Ahidjo, to employ the radio "to reach the entire population and take the voice of the government to the remotest regions," so that they would be aware of the "efforts deployed by the government to attain the goal which it has assigned itself: the making of the Cameroonian nation" (Nyamnjoh 2005:130). One observer has suggested that in Cameroon, "there was a general tendency to accept as gospel truth anything said on the radio" (Fombad 2003:236). In Senegal, a national survey conducted in 2002 found that 62 percent of those questioned said that the radio was their main source of information, as opposed to 2 percent who relied on the written press (Gellar 2005:165).

In the mid–twentieth century, television appeared and gave leaders the ability to project not just their voice but also their image, together with various national symbols, to a broad population. Citizens could not only see their leader as he spoke, but also see him surrounded by the symbols of the nation—the flag, military officers, the White House, the Élysée Palace. As de Gaulle put it, "Here, suddenly, was an unprecedented means of being present everywhere." As more homes acquired televisions, leaders moved directly and personally into the lives and living rooms of an increasing number of their fellow citizens. De Gaulle's view, perhaps self-serving, was that in using television, he was not embracing the "time honored recipes of demagogy"; instead he was endeavoring "to unite hearts and minds on the basis of what they had in common, to make all feel that they belonged to the same whole, to rouse the national spirit." As a result, "the people lifted up their heads and looked towards the heights" (de Gaulle 1971:289–290).

De Gaulle's goal was to use his position as president and national hero to remind his people of their shared French identity, their glorious history, and their joint investment in the welfare of the French nation. Whether or not these efforts fit the definition of demagoguery can be disputed, but what seems indisputable is that the message that he was communicating was aimed more at the emotions than at the reason of the French public, and that it was a message that explicitly tied the future of France to himself. During his presidency, the state exercised significant control over television, control that enabled de Gaulle to constantly speak to the public through televised press conferences, formal addresses to the country, and ubiquitous reporting of his visits throughout France and abroad. Although privatization of French television occurred in the mid-1970s, de Gaulle's successors have still played a dominant role in the media, in large measure because the "style of French political television journalism tends toward a personal, leader focus" (Clift 2005:234).

US presidents embraced television with the same vigor and with much the same purpose that de Gaulle displayed. Although President Dwight Eisenhower was the first to have his press conferences filmed and televised, President John Kennedy was the first to have virtually his entire presidency televised. With a television in almost every US home by the time he ascended to office, nearly every aspect of the Kennedy presidency was open to direct view by the people—from his famous debate during the presidential campaign with Richard Nixon, to his eloquent and much quoted inaugural address, to televised tours of the White House conducted by the first lady, to live televised press conferences, to televised speeches from the Oval Office at times of great challenge, right up to his assassination in Dallas. Since Kennedy, the enduring vision that most Americans have of each of their presidents has been televised—Lyndon Johnson announcing that he would not run for reelection in 1968, Richard Nixon's farewell in 1974, Ronald Reagan's speech at the Berlin Wall, George W. Bush's "mission accomplished" landing on an aircraft carrier. Reagan—the only US president to have made his career first as a performer before entering politics—raised all of this to an art form, with masterfully delivered speeches to the nation and carefully staged photo opportunities for the press, all of which earned him the sobriquet of "the great communicator." Barack Obama's capacity to move his audiences with similar techniques, at least during his first campaign for the presidency, is broadly acknowledged.

Early in 2010, President Nicolas Sarkozy of France, seeking to counter an emerging image of himself as arrogant and out of touch, staged a two-hour primetime television show in which he discussed issues with eleven ordinary citizens, including a dairy farmer, a teacher, and a mechanic. The president responded to the concerns of each, sometimes giving less than popular answers concerning budget cuts and taxes. The event was seen by approximately 9 million people, about a third of those who were watching television at the time. And according to a poll released shortly after the event, 57 percent of those watching found him convincing.[3]

In countries where television is privately controlled, profits come from attracting as many viewers as possible. Thus, early in the television age, it was determined that visual rather than verbal stories were more popular with viewers. This worked to the advantage of presidents, who were much more capable of generating photo opportunities than were members of the legislature. It also became clear that the sports programming that was so popular with viewers contained lessons that could be applied to political news. Television coverage of elections thus tended to focus on the horse race issues—what the polls look like, who is winning, who is losing, who is gaining an advantage from a particular issue or event, what the latest scandal might be—rather than on the weightier questions involving policy and candidate ability. Similarly, news stories during an administration tend to have the same tone—what the political advantage (or disadvantage) to the president of a particular policy position, or event, is and how it will impact the next election. And because television usually can devote no more than a minute or two (sometimes less) to each story, short sound bites and seductive catch-phrases become more important than careful policy discussion. Presidents and their advisers are of course aware of these media biases and tailor their communication strategies accordingly.

In countries where the media are heavily influenced by the regime, ratings are less important than satisfying government officials. In these cases, television serves to convey governmental messages to citizens and can become a powerful instrument of presidentialism. In Cameroon during the one-party era prior to 1990, presidents, according to one observer, used television as well as other media "to manipulate the people into compliance with statist notions," and the role of the media was "always that of explaining government's actions and policies to the population" (Nyamnjoh 2005:136–137). The environment for the electronic media was one in which journalists were expected to "serve the government and propagate its policies as outlined by the head of government" (Fombad 2003:238). In Mexico, television was for many years in the hands of a private monopoly controlled by allies of the ruling Institutional Revolutionary Party (PRI), and therefore was a faithful messenger of presidential and governmental viewpoints (Skidmore 1993:7). In Venezuela, President Chávez responded to the role that television had played in the attempted 2002 coup against himself by financing a large network of community radio and television stations that were aligned with the government (Hawkins 2010:192). All radio and television stations in the country were required to broadcast his speeches and ceremonial events live, and he established his own television show, *Alo Presidente,* that ran for four hours on Sundays. In 2007 he reduced the show's length to ninety minutes and switched its broadcast to Thursdays, but added a live daily radio show. These shows were devoted to highlighting his achievements and criticizing his opponents; he also took calls from members of the public to discuss their grievances. He had even opened a Twitter account so that his followers could keep up with him on a minute-by-minute basis. He viewed all of this as part of a "media war" to win the hearts and minds of voters.[4]

In post-Soviet Russia, television has become the major way in which government communicates with its citizens. In the words of one observer,

Russia went from a "nation of readers" to a "nation of television watchers" (Ryabov 2004:187). One estimate is that 70 percent of the Russian people get their news from television. Although government control of newspapers diminished rather quickly during the post-Soviet period, "television remained close to state authorities and subject to oversight." Nonetheless, both the newspapers and television worked closely with President Boris Yeltsin and played an important role in helping him to gain ascendancy over the remnants of the old regime. With Vladimir Putin's succession to the presidency, the media, for the most part, returned to their subordinate role of supporting the political predilections of the government.

According to two scholars of Russia, "the personalization associated with televised political campaigns amplified and enhanced the traditional Soviet focus on the individual leader" (Mickiewicz and Richter 1996:124). Putin strives to cultivate the image of a strong leader; at various times he has ridden a horse bare-chested, wrestled, deep-sea dived, and staged meetings during which he has scolded lazy bureaucrats—all in front of television cameras (Stanley 2012a). A critical observer concludes that Putin and his aides use television in such a way that the "values, interests, and ideas that are at the heart of liberal democracy" are replaced with "the media representation of a non-existing political reality that is at the core of managed democracy" (Krastev 2006:57–58). State-controlled television news, in the view of one reporter, is charged with spreading "Putin's message of stability and prosperity at any cost" (Stanley 2012b). In Senegal, as in Russia, there has been a widening of public discourse in recent years, with independent print and radio media often intensely criticizing the government in general and the president in particular. Television in Senegal, however, "remains the last bastion of state monopoly over the media" and "gives a disproportionate attention to the activities of the president and his entourage" (Gellar 2005:165).

Presidential Elections

Contrary to the wishes of the designers of early representative systems, today the right to vote is nearly universal. Restrictions on the franchise based on gender, race, and wealth have largely disappeared. Although those who supported such restrictions did so in part because they wished to protect their own privileged positions in society, they also argued that well-educated people were more apt to choose wisely among candidates for office. Those who wrote the US Constitution were convinced that the general public would never be able to choose a president who was capable of providing leadership, and they feared that mass publics would be vulnerable to manipulation by demagogues who appealed only to the emotions of the people and who promised things of pecuniary value in return for votes.

Although there are some who continue to share these concerns, today, in every nation, participation in presidential elections is typically open to all citizens, and these elections always are occasions for the largest turnout of voters. On any election day, it is the candidates for president who receive the most attention from both the voter and the media. Even if numerous legislative seats are being contested on the same day, the presidential race typically receives the lion's share of attention and coverage. The question of how much the personal characteristics and the rhetorical style of candidates affect how people vote in presidential elections has been subject to a great deal of research by political scientists, especially in the context of a scholarly consensus that citizens for the most part have little specific knowledge of the policy challenges that the nation faces and relatively little awareness of how candidates for office would deal with these issues.

In those nations in which political parties have well-defined ideologies and policy stances, citizens may choose a presidential candidate based on their own party identification—that is, the candidate toward whose party the voter feels the greatest policy affinity. Others will vote retrospectively, basing their decisions on their sense of the state of the nation and whether they perceive that times are good or times are bad. And still others will base their votes on the personal characteristics of the candidate and the degree to which they can identify with him or her. No matter which of these approaches makes the most sense for a particular individual, election, or nation, presidential elections always involve an outsized voter focus on the candidate.

In most countries, presidential elections have become much more oriented toward candidates as the partisan allegiances of citizens have become weaker and more transitory. In the words of one scholar writing about the US political system, "long term influences on politics, like party identification" have been replaced "with short-term influences, like current events." This has "boosted the importance of personalized aspects for politics, such as candidate traits, over long-standing political organizations, like political parties" (Cohen 2008:19). This decline in public partisanship has been attributed to a number of factors, including the breakdown in class structures, the declining relevance of left-right distinctions in the aftermath of the fall of the Soviet Union, and the declining importance of religion—in other words, the major divisions that had for so many years structured partisan divisions, particularly in

Europe and also in Latin America. As for the United States, today a plurality of US voters identify themselves as independents rather than as Democrats or Republicans. Rather than functioning as exponents of a particular ideology, political parties have become primarily electoral vehicles designed to gather as many votes as possible for their candidates. In such a context, the personal characteristics of a presidential candidate (as well as legislative candidates) will become more important, and this will be reflected in the nature of political campaigns.[5]

At one time, political party activists played the crucial role of identifying candidates for office, particularly presidential candidates, but in many countries this is no longer the case. In the United States, presidential candidates of the two major parties are nominated in an extended, exhausting, and disorganized process involving primaries and caucuses in each of the states, conducted in a seemingly random order and under different rules depending on the state or the party in question. The most important requirements for prevailing in such a process are money, stamina, rhetorical skills, and an ability to appeal to the decreasing number of highly partisan citizens who participate in the process. Policy knowledge and experience tend to be secondary. Candidates can be nominated who are not necessarily the favorites of party elites and who have not had extensive governing experience, but who, like Barack Obama, are well financed, convey an attractive media presence, and possess an extraordinary ability to move an audience.

Such a selection process, even in those countries where parties play a somewhat stronger role than they do in the United States, creates a specific set of personal qualifications for those who wish to be president. Certainly, the ability to speak persuasively to large audiences has become very important. How someone "looks" on television and their ability to project an image to which people can relate are also important. So too is a personal flair of some sort, or some other characteristic that makes a candidate stand out, at least visually, from others. An ability of the candidate to "connect" with voters at a personal level—to evoke a comfort level with citizens—is a valued characteristic of serious candidates. What all of this means is that presidential candidates come to resemble commodities to be marketed to consumers in much the same way as automobiles and other consumer goods are advertised and sold. The challenge for aspiring candidates is to package themselves (or to hire professionals to package them) so that they can appeal to the voter-consumers whom they are trying to attract. There are tried and true techniques to accomplish this: appealing visual presentations (with great attention to backdrops), air-brushed depictions of the candidate and his or her background and personal history, and packaged remedies for whatever ails the country or troubles its citizens, reduced to slogans and sound bites. Modern presidential campaigns are characterized by the growing importance of professional political advisers, pollsters, and speechwriters. And although this approach to campaigning may have originated in the United States, it is instructive to note that many of these campaign managers now organize themselves as international agencies, hiring themselves out to run campaigns in countries around the world. When people in other countries refer to the "Americanization" of their political campaigns, this is what they mean.

Televised debates, long a staple of presidential elections in the United States and gaining in popularity in other countries as well, are seen by candidates as opportunities to appear "presidential," and to demonstrate their coolness under fire; avoiding an embarrassing gaffe and turning a memorable phrase or two are the indicators of success. Less frequently, they provide opportunities to debate contrasting policy positions. In France, "the centerpiece and symbolic culmination of each campaign is the head-to-head televised debate." The two-and-a-half-hour debate between presidential candidates Nicolas Sarkozy and Ségolène Royal on May 2, 2007, was watched by more than 23 million citizens, a number matched only by the viewership for World Cup soccer games.[6]

In Poland's first presidential election after the collapse of the Soviet Union, "the campaign was fought largely on television" because "political parties or movements backing the six candidates . . . were either very new or in disarray, so they were incapable of mounting full-fledged campaigns." The candidate who finished a surprising second to Lech Walesa, the Solidarity leader, was Stanislaw Tyminski, a Pole by birth who had spent most of his adult life in Canada and had returned to Poland only after democratic procedures had been instituted. In the words of one observer, "Tyminski's candidacy and popularity were almost entirely creatures of television. . . . [H]is views and appearances on television struck a chord with disaffected voters." Through television, he projected an image of an independent candidate, a successful businessman, a man of the world—"honest, truthful and disciplined" (Jakubowicz 1996:142–144). Although Tyminski lost to Walesa on the second round of balloting, his campaign illustrated the way in which loose party structures, multiple candidates, and television can turn a virtual unknown into a viable and almost winning candidate.

In Argentina, personalism had always been a part of politics and political culture, with Peronism being the archetypical example of party identification with and subordination to an individual leader. But in 1983, when democracy returned to Argentina, television provided a new dimension to the personalized campaign, with legally mandated free television time allowing candidates to reach voters "through their roofs rather than ringing their doorbells." Campaigns utilized all television genres in order to get their candidates before the public, including guest appearances on situation comedies, game shows, and talk shows. "Entertainment shows have provided unmatched opportunities for candidates to shed their image as traditional politicians and wrap themselves in mundane guy-next-door clothing" (Waisbord 1996:214–215). At the same time, old party loyalties began to atrophy as voters moved to a less ideological, more pragmatic approach to politics driven largely by the economic problems confronting the nation. Candidates, having secured their party's nomination through a primary system by demonstrating their party loyalty, then moved to position themselves in the general election as party outsiders "removed from party bickering and politics as usual"; they tended to emphasize nonpartisan themes and rely on their own personal allies to organize their campaigns (Waisbord 1996:218). US presidential elections can be described in similar terms. Bill Clinton, it will be remembered, played his saxophone on a late-night television show during his 1992 campaign, and both Barack Obama and John McCain appeared on such shows during their 2008 contest.

Some have suggested that even the parliamentary systems of Western Europe are showing increasing signs of the personalism associated with presidentialism, a process driven in part by the diminishing role of political parties. As a result, public attention in these systems is becoming more focused on the head of government than on the collective membership of the governing party, and elections in parliamentary systems are becoming increasingly personalized, with greater attention paid to the personality and policies of the party leader who presumably will become prime minister than to the ideology and positions of his party organization (see Poguntke and Webb 2005). One indicator of this phenomenon occurred during the 2010 British election, when, for the first time, the leaders of the three largest political parties that were contesting the election engaged in three televised debates. Interestingly, the election was affected to a significant degree by the personality and debate performance of Nick Clegg, the leader of the smallest of the three parties, the Liberal Democrats, and a virtual unknown before the campaign began. Post-debate polls suggested a surge in support for the Liberal Democrats based, it would seem, more on Clegg's presentation of himself as a fresh new candidate than on any familiarity with the Liberal Democratic Party and its positions on the major issues facing the country, or with Clegg himself and his own record.

Televised election campaigns focusing on candidates and their personalities are heavily laden with symbolic politics. "Chronic repetition
of clichés and stale phrases that serve simply to evoke an uncritical
response is a time honored habit among politicians and a mentally restful one for their audiences" (Edelman 1982:124). Symbolic politics is
mentally restful because the candidate is not saying anything with which
the voter can disagree, or anything that requires the voter to engage with
the issues, or to think and reason in a sustained or critical manner.
Although voters often claim that they want to hear detailed policy proposals from candidates, it isn't at all clear that they respond well to such
presentations, are able to absorb such information, or are able to put that
information to any practical use.

In this context, the real purpose of the campaign is to bind the people to their candidate and future leader, to make him a vehicle for their
own fears and aspirations, and an instrument for the reassurances that
they need. When the winning candidate emerges from the electoral
process, he does so with the endorsement of a national electorate. He,
more so than any other political leader, is in a position to claim a popular, democratic mandate to govern, conferred upon him by a national
electorate, in contrast to the narrower mandates that a legislator can
claim from the smaller portion of the public that resides in the geographic constituency that he or she represents. The victorious candidate also
can claim that his election means that it is through the will of the people
that he governs. Although he may have said little that is specific in
regard to public policy, the winner also will claim, sometimes against all
reason, that his election means that the public supports each and every
one of his policy priorities.

Presidential Qualifications

This approach to presidential campaigning suggests that the outcomes of
presidential elections will turn more on these personal factors than on
those qualifications that focus on governmental experience, policy intelligence, and the development and articulation of real policy proposals
that will deal with the huge and complex challenges that the nation faces.
Recent presidential elections in the United States and elsewhere have
provided some illustrations of this point. In the US presidential election
of 2000, Al Gore received a slightly larger number of votes for president
than did George W. Bush, but because of the workings of the Electoral
College, Bush became the forty-third president. Those who voted for

Bush picked a person with no national governmental experience and with large, publicly visible gaps in his knowledge of the world, over a person who had served sixteen years in Congress and eight years as vice president of the United States, and was acknowledged to be something of a policy expert, especially on environmental issues. The Bush campaign emphasized its candidate's commitment to something called "compassionate conservatism" as well as his informal folksy style, while the Gore campaign emphasized its candidate's moral probity, his strong marriage (in the aftermath of the Clinton presidency), and his résumé. Although a great deal went into determining the outcome of that election, it was clear that many voters felt more "comfortable" with George Bush (a person whom they'd like to have a beer with, according to some pundits) than with Al Gore, a person who seemed a dull know-it-all (despite the public's ostensible interest in policy details) with a tendency to exaggerate his accomplishments (exemplified, presumably, by the apocryphal story that he had claimed to have "invented the Internet").

Eight years later, the voters selected Barack Obama, a young senator from Illinois who had been in office for only four years, two of which he spent campaigning for the presidency, and who had very limited experience with national and international issues, over John McCain, who had served for twenty-six years in Congress. As Obama contested for the presidential nomination of his party, he bested a group of politicians nearly all of whom were more experienced and were better prepared to be president than he was. Obama, as the first person of color with a serious possibility of being elected president, was indeed a novel candidate, and his rhetorical skills, his ability to connect with voters emotionally, his obvious intelligence, and his prodigious fundraising skills turned him into a formidable and ultimately victorious candidate. John McCain, in contrast, came off as grumpy, dull, and old, with a less than inspirational speaking style and a seeming inability to connect with people outside his age cohort.

The point of this is not to suggest that Al Gore would have been a better president than George Bush or that John McCain would have been a better president than Barack Obama. The point, rather, is that a fully televised, fully democratized presidential selection process, characterized by political parties that have relatively little control over selecting their nominee, to an increasing degree turns on the ability of candidates to connect at a personal level with voters and to project an image that voters can feel comfortable with, rather than on the demonstrated ability of the candidate to govern effectively. This problem was anticipated by those who invented the presidency when they wrote the US Constitution. That is why they rejected proposals for the popular election of the president, on the argument that the people would not be sufficiently knowledgeable to make a wise choice and because the Founders worried that the public would be vulnerable to manipulation by presidential aspirants who would appeal to their emotions rather than to their reason.

Certainly, the modern presidential election process can open the door not just to those with little experience, but also to the demagogues whom the Founders feared. In France, Jean Le Pen, although he never won a presidential election, did influence election outcomes with his racist and anti-Semitic oratory. Vladimir Zhirinovsky ran similarly unsuccessful campaigns in various Russian presidential elections in the post-Soviet period, campaigns that were aided by widespread television coverage that emphasized his energetic showmanship and extreme ideas (Mickiewicz and Richter 1996:122). The fact that candidates of this sort do not always win is less important than the fact that presidential elections, and the direct connection that television establishes between such candidates and the public, provide them with a broad audience and a powerful megaphone. And in times of economic crisis or threats to security from internal or external forces, candidates of this sort can become the "man on horseback" to whom people will turn.

The presidential selection process underlines the fact that the skills associated with campaigning for office are different from those associated with governing effectively. This difference is clearest with charismatic presidents who have the strongest rhetorical skills but very little experience governing. And to the extent that presidential elections begin to favor articulate "outsiders" with only a slim record of public service, this disconnect will become more apparent. For example, the first presidents of most postcolonial African nations had little governing experience, because they had been excluded from such responsibilities by their colonial masters. Thus, Ghana's first president, Kwame Nkrumah, was a man whose "skills were those of arousing mass popular support: inspiring rhetoric, mastery of political and ideological language, and virtuoso political acting. His ineffectiveness as a ruler after African independence was due largely to his lack of the more mundane and practical skills of governing" (Jackson and Rosberg 1982:198). Lech Walesa, the courageous leader of the Solidarity movement that brought down the communist system in Poland, was thought to have been rather ineffective as president, again understandable given the fact that he could not have been part of the governing process under the previous regime (see Nye 2008:86). The gap between Barack Obama's skills as a campaigner and his frustrating first term as president has been remarked on by many, and to the extent that it exists, it is likely to be a product of his very brief experience in Washington and in political office more generally (Fallows 2012).

Going Public

One way in which presidents have tried to deal with this potential disconnect between governing and running for office is to bring to the conduct of their office the same skills and techniques that got them elected. Earlier we noted a tendency on the part of presidents to "go public" as they seek to generate support for their policy proposals (Kernell 1986). Theodore Roosevelt was the first US president to use this strategy. In 1904 he traveled around the country making speeches aimed at convincing the Senate to pass the Hepburn Act, which was designed to strengthen the ability of the Interstate Commerce Commission to control some of the predatory pricing activities of the railroads. Fifteen years later, Woodrow Wilson adopted the same strategy in his ultimately futile attempt to get the Senate to ratify the Treaty of Versailles and approve US membership in the League of Nations.

The presidential strategy of going public has created what scholars and observers of the US presidency have referred to as the "permanent campaign." This phenomenon has been described as "a combination of image making and strategic calculation that turns governing into a perpetual campaign" (Heclo 2000:2), the goal of which is "to sustain an elected official's popularity" (Blumenthal 1982:7). The permanent campaign is a "continuous and voracious quest for public approval" in which "every day is election day" (Heclo 2000:15–17). Presidents are told that they need to "control the narrative" as they package themselves and their policies, meaning control the manner in which they and what they want to do is depicted to larger audiences. In support of the permanent campaign, US presidents have expanded their staffs to include the White House Offices of Communication, Public Liaison, and Political Affairs and a virtual army of speechwriters who can produce a presidential statement for any and every occasion. The responsibility of these offices is to tailor and market the image of the president and his policies so that he and what he stands for appear to be as congruent as possible with what the people seem to stand for.

Today, the permanent campaign is a permanent part of the US presidential policymaking landscape. Presidents regularly go public, traveling around the country, holding town hall meetings, scheduling press conferences and photo opportunities, making speeches to national television audiences, carefully poll testing policy proposals and their labels, and paying meticulous attention to conveying a consistent "message" from the White House. Television, of course, plays a large role in the going public approach. Presidential speechwriters "report that the one sentence paragraphs so common in presidential messages are consciously designed to accommodate television news. With short aphorisms rather than developed arguments, presidents are more likely to get a snappy quotation on the brief segment of the evening news that they are allocated, and are less likely to be quoted out of context, because there is no context" (Tulis 1987:187).

Modern presidencies have used these techniques as well as events designed specifically for television to dramatize issues, to campaign for support for their initiatives, or simply to burnish their image of being the people's president. Thus, during his first months in office, Ronald Reagan used nationally televised speeches, calibrated to important congressional votes, to generate public support for his economic agenda. These speeches explicitly encouraged citizens to communicate with their legislators and to urge them to support the president, and a string of early victories for Reagan seemed to demonstrate the efficacy of such an approach.

Speeches before friendly audiences, televised in whole or in part, can create a sense of momentum for presidential proposals. Jimmy Carter, Bill Clinton, and George W. Bush liked to use so-called town hall meetings rather than prepared speeches. These meetings, usually televised at least locally and always in front of prescreened audiences, some of whom had been furnished with planted questions, served as a means to convey the image of presidential proximity and responsiveness to the people, while at the same time pushing for the president's agenda.

President Obama's approach to moving his healthcare proposal through Congress exemplified a number of aspects of the permanent campaign. As the debate over healthcare raged on during his first year in office, the president used both speeches and town hall meetings to communicate his views as well as his sense of urgency about the issue. Early on, he assembled a group of "ordinary citizens" in the White House for a televised question and answer session. In the fall of 2009, after a summer in which the healthcare initiative had taken a beating from Republicans and the right-wing media, he gave a primetime address to a joint session of Congress, telling the assembled legislators that they were close to succeeding, with the issues they agreed upon being far more numerous than the issues they disagreed upon, and urging them to push on to a final bill. It seemed to most observers that the speech was directed less at changing the minds of his opponents in Congress and more toward conveying to the viewing public an image of a president who was involved, in charge, and leading on this key initiative. Obama then went on the road, appearing in public forums around the country to press for the healthcare legislation, answer questions, dispel what he claimed were unfair or inaccurate characterizations of the bill, and cast his opponents as allies of the detested insurance industry. As the debate reached its climatic moments in February 2010, Obama invited members of Congress from both parties to meet with him in a televised summit so that he could hear suggestions about how his proposals might be improved. Little of substance came from the event—in the end, no Republicans voted for his healthcare proposal—and because the session was held in the middle of a workday, it isn't clear how many people actually watched it. But the summit achieved its purpose, because it was widely reported and commented upon, and conveyed the image to the American public that the president was willing to listen to his opponents even if they were not willing to listen to him, that he was able to respond to their concerns, and that he was open to considering (minor) adjustments to his proposal in light of their suggestions.

The New Media

For presidents and presidential candidates who seek to use the media to control their messages, enhance their power, and advance their policies, recent changes in the nature and role of the mass media have created both challenges and opportunities. For example, the number of television outlets has increased. At one time, television in the United States was dominated by the three major networks, and their nightly news programs were a primary source of information for voters. Today, cable television has multiplied the number of channels, increasing the number of news-oriented stations but also providing more choices for those who don't care to watch the news. Many of the new stations also feature political talk shows whose hosts take simplistic and extreme positions, mostly on the right but occasionally on the left, on the issues of the day. Whether these shows are more about politics or entertainment is open to question. As is the case with entertainment, the pay of those who participate in political talk shows is based on the number of people who watch, and to the extent that viewers are attracted by outrageous assertions, fame and fortune may well ensue.

Most recently, the Internet has become an alternative source of information and represents, in some respects, the ultimate democratization of political news. The Internet has become a home for countless bloggers, some who offer little more than gossip, others who devote themselves to specific political biases, and still others who make an effort to do genuine reporting. Anyone with access to a computer and to the Internet can create a website and start blogging about his or her personal views. Anyone can report any rumor and have it read by millions and even see it picked up by more established news outlets. Every embarrassing statement by a president or a presidential candidate can be caught on cell phone cameras, uploaded to YouTube, and become an overnight sensation. Mitt Romney, the Republican presidential candidate in 2012, learned this when, in the final weeks of the campaign, a cell phone video surfaced in which he, while speaking at a private meeting of donors, remarked that 47 percent of the American people paid no taxes and were dependent on government handouts. Although this was not necessarily the deciding factor in his loss to President Obama, Romney had to devote significant time to explaining and ultimately apologizing for this remark.

All of these technological changes have been accompanied by the steady decline of newspaper readership. At one time, the print media, and especially the major newspapers, could be relied upon for more careful and detailed accounts of politics and public policy. But newspaper readership continues to decline as the influence of cable television and the Internet expands, and many of the newspapers that still seem to be thriving are those that adopt the same soft-news, personality-driven approach that characterizes cable television and the Internet.

All of this has complicated presidents' efforts to go public. This multiplication of news sources makes it possible for presidents to reach a varied audience, but makes it much more difficult for presidents to "control the narrative" or even to ensure that their narrative is fully covered. Because the competition among these multiple news sources is so intense, rumors, scandals (real or imagined), political invective, and soft-news features that attract larger audiences have crowded out the hard-news stories that presidents had typically dominated. And when presidential issues are covered, negative and critical comments—sometimes uninformed by the facts—tend to be more apparent than they were previously. Presidential news conferences, which at one time a president was able to dominate quite easily, now are characterized by more hostile "gotcha" questions than they were in the past (Clayman and Heritage 2002; Clayman et al. 2006; see also Cohen 2008). Not surprisingly, all of this has contributed to voter confusion, because there is no longer a hierarchy among media coverage. During the 1960s, Walter Cronkite, the host of *CBS Evening News,* was thought of as "the most trusted man in America." When he ended his nightly news broadcast by saying "and that's the way it is," most Americans agreed that that was indeed the way it was. In today's noisy, chaotic, and often vitriolic news environment, there is no one who could be viewed, in terms of trust, the way Cronkite was viewed.

US presidents are aware of the potential of the new media to keep them connected with the people. In Barack Obama's case, his election campaigns made revolutionary use of social networking websites and the Internet to generate money and support (Gulati 2010). Once he took office, this effort was continued by groups who were allied with the president. The Obama presidency was the first in history to have a Twitter feed on the White House website. In the United States, all presidential candidates now have websites and staff who monitor the various media outlets and "tweet" their reactions to the latest news tidbits.

The multiplication of media sources focuses even more attention on the person of the president rather than on the nature of his public policies. If presidents are to break through in this new environment, they must place an even greater premium on quotable sound bites and on personality rather than substance. They must be prepared to respond to rumors that "go viral" on the Internet—rumors that in the past they might have simply ignored—but that are now picked up by the more respectable print media. In the United States, President Obama learned this during the healthcare debate when opponents of his proposal claimed that it would set up "death panels" that would decide who were to receive care and who would not. The initial White House posture was to ignore this charge; nothing like this was contained in the president's proposal and the thought that this would be something that the administration was considering seemed absurd. But it did not take long for these imaginary panels to become real in the minds of US voters, and by the time that the administration took this misperception seriously, many minds could not be changed.

The Internet is, of course, an international presence that impacts presidential candidates and presidencies in other nations besides the United States. Social networking sites were instrumental in organizing protests against authoritarian leaders during the Arab Spring of 2011. In Russia, although Vladimir Putin has been able to control the television networks, protests against him that began in 2011 and continued into 2012 and beyond have been greatly facilitated by the Internet. Russian bloggers and political websites "not only contradict government-tailored newscasts, they also offer an alternate, unscripted reality" (Stanley 2012a).

Politics and Entertainment

But in addition to posing a challenge to presidents and other leaders, the media, old and new, also can serve as a more subtle instrument to pacify citizens and build confidence in a political regime. Broadcast media such as radio and television are not simply about informing the public or influencing the outcome of elections. As one scholar put it, the media "are part of the larger drama of social interaction in the nation-state: a process of feedback between elite and mass, leader and led, but also within a complex emotive network where the symbols, actions, and words coming from television form an essential part of the ritual that mirrors and in turn shapes the relationship between state and society. Television becomes the preferred medium for the playing out of society's fears and hopes, independently of how the viewers may vote. The line between entertainment and information blurs, as the interaction of the medium and the viewer substitutes for what was not so long ago the more intimate relations on the village or community level" (Skidmore 1993:11).

Television is the perfect medium for symbolic politics. "By its very nature, television tends to focus on personality rather than program in order to reduce the complexity of political issues, and politicians frequently respond by concentrating on symbolism rather than substance and detail in order to cater to the media's inherent need." Presidents and other government leaders thus make a conscious choice "to exploit the visual media's potential for simplification and symbolism for their own ends" (Poguntke and Webb 2005:15). This is apparent in the "nonpolitical" component of television. Dramas depict heroes and villains, and the good guys tend to win, usually in one hour. Sporting events, soap operas, reality shows, and situation comedies entertain and soothe, distracting us from the anxieties that plague our everyday lives. Game shows convey the ideas that there are winners and losers who are determined largely by chance and skill rather than by society's political or economic structure. And the advertisements that accompany the entertainment emphasize the tenets of the consumer society, assuring us that by purchasing particular products, we will feel better, look and smell better, live longer, and be safer and happier. The Internet also plays its part here, as it provides citizens with access to a variety of products, allows people to keep in touch with each other about trivial aspects of their own personal lives, and concentrates popular attention on the latest "app" rather than the latest policy proposal emanating from government officials.

Even in more authoritarian nations, where government leaders tend to regulate news programming as well as the Internet, entertainment shows are much more broadly tolerated, sometimes as a way to spread subtle or more direct political messages and other times as a way to simply distract the population from current events. In many ways, they are the electronic equivalent of the "circuses" that the Roman Aediles found so useful two millennia ago. One example of the permeable boundary between entertainment and politics is the Brazilian *novellas*. Akin to soap operas, *novellas* constitute a major portion of television entertainment, draw a wide audience, and have enormous cultural importance. In the run-up to the 1989 presidential election in Brazil, several of these *novellas* presented a view of the country as "a kingdom of political corruption run by professional politicians." These shows helped to construct the scenario for the national launching of an "outsider," a young, unknown, modern "hero," a "savior of the country" (de Lima 1993:105–106). Luiz Inácio Lula da Silva, at the time a relatively unknown union leader, came from nowhere that year to run a competitive race for the Brazilian presidency, using the electronic media and the law that provided candidates with free access to television to mobilize mass support. And rather than simply talking to the people, he used popular musicians and other entertainment-oriented approaches as a way to attract large audiences (Zuleta-Puceiro 1993:79).

Whether or not the winner of the 1989 election, Fernando Collor de Mello, fit the description of national hero better than Lula did is open to dispute, but the key point here is that television entertainment as well as cinema, whether in Brazil or anywhere else, have a disposition toward the hero, the detective who solves the crime, the champion who saves the town from the bandits or saves the nation from those who threaten it, the special agent whose courage and insight foils a terrorist plot, and the honest person who comes to office to clean up the mess created by the professional politicians. To the extent that this role becomes fixed in the national psyche, it is the singular president who fits the part. On the other hand, collective bodies such as legislatures or bureaucracies seldom fare as well as these singular leaders. In the iconic American film *Mr. Smith Goes to Washington,* Congress and its members are depicted as corrupt and self-serving politicians, and it is the citizen hero, played by Jimmy Stewart, who challenges their ways. No television show about the US Congress has ever succeeded, but *The West Wing,* focusing on an exceptionally talented president and his White House staff, lasted for eight seasons and garnered countless awards for the show, its stars, and its producers. To the extent that we believe (or need to believe) in political heroes, we believe in presidents, for the president is the public servant who is most able to meet the requirements of the role of hero as established by the media.

The Presidency and the People

Jeffrey Tulis argues that the strategy of going public, or the permanent campaign, means that the original concept of the US presidency endorsed by the Framers, one that posited a healthy distance between the president and public opinion, has been replaced by a de facto "second constitution" that "puts a premium on active and continuous presidential leadership of popular opinion" (1987:18). This second constitution highlights the importance of the rhetorical skills of the president and his ability to deploy those skills to raise public support for his policy initiatives. As will be recalled from Chapter 2, it was exactly such an intimate relationship between public opinion and the presidency that the Founders wished to avoid. Alexander Hamilton, writing in the 1st Federalist Paper, warned "that of those men who have overturned the liberties of republics, the greatest number have begun their career by paying an obsequious court to the people, commencing demagogues and ending tyrants" (1:35). Tulis points out that this switch from the vision of the Founders is not just a matter of style. Rather, it constitutes a rethinking of the relationship between public opinion and political leadership, one that reduces political debate "to assertions of policy stands, focusing attention upon what sides citizens take, and how many of them take them, rather than on the complexities of what they stand for" (1987:188). This also means that rather than the president responding to public opinion, his goal is to shape and arouse public opinion to support him and his priorities. The staff and resources that US presidents devote to that enterprise is reflected in other nations as well. One observer of Latin American politics reports that in Brazil and Mexico, there are cabinet-level offices "dedicated to measuring, analyzing, and shaping public opinion" (Hughes 2010:272).

Another way of characterizing the permanent campaign is that it moves a nation and its leadership toward plebiscitarianism. Although plebiscitarianism narrowly refers to placing policy options or even incumbent presidents before the voters and asking them to vote yes or no on these options or incumbents, it has taken on a broader meaning that refers to the inclination of presidents to manipulate public opinion and to cite public opinion polls or mass demonstrations as indicative of support for their policy positions. In other words, presidents employ democratic rhetoric to achieve their policy goals by arguing in effect that they are the sole expression of the popular will, that it falls to them to represent "the people" (see Barr 2009:36; Hawkins 2010:58–61).

Presidents who rely on this approach base their government "on a seemingly direct connection to their largely unorganized mass base, bypassing established parties and interest organizations; attacking the political class and other established elites; using opinion polls, (the threat of) plebiscites, and other populist instruments for overcoming opposition; strengthening their personalistic leadership; concentrating power and reinforcing the majoritarian elements of constitutional arrangements." These presidents work "to skew the separation of powers so as to privilege the executive branch over congress and the judiciary" and thus diminish the extent to which checks and balances can restrict their own authority (Weyland 2003:1102, 1107). Using television and other techniques to create direct contact with their people, such presidents "delegitimize party systems and discredit legislative assemblies," and "displace parties as the primary vehicle of the expression of the popular will" (Mainwaring 2006:18; see also Pérez-Liñán 2007:85). There is also reason to believe that these presidents, by distancing themselves from collective institutions such as political parties and legislatures and relying only on popular support, run a greater risk of being forced from office prematurely or being denied reelection. If the people decide to turn against them, these presidents will find little support among the political class, some of whom may seize the opportunity to force incumbents from office and advance their own ambitions (Hochstetler 2006; Pérez-Liñán 2007:37).

Evo Morales of Bolivia and Rafael Correa of Ecuador are examples of populist outsiders who rose to the presidencies of their countries by arguing that the functioning representative institutions were designed to maintain the existing class structure and distribution of wealth. In the case of Correa, during his campaign he regularly characterized the Ecuadorean Congress as a "sewer" of corruption, and his party ran no candidates for legislative seats. After his election, Correa, like Morales, sought to replace existing institutions of representative democracy with a more plebiscitary form of democracy, focusing on them personally and on their agenda for change. Steps were taken to enhance presidential power and to create new legislative bodies that were more broadly representative of the population, particularly indigenous people, and more likely to support presidential initiatives. In the case of Morales, he proposed transforming the legislature into a unicameral body, thus abolishing the Senate, in which his party did not have a majority of seats; allowing the reelection of the president for a second five-year term; and eliminating the provision that allowed Congress to appoint the president if no candidate received a majority of the popular vote, substituting instead a provision for runoff elections (see Corrales 2009). Although Morales ultimately compromised on some of these goals, the resulting Constitution significantly expanded the power of the presidency. To achieve their goals, both Correa and Morales constantly returned to the people, scheduling referenda on their proposals and organizing street demonstrations to persuade (or intimidate) opponents.

This approach is not peculiar to Latin American. In the United States, one observer has suggested that "for most Americans, the presidency has come to be nearly all there is to democratic politics" (Miroff 1982:219). Political scientist Theodore Lowi argued that the US presidency has become an office of "tremendous personal power drawn from the people" and that a "new democratic theory" has developed, one in which "the presidency with all powers is the necessary condition for governing a large democratic nation" (1985:20). In France, when Charles de Gaulle assumed the presidency of France, he also went to the electorate to solicit their endorsement of him and his policies. From his point of view, one French political scientist argued, "presidential power [was] permanently resourced by public opinion. The electorate's endorsement of his personal power, whether in referenda which he regarded as plebiscites on his own presidency, or in the 1965 direct presidential election, functioned as national confidence votes in the president" (Clift 2005:233–234). In the United States in 2008, Barack Obama too ran as an antiestablishment candidate during his successful campaign for the presidency. He condemned the way in which Washington worked (or did not work), the level of acrimony that seemed to characterize the relationship between the two parties, and the seeming inability of existing political arrangements to deal with the major problems confronting the nation. In contrast, he promised an end to "politics as usual," a renewed effort at bipartisanship, and, of course, "change."

To an increasing degree, US presidential candidates present themselves as outsiders on a mission to "clean up the mess in Washington." Even candidates who have spent decades in Washington, like Senator McCain, attempt to repackage themselves as "mavericks" intent on disrupting the status quo. The importance of the outsider image is suggested by the fact that candidates for the US presidency now tend to come from the ranks of governors (Carter, Reagan, Clinton, George W. Bush, Romney) rather than from those who have had extensive (or any) experience in national politics. In the 2012 Republican nomination fight, the eventual nominee, Mitt Romney, proudly proclaimed that he was the only candidate in the race who had never served in Washington.

Conclusion

At one time the legitimacy of an executive leader was based on tradition or on divine right or even on wisdom and age, but today presidential legitimacy is rooted almost entirely in democratic principles. Now all presidents are popularly selected by an electorate that includes virtually every adult citizen of the nation. To an increasing degree, presidential candidates reach this electorate through the electronic mass media, particularly television and now the Internet. While at one time political parties played the key role in selecting and electing presidential candidates, they are becoming increasingly marginal to that process. Presidential campaigns are highly personalized operations, run by the candidates themselves and focusing on their personal qualities, their rhetoric, and in some cases their charisma, rather than on their policy positions and their qualifications for the office. An election process of this sort can facilitate the presidential candidacies of politicians who are not well prepared for the responsibilities of office but who possess a capacity to connect on a personal rather than a policy level with large segments of the population.

As they connect with the people, either as candidates or as incumbents, presidents exploit the latent disposition of the population toward a strong, singular leader, especially in difficult or confusing times. Presidents and presidential candidates articulate themes that appear to ally them with the mass public, that evoke patriotic or nationalistic symbols, and that emphasize simple solutions for complex problems. In the most extreme cases, they have a disposition toward vilifying their opponents and claiming that they alone embody the will of the people and that they alone stand as the guardian of the nation and its traditional values.

Once elected, they work diligently to foster and maintain public support for themselves and for their policies, employing whatever tools might be available to them to shape public opinion. Presidential administrations are to an increasing degree characterized by a "permanent campaign" atmosphere that requires the president to be constantly at work selling his policy proposals as well as himself to a broad public. In that context, public support tends to become the primary criterion for judging the wisdom of policy proposals. As they seek to generate such support, presidents attempt to exploit their constitutional position as head of state, a position that implicitly connects them with the patriotic and historical symbols of nationhood. They also use the media to generate support, through control and intimidation in hyperpresidential contexts, and in more subtle ways in more constrained systems.

This intimate relationship between presidents and the people—largely a product of the twentieth century—was something that those who created the US presidency wished to avoid. They feared that the people would make bad choices in their selection of the president and they feared that presidents who were dependent on the people would use demagoguery to manipulate public opinion or, failing that, would be inclined toward actions that were popular rather than in the public interest. They feared as well that populist presidents would ultimately constitute a danger to liberty, because they would use the support of the people to move in a tyrannical direction. Today, presidents justify attempts to expand their power by citing their connection with the people, and they claim that the goals that they wish to accomplish reflect the popular will. As they make that case, they benefit from the public's skepticism toward legislative bodies and their susceptibility to strong decisive leaders who are able to provide reassurance in a difficult and uncertain world. However, they also run the risk of a sudden loss of power and office if the public upon whom they so heavily rely turns against them.

Notes

1. "South Africans's Ratings of Government Performance," Afrobarometer Briefing Paper no. 44, 2006, www.afrobarometer.org.

2. "The Status of Democracy, 2005–2006: Findings from Afrobarometer Round 3 for 18 Countries," Afrobarometer Briefing Paper no. 40, 2006, www.afrobarometer.org.

3. "Rebranding Nicolas Sarkozy," *The Economist,* January 28, 2010.

4. "Chavez Show to be Broadcast Daily," *BBC News,* February 13, 2007; "Hugo Chavez Embraces Twitter to Fight On-Line 'Conspiracy,'" *The Guardian,* April 28, 2010.

5. Whether or not the current period of party polarization in the United States presages a resurgence of party strength is an open question. While party platforms have become more ideologically distinct and party unity scores in Congress have risen (see Jacobson 2013:261), candidates continue to win party nominations by efforts that they mount independent of party leaders and still feel free to disagree with party policy positions either for ideological or electorally convenient reasons. And presidential campaigns continue to be candidate-centered, run by the candidate and his own personal organization rather than by his or her political party (see Wayne 2012).

6. "Royal Ignites Election Debate with Attack on Sarkozy," *The Guardian,* May 3, 2007. The Sarkozy-Hollande debate five years later drew 17 million viewers. "Presidential Sweet: Nice Guy Hollande Outshines Sarkozy in French TV Debate," *The Guardian,* May 3, 2012.

7

The Perils and Promise of Presidentialism

Social scientists who take a functionalist approach to understanding political systems would conclude that the executive is the one essential institution for any political system. No matter how a nation makes its political decisions, they cannot be self-implementing; someone has to execute the will of the state. Whether a law is promulgated by an absolute monarch or debated and voted upon in the Roman Senate, whether decreed by the president of Brazil or enacted by a New England town meeting, someone has to carry out its provisions—to execute it—and doing so is the core executive function. Governments without an executive, if one could imagine such a creature, would not be worthy of the name; without someone responsible for carrying out its laws and for sanctioning those who disobeyed, the law would have no force. In effect, there would be no government at all, civil society would cease to exist, and we would return to some form of the state of nature in which all would be free to do as they please and only the strongest would survive.

States require the ability not only to carry out the law, but also to act in a timely manner. In dangerous times or when faced with a crisis, the political system must have the capacity to act expeditiously. It is self-evident that the larger the number of people who need to consent to a decision to act, the less quickly such a decision can be taken; a smaller number of people can reach agreement more quickly, and, of course, one person can act most quickly. Governments with an executive who is incapable of acting expeditiously may not be able to provide individual citizens with protection against predators, nor provide the nation as a whole with protection against external forces that might threaten it. Finally, all nations require leadership—someone to set the national agenda, to speak for and to its people, to evoke a spirit of national unity and purpose, and in troubled times to provide reassurance and direction, and to convey the sense that someone is in charge.

Although the executive power is indispensable, it also is potentially dangerous. An executive with a tyrannical bent can make arbitrary decisions about what the law is, can decide to implement it in a brutal manner, and can avoid being held to account for his actions. Such a person could assume not just the role of executor of the law, but also the roles of determining what the law is and judging the guilt or innocence of those charged with violations, tasks that modern political systems typically assign to nonexecutive agencies such as legislatures and judiciaries. Like Machiavelli's Prince, such a despot would not be simply above the law; he would embody the law. The great task of constitutional government as it arose during the period of the Enlightenment was to constrain the discretionary power of the Prince by requiring his actions to conform with the law and by identifying institutions and actors beyond his control who would be in charge of deciding what the law is. On the other hand, if the executive was so constrained that he lacked the ability to take the initiative and to act, especially when confronted with an emergency, that might be as dangerous to the nation as an executive with unconstrained power. In other words, the seemingly contradictory constitutional challenge was to simultaneously empower and restrain executives.

In addition to constitutionalism, the Enlightenment period also established the principle that the governed—those who lived under the law—should have a role in its creation. This led to the development and empowerment of representative institutions that would reflect the interests and opinions of citizens, that would be charged with making laws that would govern the behavior of both citizens and their rulers, and that would have the capacity to constrain the executive. The scheme to restrict or check the absolute power of the executive with an institution whose legitimacy is based upon the participation of the citizenry began to take form in Europe during the eighteenth century with the rise of parliamentary government. Although the monarch (i.e., the executive) would possess a number of prerogatives that he was entitled to exercise on a unilateral basis—particularly on issues of war and peace—he was to be accountable to a legislative body and, through that body, to the people of the nation.

In the United States, the more complicated challenge was to create a republican executive—a nonmonarchical office that would nonetheless possess a range of executive powers. The efforts of the Constitutional Convention culminated in the creation of the presidency, an office with the full responsibilities of the executive, but restricted in what its occupant could do by a written constitution, by an independent legislature and judiciary, and by the power of the former to remove the incumbent if he transcended the constitutional limits of his power. This constrained presidency also would be accountable indirectly to the citizenry at large, because voters would have a voice in deciding who would hold the office and because the president would serve a fixed term rather than the unlimited tenure that his monarchical counterparts enjoyed.

The US presidency served as a model for the development of presidential systems in other parts of the world, first in Latin America, where it directly influenced the views of early constitution makers such as Simón Bolivar, and more than a century later in the African and Asian countries that gained their independence from European colonial powers. Although most countries placed fewer constraints on their presidents than did the writers of the US Constitution, all of the documents that created such presidencies provided for some degree of power-sharing between the legislature and the executive. Of course, many constitutions did not accurately reflect the real allocation of political power. In some instances, legislatures that seemed constitutionally to possess significant power were in practice subordinate to presidents who exercised a great deal more authority than the Constitution seemed to provide, with only minimal checks from other political institutions.

Rather than simply lamentable deviants from the more constrained arrangement provided in the US Constitution, these systems with strong presidencies were harbingers of how all presidential systems, including the US system, would evolve. The centuries since the US presidency was created have witnessed a general weakening of constitutional and political constraints on the executive and a movement toward greater presidential power. This process was driven by forces that those who wrote the US Constitution did not and could not have fully anticipated. The first was the extraordinary growth in the role of the state in the lives of its citizens, a process that began in Europe in the last decades of the nineteenth century and in the United States some years later. Absolute, authoritarian governments always exercised a great deal of control over the lives of their citizens, but representative governments were supposed to limit the role of government and maintain a larger sphere of individual autonomy. But while republican governments respected and even enlarged the individual liberties of their citizens, they also began to develop public policies that addressed an increasing number of social, economic, cultural, and scientific issues that their nations confronted. As the number of public policies embodied in legislation expanded, and as the policy areas addressed became increasingly specialized, the task of executing the law became larger and more complex. In order to handle this job, the executive component of government under the direction of the president expanded both in size and in its discretionary power. As government grew, in other words, presidents had more policies to implement, more leeway in how they would be implemented, more money to spend, and more people working for them. Inevitably, this meant more power for the president.

The second factor that drove the movement toward increased presidential power was the growing importance of every nation's interactions with other countries. External affairs, a primary concern of every government, have been a traditional responsibility of the executive. At one time, such interactions usually involved only a nation's most immediate neighbors, but in the modern world nations have relationships with countries around the globe, and wars, when they occur, have been fought on a regional and sometimes on a worldwide basis. The number of people permanently under arms, the number, quality, and destructive capacity of the weapons at their disposal, and the speed at which these people and weapons can be put to use are far beyond the realm of what earlier generations could have imagined. All of these people and their equipment are under the control of the executive, who is essentially free to deploy these resources as he wishes.

In addition, issues that at one time might have been purely domestic have acquired an international dimension because of revolutions in transportation and communication and the resulting globalization of the world's economy. Today, trade, budgetary issues, monetary policy, and the general state of country's domestic economy are all issues that are affected by and connected to international institutions, events, and actors. In 2011 and 2012, the debt problems of the Greek government were felt throughout Europe and also on Wall Street and therefore on the balance sheets of Americans' individual retirement funds. Environmental and immigration issues, terrorism, and access to supplies of energy and raw material all present international challenges that have immediate and significant domestic consequences. No country in the world is completely or even nearly self-sufficient and therefore all are affected by what others outside their borders do. To the extent that these erstwhile domestic policy issues became international, the responsibility for dealing with them moved toward the president.

Finally, the world has become democratized, at least in terms of access to the franchise. In virtually all countries that have elections, all citizens, regardless of gender, race, income, or education, are permitted to vote, and nearly all presidents gain office through the voting decisions of this broadened electorate. More than ever, presidents claim that their ascension to office and their right to govern as they please derive from the will of the people. In this sense, democratization can undermine constitutionalism when presidents claim that their democratic legitimacy allows them to supersede the restrictions imposed upon them by their nation's constitution.

The direct ties between the president and the population that the electoral process implies have been further strengthened by the electronic mass media, which constantly and intimately connects presidents as well as presidential candidates to the people. In addition, political parties today play a weaker role in selecting and electing presidential candidates than they did in the past, and they have relatively little ability to constrain presidents once they are in office. This has resulted in the personalization of government and politics, a situation characterized by an intense focus on the president himself—either candidate or incumbent—and an increased emphasis on charisma rather than demonstrated competence, on rhetoric rather than deeds, on image rather than substance, and on passion rather than reason. This concentration on the presidency encourages many citizens to think of the president and the government as being one and the same thing. When new presidents are elected, they assume office in the context of extraordinarily inflated and hopelessly conflicted expectations on the part of the electorate, who assume that the president can and should tackle all of the problems that the nation faces, and do so successfully. Presidential campaigns, largely conducted through the electronic media, contribute to these unrealistic expectations by their focus on the candidate and his style and personality. The candidates emphasize their own commitment and ability to bring about needed change, implicitly marginalize the role of the other political institutions and actors with whom they will need to work, and minimize the intractability and durability of many of the problems before the country.

In challenging or difficult times, in times of danger or crisis, people are especially inclined to turn to the president for leadership, protection, reassurance, and answers, and in return they are often willing to accept broad discretionary presidential power. The political institutions that are supposed to constrain executive power tend to be overwhelmed by such a public mood; at the extreme, executive power can come nearly full circle, back to the original model of unconstrained prerogatives, or hyperpresidentialism—the untamed prince, but this time a prince that governs not just by virtue of the brute force that he controls, but one whose power is legitimized by his democratic claim that he represents the voice and the will of the people.

The movement toward presidentialism, driven by the size of government, globalization, and democratization, and facilitated by technological advances, appears to be inexorable but, despite its perils, not entirely without advantages. There always have been good arguments for strong leadership that is capable of decisive action, especially in difficult times. There are many examples of strong leaders who have been able to accomplish great things for their people and for their nation. It also is the case that the aggrandizement of presidents reflected in the movement toward presidentialism is not solely the product of executive attempts to usurp the powers of other institutions. Legislators, judges, and other elites, as well as average citizens, have been quite willing, even eager, to devolve authority and attention upon the president, and often with good reason: legislatures are singularly unimpressive in their ability to move decisively or to provide political leadership and judges are always conscious of their inability to enforce their decisions without the assistance and support of the executive. Nonetheless, presidentialism entails significant risks for political systems, many of which have been alluded to in earlier chapters. As we address these risks, it will become clear that there are no easy answers, and that in some instances the systemic risks associated with presidentialism may well be offset by important benefits for the nation. It is also possible that the noble goal of "taming the prince" will turn out to be something of a fool's errand.

Authoritarianism

The most obvious risk associated with presidentialism is that highly personalized leadership in which substantial formal power comes to reside in the hands of the president, especially decree and emergency powers, can lead to an authoritarian political system. In such an environment, political decisionmaking becomes more centralized, partisan and parliamentary voices become more marginalized, civil society in the form of interest groups, nongovernmental organizations, and the media becomes intimidated, and dissent, along with other basic civil liberties, is put at risk or restricted. Presidents who believe that they represent the will of the people, that they have widespread popular support, and that the destiny of their nation is in their hands may be less tolerant of those in the mass media or among their political opponents who disagree with them. Inevitably, it is argued, such presidents will seek to control the judiciary and the media, harass their political opponents, deploy the financial and military resources of the state to their political and electoral advantage, and, if they think it necessary, exceed existing constitutional limitations on their power.

As Russia moved from authoritarianism to a more democratic political system, its presidency under Boris Yeltsin was relatively constrained. But after Vladimir Putin became president in 2000 upon Yeltsin's resignation, the regime gradually moved in a more authoritarian direction—not to the extent of the old system, but with increasing incidents of intimidation and harassment of political opponents and the full utilization of state resources to ensure that Putin and his supporters would remain in control. In Venezuela under Hugo Chávez, the process also was gradual as intimidation of dissenting parties and the mass media became more frequent and more heavy-handed, and as increasingly more power flowed to the president. The legislature became less independent and much more responsive to Chávez's wishes, and the judiciary slowly lost whatever independence it might have had (Hawkins 2010:20–25).

Clearly, this process is not always as malevolent as the critics of presidential power assert. There have been examples of presidents who have acquired a great deal of power, but have used it to do some exceedingly good things for their countries and for their people without infringing on civil liberties. As we observed in Chapter 4, presidents such as Evo Morales in Bolivia and Rafael Correa in Ecuador in the view of many have been able to move their countries toward a more equitable and just distribution of national resources while appearing to maintain democratic liberties. However, there are those who are skeptical that presidentialism of this sort can avoid authoritarianism. In his discussion of electoral caudillos in Latin America—strong presidents who come to power via elections rather than force of arms, a category that would include both Morales and Correa—Kalowatie Deonandan concludes that the politics of such leaders tend to be characterized by "centralization, personalization, verticalism, oppression, corruption, patron-client bonds and a willingness to resort to extralegal practices" (2004:45). In the case of Bolivia, one observer reports that the president's continuing battles "with the opposition in Congress and with the judiciary [have] led to widespread accusations that President Morales is attempting both to rein in the opposition and to pack the courts" with justices who will support him and his policies (Gamarra 2008:148). In Ecuador, courts have convicted journalists for libeling President Correa, who has said that such verdicts have "demonstrated that no one has the right to tarnish the truth" (Ayala 2012). Examples such as these suggest to some that these new populist reformers may not differ very much from the strong, militarily backed presidents who were generally credited with rescuing their countries from the economic ravages of hyperinflation, but at the cost of civil liberties and other democratic procedures. But unlike their militarily backed predecessors, these new leaders have a stronger claim to democratic legitimacy; they cite the high level of popular support that they received from the people during elections as well as the policies they are pursuing that appear to benefit the poor and dispossessed majorities of their nations.

A national decision to accept expanded presidential power in order to accomplish needed systemic change, either neoliberal or neopopulist, as rapidly as possible, must consider the possibility that this power will remain with the presidency even after short-term policy goals are achieved and that such presidents, in order to retain their power, will resort to authoritarian methods. And the danger of authoritarianism is not restricted to those "less developed" nations in Latin America and Africa that face extraordinary economic challenges and have less institutionalized political systems.

In 1973, historian Arthur Schlesinger Jr. wrote of "the imperial presidency"; he worried that the increasing concentration of power in the hands of the US president had transformed the energetic but constrained executive that the Framers had created into something akin to an elected emperor. These virtually unlimited powers seemed to Schlesinger to be most apparent and especially dangerous in the area of foreign and defense policy and could potentially be used to expand the president's power in the domestic arena beyond the limited role anticipated in the Constitution. Schlesinger's prophecy seemed to be verified in the wake of the September 11, 2001, attacks. At the time, President George W. Bush said that in the war on terror "one of the most critical battlefields is the home front" (Kleinerman 2009:2). That view provided the White House with justification for a number of intrusions on the civil liberties of Americans as well as for Bush's decisions, reflected in his signing statements, to ignore various congressional actions that he asserted would impede his efforts to fight terrorism. Bush proceeded on the assumption that as president he was utilizing his constitutional authority as commander in chief to protect the nation and therefore that whatever he did in this respect was by definition within his constitutional powers, and that congressional or even judicial attempts to limit his actions were therefore unconstitutional. Vice President Dick Cheney suggested that these domestic manifestations of the president's commander in chief role would likely become a permanent part of American life—what he called "the new normalcy" (Kleinerman 2009:3).

Some of the actions of the Obama administration have provided ample support for Cheney's viewpoint. As president, Obama expanded the use of unmanned drones to kill suspected terrorists and indicated that he personally approved each name on the "kill list." Often, such attacks took the lives of innocent civilians as well as the targeted person. In September 2011 in Yemen, a drone targeted and killed Anwar al-Awlaki, a citizen of the United States who had become a leading figure in the al-Qaeda affiliate in Yemen. Another American traveling with him also died in the attack. In response to public concern that the president had ordered the killing of an American citizen without any semblance of due process of law, the White House indicated that the Justice Department had produced a memorandum providing legal justification for such a presidential action. However, the memorandum has never been released to the public. When the *New York Times* went to court to seek the release of the memorandum, the judge ruled against the newspaper, citing precedents that "effectively allow the executive branch of our government to proclaim as perfectly lawful certain actions that seem on their face incompatible with our Constitution and laws while keeping the reasons for their conclusion a secret" (Carr 2013). In February 2013, the White House agreed to share the memorandum with members of the congressional intelligence committees but not with the broader public.

Similarly, the theory of the unitary presidency, argued most aggressively by President Bush, but also endorsed in whole or in part by several of his predecessors and his successor, views the president as being in complete control of the entire bureaucracy. Critics of this position argue, among other things, that it undermines Congress's role in assigning specific responsibilities to government agencies. For example, an act of Congress delegating final decisions about eligibility for certain federal benefits to administrative-law judges could be construed as infringing upon the president's ability to control the unitary executive. Also in question would be the status of independent regulatory agencies housed in the executive branch. Could a president, for example, remove the head of the Federal Reserve board or the chair of the Federal Trade Commission if he disagreed with their decisions? The Supreme Court has said no to that question, but as we will recall, President Bush's version of the unitary theory argument seemed to restrict the courts from second-guessing the president's interpretation of his executive power (see Krent 2008).

Arguments for the unitary presidency aside, the threat of presidential unilateralism is further enhanced by the worldwide rise of the bureaucratic state under the formal control of presidents, and the exponential increase in the volume and reach of government rules and regulations that emanate from the executive. Because neither legislatures nor courts have the expertise, time, or inclination to review each of the countless decisions made under the countless statutes from which these rules derive, there is a legitimate concern that excessive power is now in the hands of the bureaucracy and by extension the president. In the United States, the predominantly procedural approach that the judiciary has taken to the task of reviewing the application of federal statutes and regulations suggests that the courts will intervene only when formal administrative procedures have been violated or if the decisions in question can be viewed as contrary to the Constitution. If neither of these conditions apply, the general rule has been to defer to the substantive content of agency decisions. The comparative strength of the US judiciary compared with its counterparts elsewhere in the world suggests that judicial checks on executive power are unlikely to be more effective elsewhere (see de Groot–van Leeuwen and Rombouts 2010). We also have observed the hit-and-miss approach that all legislative bodies tend to take toward oversight of the bureaucracy, an approach dictated by the competing policy and political demands on the time and expertise of representatives. So without effective control from either the legislative or the judicial branch, the result, many fear, is too much unchecked power in the hands of the president and his administration.

Presidentialism and Democracy

Whether or not such presidential unilateralism is undemocratic depends on how one views the concept of democracy. Some have distinguished between liberal and illiberal democracies, the latter characterized simply by "procedures for electing leaders that involve the participation of the people," but with the former also offering "protection of individual and minority rights" and ensuring "that rulers are not above the law" (Gellar 2005:175–176). In a similar vein, Guillermo O'Donnell discusses liberalism and republicanism, two concepts with which democracy is often erroneously conflated. He argues that liberalism and republicanism share a commitment to what he calls "horizontal accountability," which means "state agencies that are authorized and willing to oversee, control, redress, and if need be sanction unlawful actions by other state agencies," most notably the executive (1998:118). Democracy, on the other hand, focuses almost exclusively on procedural issues such as the holding of free and fair elections, the maintenance of only those civil liberties that are necessary if elections of that sort are to take place, and empowering those who emerge victorious in such contests to make government decisions. Presidentialism reflects a movement away from republicanism and toward this procedural view of democracy; simply because a president is popularly elected, the argument is that he should have the right to rule.

Some note that this procedural definition of democracy is too narrow, a version of what political theorist Benjamin Barber (1984) refers to as "thin democracy." This is a view of democracy that concentrates exclusively on electoral procedures and assumes a passive, ill-informed, and inarticulate citizenry. Barber contrasts this perspective with what he calls "strong democracy," which rests on the vigorous participation of citizens in civic affairs. Thin democracy as it applies to the presidency is, in the view of one scholar, contrary to more robust democratic principles. He concludes that it is "downright embarrassing . . . to ask free and equal citizens to place so much trust in the personal integrity and ideals of a single human being." It is preferable, in his view, to see citizens "debating which of the existing political parties best expresses their collective ideals, working to revise these ideals to change with the times, and forming sensible coalitions when no single party gains the support of the majority" (Ackerman 2000:663).

O'Donnell believes that a "minimalist" definition of democracy (or, if you will, Barber's thin democracy) can give rise to a "monistic bent" that concentrates too much power in the hands of elected presidents (1998:119). When one defines a democratic system in such a narrow way, it "enables old authoritarian practices to reassert themselves" (1996:45). One student of Latin American politics concludes that the plebiscitarian approach of appealing directly to the people, an approach favored by the new generation of democratically elected presidents, actually "chips away at democratic institutions, and sometimes paves the way to authoritarian or semi-authoritarian regimes, as occurred with Peruvian president Alberto Fujimori in the 1990s and Venezuelan president Hugo Chavez after 1998" (Mainwaring 2006:18).

Similarly, in Africa, one observer has cited the rise of "elective dictatorships"—political systems in which "unchecked executive power prevails over parliamentary sovereignty and judicial independence" and in which civil liberties are at serious risk (Woldemariam 2009:5). These so-called facade democracies, some argue, were created largely in response to the fall of the Soviet Union and the withdrawal of Russian support from many states in Africa. These events forced African countries into a much greater reliance on Western donor nations and on organizations such as the World Bank and the International Monetary Fund, all of which demanded democratic political reforms along with a greater commitment to fight corruption as a precondition for aid. Thus, by 1997 there were only four countries in sub-Saharan Africa that had not held competitive elections during the 1990s. However, incumbents or their chosen successors seldom lose such elections, and the winners have often moved to restrict civil liberties (Gellar 2005:174).

In other words, a tendency toward presidential unilateralism can be nurtured in states whose commitment to democracy extends only to electoral procedures. Such a perspective highlights the potential tension between democracy and constitutionalism (or what O'Donnell referred to as republicanism), a tension that those who wrote the US Constitution clearly recognized when they took pains to distinguish between democratic government, which they opposed, and the republican form that they had created. The great task of these constitution writers and those in other countries who followed them was to develop mechanisms for restraining the actions of governments in general and executives in particular. But a view that equates democracy with popular election of the president can embolden presidents to take actions that move beyond these constitutional restraints, steps that they will justify as reflecting the will of the people.

The movement of governing power toward the president also has been abetted by the more marginal role that political parties play in the process by which modern democracies elect their presidents. As the electoral role of the parties has diminished, the role of individual candidates and their own personalities and resources has increased. Two scholars of the US presidency suggest that the current nomination and election process has produced presidents who are more willing to extend the powers of their office. As the business of becoming president has become more demanding, candidates must have "fire in the belly" before they commit to the rigors of such a campaign. Rather than a party workhorse, therefore, the process produces a "candidate driven by ambition of world-historical dimensions," a candidate who seeks election "not just to hold the office, but to make history." Once in office, such presidents become "impatient with its bounds and limits, and their efforts to overcome them provide much of the animating force that drove the expansion of presidential power" (Crenson and Ginsberg 2007:353).

Defenders of presidentialism make the case that from the perspective of accountability, concentrating power in the hands of the president is more desirable than the republican option of constrained presidential power. It is commonplace for democratic theorists to argue that citizens cannot exercise control over their political leaders if they do not know who is responsible for the policies under which they live. In a system of shared power between an independent president and an equally independent legislature, it may be difficult for citizens to affix responsibility accurately, as political leaders attempt to shift the blame for what has gone wrong to others and as they contest with each other for the credit for successes. On the other hand, presidential power, with all of its dangers, at least leaves citizens with no doubt about whom to hold responsible. And given the fact that citizens tend to hold presidents responsible for the state of the nation, no matter what the constitutional power-sharing arrangement in the country might be, some degree of unilateralism can be seen as conforming to the expectations of citizens in the sense that it will at least allow presidents to actually exercise the sort of control that citizens believe that such leaders have. In this connection, there is some evidence from one study of Nicaragua that suggests that strong, popularly elected presidents have been constrained and held accountable by civil society and popular mobilization efforts, and that these constraints have been at least as effective if not more than those that legislators have attempted to apply (Anderson 2006). To the extent that enhanced presidential power leads to enhanced public accountability, it can be argued that popular sovereignty and the principles of democratic government are advanced (see Samuels and Shugart 2003:55).

In any event, few would make the argument that because US presidents now exercise more power than the original constitutional design anticipated, the United States should no longer be classified as democratic. Similarly, despite the fact that presidents in countries such as Bolivia, Ecuador, and Senegal have consistently rejected any attempts by the legislature to invoke their ostensible constitutional powers to check their actions (see Beck 2008:223), all are still classified as democratic political systems by Freedom House.

Although it is relatively easy to make the case for the authoritarian dangers of presidentialism, it is important to note that in many countries presidents are effectively limited, at least in domestic policy matters, by other political institutions. The theory of the unitary presidency notwithstanding, it likely would be difficult to convince Barack Obama that the most important institutional challenge facing Americans is the danger of presidential authoritarianism. With much of his domestic legislative agenda stalemated by the unified resistance of Republican senators and, after the 2010 election, by the Republican House majority, it is easier to make the case that when US presidents seek to make significant changes in existing policies, the problem is a lack of presidential power rather than too much power (see Calabresi and Lindgren 2006). And even in countries where presidents do have decree power, like Brazil, they must engage in significant compromises of their electoral platform in order to generate a congressional majority. More generally, John Carey has noted that during the 1990s, presidents in Brazil, Venezuela, Guatemala,

Ecuador, and Paraguay were removed from office during their terms not by military coup but by "extraordinary legislative action—impeachment or quasi-impeachment"—events that, in his view, may mark "a regional resurgence of checks and balances over *presidencialismo*" (Carey 2003:12; see also Hochstetler 2006). Aníbal Pérez-Liñán (2007:3) suggests that impeachment has become the functional equivalent of a no-confidence vote—a tool for a belligerent legislature to deal with a president with whom it is at loggerheads.

Corruption

Writing in the late nineteenth century, Lord Acton enunciated his oft-quoted dictum that power tends to corrupt and absolute power corrupts absolutely. As a nation moves toward hyperpresidentialism, it often comes to be identified with corruption and cronyism, in part because the institutions that typically provide a check on corruption, such as the legislature, the judiciary, and the mass media, are marginalized, intimidated, or co-opted. Especially in systems with weak political parties, one way that presidents can consolidate their power is by distributing the legal as well as the illicit benefits of office to their close circle of friends and supporters and taking a portion for themselves and their families. One comparative study of corruption finds that parliamentary systems, in part because they are characterized by strong political parties, experience lower levels of corruption than do presidential systems. (Gerring and Thacker 2004:315). It also has been suggested that presidential systems in younger, less institutionalized democracies are more vulnerable to corruption than are more established presidential systems (Persson and Tabellini 2003:193).

The problem of corruption may be further compounded in political cultures characterized by clientelism (Gerring and Thacker 2004:320). In Africa, the so-called presidential kleptocracies are examples of this worst-case scenario. Polls conducted in African countries regularly indicate a public perception of widespread corruption across the continent. In countless cases, African presidents and their friends and families have risen from modest circumstances to become people of great wealth, living lifestyles that stand in stark contrast to the poverty that characterizes the lives of most of their citizens. Although it can be argued that corruption can be important to nationbuilding if the money stays within the country, in the cases of these presidents, more often than not a great deal of their ill-gotten gains ends up in European banks and real estate. Frederick Chiluba, who served as president of Zambia from 1991 to 2002, was estimated to have looted $57 million from his nation's treasury (Howden 2009) and former president Mobutu Sese Seko of Zaire was estimated to have embezzled $5 billion over his three-decade presidency. Early in 2009, Transparency International's office in France filed anticorruption suits against President Omar Bongo of Gabon and President Denis Sassou Nguesso of the Congo, accusing the former of having seventeen properties and eleven bank accounts in his name in France and the latter, fifteen villas and apartments in his and his family's name.[1] Meanwhile, these presidents run their own countries with an iron hand, utilizing their control of the military and the police to intimidate opponents, and their control of the nation's budget to maintain the support of their friends and punish their enemies. One scholar's succinct summation of these systems is that they are "a vast unproductive network of corruption lorded over by presidential monarchs who dispense favors, resources, and money to gain loyalty, obedience, and submission" (Fatton 1990:461).

Latin American presidencies also have been marred by this same combination of concentrated power and corruption, with President Arnoldo Alemán of Nicaragua and President Alberto Fujimori of Peru, among many others, having been accused of various schemes designed for personal enrichment. Although some corruption is apparent in virtually every nation, in Latin America and particularly in Africa it seems to be chronic, involving not just the president but lower levels of government as well. One Afrobarometer public opinion study of twelve African nations found that majorities of citizens perceive corruption among all public office holders and officials, with slightly larger majorities perceiving corruption among unelected officials such as police officers and tax officials compared to elected leaders (Armah-Attoh, Gyimah-Boadi, and Chikwana 2007). An earlier study, also based on Afrobarometer data, found that 52 percent of the respondents thought that corruption among public officials was common, while only 35 percent thought of it as rare.[2]

And contrary to the idea that authoritarianism alone breeds corruption, there is some evidence from studies of Latin America that corruption has increased as political systems have become more open and less authoritarian. As power becomes dispersed, the argument goes, more decisionmakers have the opportunity to use their positions to convert their responsibilities into profits. Also, the move to the more open, market-oriented economy that typically has accompanied democratic reforms increases the likelihood of corrupt arrangements between business enterprises and government officials (Weyland 1998). Certainly, there is little doubt that as Russia moved toward a more economically open and more politically democratic system, corruption increased. Transparency International concluded that corruption in Russia is now endemic. In one of its surveys, public officials and civil servants were perceived as the country's most corrupt segment of the elite, with 31 percent of respondents reporting that they had paid a bribe in the previous twelve months. Russia's score on Transparency International's Corruption Perception Index puts it on a par with Zimbabwe and Sierra Leone.[3] According to one analyst, President Vladimir Putin's governing party is literally held together by corruption, with government bureaucrats who benefit from corruption forming the base of the party. It may be that Putin's intimidation of the media is designed less to discourage political opposition and more to quash embarrassing stories about corruption (Orttung 2006).

As indicated in Chapter 1, certain of these presidencies, particularly the African examples, are in principle beyond the scope of this discussion of presidentialism, because it would be difficult to think of the presidents in the countries as elected leaders. In the past, many of these presidents have been confirmed in plebiscites, sometimes with the only option on the ballot being a yes vote; it was not unusual for the single candidate to receive 99 percent or more of the vote (see Jackson and Rosberg 1982: 270). In the current wave of democracy in Africa, most elections are now contested, but tremendous advantages, many based on access to state resources and state-controlled media, accrue to the president's party.

Ironically, popular election of the president, just like economic liberalism, may exacerbate the issue of corruption. Democracy can be more expensive than the authoritarian alternative. Winning a competitive election in a nation with universal voting rights will cost a great deal of money, regardless of the country in question, and it is therefore reasonable to expect that more intimate ties will develop between politicians and those who have the resources to finance their election (see Weyland 1998; Pérez-Liñán 2007:chap. 4). In Russia, the resources of the governing party, largely the product of corruption, have been instrumental in helping Putin and his allies win election. And certainly in the United States, the accelerating cost of presidential elections has created an ever stronger bond between successful candidates and those who provide the money that they require to win.

Demagoguery

Although the original Greek term "demagogue" meant simply "leader of the people," its meaning has changed over the centuries. At one time, a demagogue could best be defined as champion of the power of the people (as opposed to the power of elites or aristocrats). But as the authors of the US Constitution used the term, it had a more negative connotation, suggesting a leader who succeeded by appealing to the passions or emotions of the voters rather than to their reason (Tulis 1987:28). One reason why the Founders were skeptical about democracy was their concern that such political leaders would gain power because they were able to manipulate public opinion and the electoral decisions of voters and not because of their principles or their capacity to govern in the national interest. Once in office, such leaders would tend to equate good public policy with popular public policy.

Were the Founders in Ecuador or Bolivia today, they might well characterize the presidents of these countries as demagogues, given the nature of their popular appeal based on class or ethnicity. And they would see as well aspects of demagoguery in the United States, as some candidates for the presidency as well as other offices make class-based appeals to voters, or appeal to the resentments that some citizens have against economic forces that they can't control, or rail against racial, religious, and ethnic minorities that, they argue, are changing the nation for the worse and are primarily responsible for the ills that the country faces.

Presidents and presidential candidates are well situated and strongly tempted to play the role of demagogue. After all, they must compete in a winner-take-all electoral system in which the person with the most votes wins all of the executive power and few seem to care about the means used to harvest these votes. In addition, candidates are seeking the votes of a citizenry that for the most part is uninformed about and not particularly interested in the details of public policy. In such an environment, rhetoric and symbols are generally more important than policy substance. Campaign advertisements in particular, whether on television or the Internet, reduce difficult and complicated issues to thirty-second sound bites, and those who are paid to compose these sound bites do so with an ear toward finding the most direct route to the emotions and passions of the voter.

Presidents typically tone down this campaign mode once in office, but they do not abandon it entirely. They may not run television advertisements in support of their policy initiatives (although their supporters frequently do, with implicit support from the White House), but they do engage in speech-making on behalf of their proposals, and this oratory can deteriorate in the direction of demagoguery as the president seeks to find a way to rouse public indignation and direct it against his political opponents. As President Barack Obama made his final public push for his healthcare proposal with a series of speeches around the country, he took on the health insurance industry at every stop, claiming that Congress was facing a choice between doing what was good for the people and doing what was good for the insurance industry. This is not to say that the industry didn't deserve to be criticized. Rather, the point is that questions about, and opposition to, the healthcare plan were motivated by a number of concerns, many having little to do with the profits of the insurance industry; however, attacking these companies—which are among the least-admired organizations in the United States—proved to be a potent way to appeal to the emotions and rouse the enthusiasm of those to whom the president was speaking. And in fairness, the president's defenders could say that he was fighting fire with fire, combating the hyperbolic claims of his opponents about death panels and government-run healthcare. Similarly, as President George W. Bush encountered increasing criticism of the war effort in Iraq and the steps that he had taken to protect the nation against terrorism, his speeches, and more often the speeches of his vice president, began to depict his opponents as less than patriotic and as implicit (and sometimes explicit) supporters of terrorism.

In the permanent campaign, says one of its most severe critics, the performance of the president and his surrogates becomes less significant than what is said. The effort is not designed to educate the electorate or to solicit their views on public policy; rather, it "engages people to tell them what they want to hear in ways that will promote one's cause against others" (Heclo 2000:31–32). Political discussion becomes a matter of spin—framing issues so that public approval can be generated, exaggerating problems, demonizing opponents, and avoiding substantive policy questions. As suggested in Chapter 6, all of this moves a nation toward a form of plebiscitary democracy that holds that the most important value is the congruence of public opinion and public policy (Abramson, Arterton, and Orren 1988:19–22). In this respect, it is a realization of the worst nightmare of the US Founders, who worried so much about an unhealthy relationship between the president and the people—presidents overly dependent upon public opinion in order to advance their policies and employing the "vicious arts" to influence those opinions. And, of course, they worried in an era before the invention of television, talk radio, the Internet, and the other forms of instant and omnipresent mass communication that have created the twenty-four-hour news cycle.

On the other hand, it may be difficult to criticize demagoguery without implicitly criticizing the concept of popular sovereignty upon which democracy rests. One person's demagogue, after all, may be another person's tribune of the poor and downtrodden. If the people are to rule, we may need to accept the people as they are. It would be nice to have a citizenry who are willing to devote the time necessary to understand and debate complex policy issues, willing to display the civic virtue that would enable them to opt for the public interest rather than their own self-interest, and willing to privilege their reason over their passions. But there is little evidence that we have or can have such an idealized citizenry. If that is the case, as long as one is committed to the democratic principle of popular election, some degree of demagoguery among candidates for the presidency as well as incumbents may be inevitable.

Presidential Personality

Presidential power, as we have noted, is personal power, in the sense that when it comes to actions of the executive branch of the government, it is the president alone who is able to decide. He need not take votes or get anyone else's consent to tell a federal agency to develop new rules, to order troops to a dangerous location, or to establish his nation's foreign policy. And as we have seen, in the area of defense policy, presidents either claim or have been explicitly granted unilateral power not only to act, but also to act beyond constitutional limits if they believe it to be necessary.

So much discretionary power in one set of hands leads inevitably to an entire range of questions about a president: What type of person is he, how intelligent is he, how does he view the world, how does he arrive at decisions, is it his style to act impulsively or deliberately, is he secure enough to hear and give fair consideration to different or dissenting points of view, or does he respond defensively to those who question him and his decisions? As James David Barber's (1985) classic work demonstrated, presidential personalities do vary on these and other dimensions, and the sources of these variations are buried deep within the personal histories, psyches, and developmental experiences of each individual. Needless to say, these variations can have a significant impact on how a president conducts himself in office, on what he says, and on what he does.

The problem is that neither average citizens nor members of the elite know very much about a candidate's personality before he comes to office. Although new presidents may be well-known public figures in the sense that people can identify them and know a few things about them, what citizens know may have little to do with a candidate's real personality traits. Presidents may appear affable and secure to the casual voter, but just below the surface they may be a bubbling cauldron of insecurities and resentments. Also, it is unlikely that presidents have been in the position of exercising so much power, and therefore citizens do not know how a president's personality will affect the manner in which he deals with the extraordinary responsibilities and discretionary authority that he inherits upon assuming office.

With the deteriorating role of political parties as gatekeepers in the process of presidential selection and the rise in their stead of the electronic media, the door to the presidency is now open to many who have not had extensive previous political experience, who may be largely unknown to governmental or party elites, and about whom it may be difficult to make judgments as to what kind of person they are. In such a context, the lack of knowledge about candidates and their personalities can become more consequential. Had more been known about the insecurities of Bill Clinton's childhood, could the self-destructive personal behavior that nearly sunk his presidency have been predicted? To what extent did George W. Bush's complicated relationship with his father lead to his precipitous decisions concerning Iraq? How did Barack Obama's experience as a child of a biracial marriage and an absent father affect his approach to the presidency and the nature of the decisions that he made in office? In each of these cases, Americans elected people who had minimal to no political experience at the national level and who were in essence ciphers to average citizens and to others in the political or media elite. Although candidates do become somewhat better known once their campaigns begin, because the best campaigns are well orchestrated and carefully scripted, it is not easy, and perhaps impossible, for voters to get a genuine sense of what a candidate is like. Obviously, these challenges are not peculiar to the United States. The personalities of presidents as diverse as Yeltsin, Putin, Mugabe, Sarkozy, Chávez, and Mbeki have at various times been identified as explanations for the direction in which their respective countries have moved. The point is that presidential systems by definition mean that the personality of a single leader will have an outsized impact on crucial public policy decisions.

The challenge is not to do away with variations in presidential personality or—although it would be interesting—to develop more effective ways to find out about their personalities before they come to office. The Americans who invented the presidency realized that there was no way to know what kind of people would succeed to the office in the future. Their remedy was to restrict the number of people involved in the selection of the president and to check the power of the president so that the damage to the body politic resulting from whatever demons or deficiencies the holder of the office might be wrestling with could be minimized. But eligibility to vote in presidential elections is now unrestricted, and as political systems move toward greater degrees of presidentialism, the potency of the institutional checks on the presidency have diminished as presidential power has increased. In addition, the role that political parties once played in vetting presidential candidates has atrophied with the rise of "outsiders." The result is an unnerving amount of power in the hands of one inevitably flawed, inevitably human individual.

The greatest risk associated with so much power in the hands of a president comes with decisions about going to war. It is in this arena that presidents have virtually unilateral power, because of their position as head of their nation's military establishment. As James Madison (1793) observed, war evokes "the strongest passions and most dangerous weaknesses of the human breast; ambition, avarice, vanity, the honorable or venial love of fame." Although he did not use the term, he was writing here about "human nature," or personality, and he concluded that "the trust and the temptation would be too great for any one man." Certainly, a president who is pursuing an unwise economic or budgetary strategy can do serious damage to the welfare of his country and his people, but the damage would be relatively minor compared to what could be wrought by an unnecessary or unwise war undertaken for the wrong reasons and at the wrong time. In the period from 1960 onward, the US economy has had good years as well as poor years, but the latter have left no permanent scars on the body politic. On the other hand, the war in Vietnam committed tens of thousands of Americans to death or permanent mental or physical disability, cost many times more Vietnamese than American lives, split the United States into warring camps, and lingered as a malevolent shadow over US foreign policy and the American psyche well into the next century. Each of the four US presidents who made the key decisions in regard to Vietnam made errors, and there is nothing to say that someone else in their position would not have done as they did. The point is that it was *their* decisions that took the country step by step into the Vietnam quagmire. Similarly, George W. Bush's single-minded focus on Iraq and its leader, Saddam Hussein, seemed to propel the country toward a war that did not have to be fought and in the end did great damage to the United States as well as to Iraq without in any way stemming the tide of terrorism—one of its ostensible purposes.

Personal vs. Institutional Power

The problem of who decides whether or not a country goes to war is indicative of a larger concern about presidentialism. It has been a given among political scientists that while leadership is important, the strength of a political system depends not only on the qualities of an individual leader but also (and possibly more so) on the durability and qualities of its political institutions. From this perspective, a political system is weaker and less stable to the extent that its success or failure turns upon the actions or inactions of a single individual. Because presidential power tends to be personal power, it is almost by definition in tension with the concept of institutionalization. Presidents have a tendency to depict themselves as patriots rather than partisans, to declare themselves to be above petty partisan conflict, and to say that they represent the nation as a whole and that they draw their strength and inspiration directly from the people.

When Charles de Gaulle came to power in France, he declared that political parties were damaging to the nation and that he hoped for a constitution that would do away with them. Barack Obama, in his first campaign, decried partisanship and envisioned a new postpartisan era. In the case of African presidents, it has been said that "charisma acts as a substitute for institutionalization" and that presidents in countries as diverse as Ghana, Kenya, Malawi, and Côte d'Ivoire have fortified their personal administrative apparatus and downgraded the significance of the political parties (Chazan et al. 1992:163, 173). A similar process has taken place in Latin America, as populist presidents have adopted plebiscitarian approaches that have had the effect of sidelining political parties (Mainwaring 2006). As systems move toward presidentialism, political parties are relegated to the status of election vehicles for presidential candidates, institutions such as legislatures and courts can be marginalized, and the power and prominence of the bureaucracy under the supervision of the president grows. For political systems that do not have a history of strong institutions, presidentialism ensures that these institutions will remain weak. In more established political systems, personalized presidential power has a long-term debilitating effect on the strength of their institutions and, it is argued, on the quality of the public policies that emerge from those institutions.

Guillermo O'Donnell (1994) has written that although allowing the president to act decisively, even unilaterally—what he refers to as "delegative democracy"—may provide short-term solutions to particular problems, when presidential regimes change, such presidentially determined solutions also may be changed by the next administration. Decisions that are only the president's become personal decisions; collective decisions involving negotiations between the legislature and the president become institutional decisions that are more durable and less likely to be overturned when there is a changeover in political office holders. The difference is between decisive policy, which favors presidential unilateralism and few veto groups, and resolute or durable policy, which is ensured by the involvement of multiple veto players (Haggard, McCubbins, and Shugart 2001:320–321). This trade-off between decisiveness and resoluteness highlights and implicitly questions one of the primary arguments for presidentialism—that presidents can act with dispatch and that the necessity for prolonged debate and negotiation with others, as is required when the legislature or one's co-partisans are intimately involved, will mean that policymaking will proceed more slowly and produce heavily compromised and therefore inferior and unworkable policies.

The critique of presidential domination is based on the premise that a broadly consultative policymaking process produces better policies than those that are the product of narrower consultation, and certainly produces better policies than those that result from the will of one person. All individuals, as we have observed, are fallible; no single political leader can embody all the various perspectives on public policy that may be present in a nation; and no single political leader can be relied upon to always know what his or her nation needs. From this perspective, when important decisions need to be made, the more voices that are heard, the more people who are at the table, and the more views that are taken into account, the better the policy is likely to be.

There is evidence for and against this point of view. Sebastian Saiegh (2011) argues in his cross-national analysis that polities are more stable when the legislature is involved in the policymaking process, compared with systems characterized by unilateral presidential actions. At the outset of the twenty-first century, Brazil and Chile elected reformist presidents who, working within their political systems' constitutional constraints, produced policies through negotiations with their own and opposition parties in their congresses. In the case of Chile, President Michelle Bachelet had to operate within a constitutional context that limited the role of the state in the economy and maintained some representation of the military in Congress. Nonetheless, she appeared to be highly successful and concluded her term in office with a public approval rating above 70 percent. Her popularity seemed to be due to her handling of the economy, which allowed the country to come through the world financial crisis of the early twenty-first century relatively unscathed (Barrionuevo 2009). Similarly, in Brazil, President Luiz Inácio Lula da Silva also enjoyed relatively high levels of popularity due to his handling of the economy and also to his success in delivering government benefits to more marginalized segments of the society. Both Lula and Bachelet had significant legislative powers under their respective constitutions, but each operated through a coalition of parties in their cabinets that reflected the divisions within Congress. Each disappointed their most ardent and ideological supporters as the gap between what they had promised in their election campaigns and what they were able to accomplish grew. Nonetheless, the politics of each nation was characterized by relatively high levels of stability and a solid commitment to civil liberties.

On the other hand, Rafael Correa in Ecuador and Evo Morales in Bolivia have made significant progress on their agendas for systemic and social change of a dramatic nature, and have done so largely over the opposition of their legislatures, consulting for the most part with a small circle of advisers and technocrats and drawing in a highly personalized manner upon their support from the people of their countries. Such an approach may not be inconsistent with the needs of the country or the wishes of its citizens. Writing about the period leading up to the installation of these presidents, one scholar points out that poor state performance in terms of economic progress, government corruption, and dealing with security concerns has led many citizens to state in survey responses "that they would welcome abolishing legislatures and would accept a 'strong' leader if state capacity improved" (Mainwaring 2006:23). On the other hand, O'Donnell's hypothesis along with Saiegh's data suggest that these reforms will prove to be more fragile and vulnerable to retraction given their association with the singular character of the president than would perhaps more modest reforms negotiated with other political actors. It is, of course, too early to make that judgment.

The uncomfortable choice seems to be between compromised albeit more durable and consensual policies rife with concessions to the particularized demands of various political actors, and more robust albeit more fragile policies developed by the executive with only minimal legislative involvement. One way out, it has been suggested, is through electoral reforms that will ensure that a president and the legislators with whom he serves are on the same page in terms of policy. This can allow for negotiations that will avoid particularistic and counterproductive payoffs and produce stronger public policy decisions. In France, the constitutional revision that placed parliamentary elections the year after presidential elections seems to have reduced the likelihood of divided party control and increased the likelihood of presidential control of the cabinet and a parliamentary majority (see Jones 2010). Haggard, McCubbins, and Shugart (2001:323) suggest that electoral reforms that combine single-member district systems with a national proportional representation list—the system that has been used in Germany and New Zealand—could serve to moderate the particularized nature of legislative policymaking that is associated with single-member district systems as well as the fragmentation that results from proportional representation systems, particularly those with high district magnitudes and relatively low thresholds. John Carey and Simon Hix (2009) find that a proportional representation system that provides for no more than five representatives per district produces fair legislative outcomes while at the same time limiting party fragmentation and producing simpler government coalitions.

Presidentialism and Instability

In a large and well-discussed literature that emerged in the early 1990s, many argued that the presidential systems so prevalent in Latin America and Africa put the political stability of these countries at risk, and that parliamentary systems of government were inherently more stable (Linz 1990, 1994; Shugart and Mainwaring 1997). Several reasons were offered in support of this point of view. First, the president and the legislature had competing claims to democratic legitimacy—for the president a national electorate and for representatives their local constituencies—and therefore tensions between them could not be resolved by appealing to democratic principles. Second, these systems suffered from "temporal rigidity"; that is, the members of Congress as well as the president served fixed terms in office and therefore changes in the state of the nation, or a loss of confidence in the president, could not result in new elections, as would a loss of confidence in a prime minister and his cabinet in parliamentary systems. Third, presidents were elected through a winner-take-all process that made it difficult to arrive at the sort of power-sharing arrangements that characterized parliamentary systems, especially those that operated as coalitions, with cabinet positions distributed among the various political parties participating in the government. Fourth, there was a tension between the president's dual roles, as head of state and head of government, with the former fostering a tendency toward presidential intolerance of opposition viewpoints and activities. Fifth, presidential systems confronted a tension between the constitutional requirement of an independent president and the suspicion inherent in all democracies of a concentration of power in the hands of one individual. Finally, presidential systems were prone to stalemate. These systems of separate institutions sharing power have multiple veto players; that is, many political leaders have the ability to stop the system from acting by saying no. An inability to act on pressing economic or social issues could contribute to instability.

Each of these factors has been acknowledged in this book and clearly each has the capacity to lead to instability. But the notion of inherent instability in presidential systems has been challenged by other scholars. Although there are data that seem to associate presidential regimes with instability, José Antonio Cheibub makes the argument that this is a spurious correlation; he finds that presidential systems seem to arise in countries that for reasons quite apart from their presidential structure have been prone to democratic breakdown. As he puts it, "some democracies emerge in countries where the probability of democratic breakdown is high, regardless of the type of democracy that exists, and presidential democracies have emerged more frequently in such countries" (Cheibub 2007:136; see also Persson and Tabellini 2003:193). Parliamentary systems in contrast have emerged in those countries where the probability of democratic breakdown is relatively low. And in an earlier paper, Cheibub and his colleagues make the point that coalition formation indeed does take place in presidential systems, perhaps not as frequently as in parliamentary systems, but not as infrequently as the critics of presidential systems suggest (Cheibub, Przeworski, and Saiegh 2004). A second critique is offered by Aníbal Pérez-Liñán (2007), who argues that at least in Latin America, the problem of temporal rigidity has been overcome by the rising frequency of legislatively led presidential impeachments. While this may create short-term governmental instability, the democratic regime survives.

A third qualification is offered by Matthew Shugart and John Carey, who conclude that the apparent instability of presidential systems depends upon how much power is in the hands of the president. They find that systems in which presidents possess very strong legislative powers tend to be less stable than systems in which presidential and legislative power are more evenly matched. In their view, the legislature "represents the diversity of a polity far better than an executive dependent on the president's whims is likely to do" (1992:165). This means that legislatures are more likely to recognize divergent views and find compromises among them. They conclude that the problem of dual democratic legitimacy shared by a president and the assembly needs to be resolved in favor of a strong assembly, with the principle being "that the assembly prevails, subject to a need for compromise with the president" (Shugart and Carey 1992:165). Thus, relatively weaker presidencies such as those in Costa Rica and the United States survive, while relatively strong presidencies, such as the Chilean presidency prior to the 1973 coup, and the Brazilian presidencies during that same period, were more fragile.

On the other hand, an argument can be made that a weak presidency with an inability to deal effectively with the challenges that the nation is facing may contribute to instability. Writing about the period in Bolivia in the years prior to Morales's election, one observer notes that the street demonstrations that occurred there and contributed to driving President Gonzalo Sánchez de Lozada out of office were sparked by the inability of the government to deliver programs that provided "tangible benefits to the majority of the people"; this observer also notes of Bolivia "that political parties of all stripes had become self-serving cliques incapable of solving national problems; that only direct action in defiance of public authority could deliver any worthwhile changes in government policy; that all institutional procedures were devices to delay and frustrate public demands" (Whitehead 2001:13). Scott Mainwaring (2006) and Kathryn Hochstetler (2006) come to similar conclusions in their discussions of political instability in Latin America.

It is also possible that the case for instability of presidential systems may have less to do with presidential power and more to do with the personalization of presidential regimes. The potential for instability in presidential regimes, it can be argued, derives from the personalized leadership that such systems seem to spawn, and from the gap between inflated popular expectations and the capacity of presidents to deliver on those expectations. Writing about Latin America, Arturo Valenzuela suggests that the "personalization of authority in the figure of the president" means that "failures of government are viewed not as failures of a party or movement, but as failures of the chief executive himself. The heavy symbolic trappings carried by the head of state, combined with often overblown folk memories concerning powerful and nondemocratic past presidents, lead citizens to expect that a leader must fix the country's problems or face bitter charges of incompetence and corruption" (2004:12). Simply put, presidentialism focuses the attention and the conflicted and inflated expectations of the public exclusively on the president. More often than not, it is difficult for him to meet these expectations, because the problems may not be amenable to a governmental solution, because he is thwarted by the constraints of the nation's constitutional and political arrangements, or because external events have intervened.

The Parliamentary Alternative

This perspective returns us to the original debate on the comparative virtues of parliamentary and presidential systems. Although there are signs of increasing personalism in parliamentary systems, nonetheless the responsibility for governing is clearly a shared enterprise among those leaders who compose the government. The prime minister, or pre-mier, is certainly head of government, is its most visible member, and exercises a great deal of power; however, ultimate responsibility for deci-sions and events is more collective in nature, focusing on the cabinet and the party or parties that compose its membership. This is because in par-liamentary systems, leaders of the executive are selected by their politi-cal parties and can be constrained or removed by those parties should they prove insufficient to the task of governing, or should they for any other reason lose the confidence of their co-partisans in the legislature. As we have observed, in presidential systems, political parties often have little to do with the selection of their nominee for president, and because the goal is to get as many votes as possible for the candidate, the person who becomes the nominee may not necessarily share the policy priorities of his co-partisans in the legislature. And, of course, once in office, the president serves a defined term and cannot be removed before the end of that term without resorting to extraordinary measures such as impeach-ment or forced resignation. Although presidents and legislators may for-mally be members of the same political party, in fact they are members of functionally separate parts of the party—a part devoted to the election of the president, and a part devoted to the election, reelection, and policy priorities of its legislative members. As two scholars who have looked at this question conclude, "parties rarely reunite what constitutions divide" (Samuels and Shugart 2010:251). In this connection, a recent empirical study finds that parliamentary systems are superior to presidential sys-tems in terms of their capacity to produce good public policy, particularly in areas of economic and human development (Gerring, Thacker, and Moreno 2009). In sum, legislative-executive conflict and the potential for policy stalemate are hard-wired into presidential systems; legislative-executive coordination and the ability to act in the face of a nation's chal-lenges are integral to the parliamentary design.

Parliamentary systems also can address some of the other perils of presidentialism that we have identified. Because citizens do not directly elect the head of government, opportunities for demagoguery in pursuit of the office may well be reduced. Because the prime minister governs collectively with his cabinet, the dangers associated with too much power residing in the hands of a single individual are reduced, although not eliminated. Presumably, a decision to go to war under a parliamen-tary system would be a collective decision taken by a cabinet rather than an individual decision taken by a singular president. A strong prime min-ister would likely have a great deal of influence on such a decision, as Margaret Thatcher did in regard to the Falklands War, but because of collective decisionmaking, the dangers associated with any personality flaws of such a singular leader would be reduced as well. Direct accountability to the legislature also should guard against any executive disposition toward authoritarian government. It is worth noting that few if any purely parliamentary systems, but several presidential systems, have acted in a clearly authoritarian manner. In Asia, for example, India and Japan have parliamentary systems and have for the most part avoided the actions that one would usually associate with authoritarian leaders. The Philippines, Indonesia, Pakistan, and South Korea, in contrast, have presidential systems, and each of these nations has at one time or another had an authoritarian government that has threatened civil liberties.

Conclusion

There is little doubt that presidential power varies cross-nationally, as well as across policy areas, and even among presidents who have served at various times in the same country's history. African presidents, as well as many Latin American presidents, seem to have exercised a great deal more power in their own nations than have their counterparts in the United States. In Bolivia, Evo Morales was able to nationalize large sections of the oil and gas industries and to strengthen the influence of the indigenous people of that country. Despite his Marxist orientation, the country experienced sustained economic growth and earned the praise of the International Monetary Fund at a time when other nations were suffering economic crises and looking for bailout money. Some viewed Morales as the strongest and most successful president in Bolivian history (Romero and Schipani 2009). In the United States, on the other hand, Barack Obama's domestic policy agenda, for much of his first term in office, was frustrated by strong congressional resistance, particularly from his Republican opponents, but also from some members of his own Democratic Party. In the United States there have been presidents such as Jimmy Carter and George H. W. Bush who were unable to exercise a great deal of power or accomplish very much of what they had hoped and promised to. But there also have been presidents such as Franklin Roosevelt and Lyndon Johnson who were able to accomplish a great deal.

These variations across and within countries might suggest that the argument of this book that there is a global trend toward presidentialism is at best problematic. Especially in the US context, the president, at least on domestic issues, is constrained by a very strong Congress, a potentially active judiciary, and a large and often conservative bureaucracy. And in any country, so much of what presidents can accomplish will depend on the skills of the president and the nature of the political environment that he faces.

But a focus on the obvious variations in the exercise of presidential power misses the impact of the long-term forces pointing toward presidentialism. Just as global temperature change has proceeded in an erratic fashion but with a generally upward trend over the long term, there is reason to believe that presidential power, while undergoing its ups and downs in different countries, also is experiencing, and will continue to experience, a long-term upward trend. Certainly, there is little doubt that the scope of governments around the world has expanded and with it the size and power of their bureaucracies, civilian and military. The various elements of this expanded bureaucracy sometimes resist presidential control, but presidents continue to work diligently to find means to overcome such resistance. Just as certainly, there can be little argument that the importance of international affairs has increased, incorporating not just the traditional issues of war and peace and command of an ever growing military establishment, but also monetary, trade, and environmental concerns, to name some obvious examples. For a variety of reasons, heads of state always have had a leading role in international issues, while they have been more likely to have to share power with other institutions and actors on purely domestic issues. So as the realm of purely domestic issues shrinks and as the number of policy issues with a significant international dimension expands, the prominence of the president also must increase.

Finally, there can be little doubt that presidents continue to be the focus of the political attention and expectations of mass publics as well as elites. Presidents dominate the news media of their countries not necessarily in the sense of state control (although we have seen examples of this), but in the sense that they are constantly present in the media and therefore a constant presence in the homes and lives of their citizens. In terms of public perceptions, such institutions as political parties and legislatures to an increasing extent have been marginalized in favor of the more highly personalized leadership and presence that the president offers. A democratized and for the most part televised presidential selection process means that those who aspire to the presidency must do all that they can to connect with the hopes and fears of the electorate, and in such a context it is not surprising that candidates inevitably will stoke those fears as they promise more than they can deliver. At the same time, an increasingly complex, uncertain, and seemingly dangerous world will arouse the latent tendency of mass publics to turn toward a strong individual leader who can provide reassurance in difficult times, even if this leader decides that it is necessary that he cut certain constitutional and statutory corners. Even in less dangerous times, citizens who are profoundly dissatisfied with the status quo may be willing to support strong executive leaders who promise dramatic changes rather than stick with the slower, more deliberative, more complicated, and inevitably more conservative decisions that emanate from collective bodies such as legislatures.

During their terms in office, presidents work diligently to maintain their contact with the public, to raise their level of personal support as well as support for their policies and thereby justify their claim to power as well as their policy preferences on the democratic grounds that the president speaks for the people. In the best interpretation, such activities seek to educate the public about the wisdom of the president's policy priorities; in the worst case, these activities can amount to demagoguery as the president plays to the population's fears and passions.

Hyperpresidentialism occurs when a president succeeds in harnessing these disparate forces—the size of the executive branch, the pronounced international dimension to so many key policy areas, his intimate, nearly constant connection with the people, and the public disposition toward strong individual leaders. When that happens, as it nearly always does on issues of war and peace as well as other international issues, presidential power is virtually unconstrained no matter what nation one is discussing.[4] On other issues, there may be a good deal more variation, depending upon the degree to which constitutions, the institutions that they establish, and other political actors are able to impose constraints on the president. US presidents are constrained to a significant degree, especially on purely domestic policy issues; presidents such as Venezuela's Hugo Chávez and Russia's Vladimir Putin are not. But what doesn't vary is the extent to which popular expectations focus on the president, regardless of the constraints under which he may operate. All presidents will fail to meet the full expectations of their people because they will face problems that are beyond their capacity to solve, and sometimes beyond the capacity of anyone to solve. Or they will be perceived as having failed because of the unrealistic and inconsistent expectations that surround them and their office, or because the solutions that they have developed are not as pain-free and simple as their campaign promises had suggested. As presidential performance continually (and inevitably) falls short of the expectations of those who elect them, a sense of cynicism will set in and this may well sow the seeds of instability.

Although it may be an exercise in mass naiveté, citizens continue to seek heroic leaders who will save their nations from catastrophe, make difficult but wise decisions, and lead their countries to a better, safer, more powerful, and more prosperous future while at the same time maintaining a high level of popular support and job approval. Few presidents turn out to be heroes, either because their abilities are limited, or because the times and the challenges that they confront and those with whom they share power make it impossible for them to achieve their most heroic goals. Some presidents, frustrated at their inability to do what their people expect of them, or what they expect of themselves, turn to authoritarian or extraconstitutional actions, sometimes citing a domestic or international emergency, and at other times simply acting and daring others to stop them. Although not every president will resort to these tactics, every president is capable of following this course, especially if he believes that he has the support of the people. From a presidential perspective, such democratic legitimacy is the gold standard for justifying each action that he wishes to take. When presidents bring all of these forces together, we may well be confronted, as Enlightenment philosophers were, with an untamed prince, but this time with a prince who relies heavily on democratic legitimacy and not solely on the physical force favored by Machiavelli.

Notes

1. "Clamping Down on Kleptocrats," November 8, 2011, www.transparency.org/news/feature/clamping_down_on_kleptocrats.
2. "Key Findings About Public Opinion in Africa," Afrobarometer Briefing Paper no. 1, April 2002.
3. "Corruption Perceptions Index," www.transparency.org/policy_research/surveys_indices/cpi/2009/cpi_2009_table.
4. But see Howell and Pevehouse 2007 for an argument that when Congress is controlled by a large and disciplined opposition, presidential latitude for deploying military force is significantly restrained.

Bibliography

Abramson, Jeffrey B. F., Christopher Arterton, and Gary R. Orren (1988) *The Electronic Commonwealth: The Impact of New Media Technologies on Democratic Politics.* New York: Basic.

Ackerman, Bruce (2000) "The New Separation of Powers." *Harvard Law Review* 113:3 (January), 633–729.

Agbese, Pita Ogaba (2003) "Keeping the African Military at Bay: Current Trends in Civil-Military Relations." In John Mukum Mbaku and Julius Omozuanvbo Ihonvbere, eds., *The Transition to Democratic Governance in Africa: The Continuing Struggle.* Westport: Praeger.

——— (2009) "Traditional Institutions and Governance in Africa: Chiefs, Constitutions, and Politics in Nigeria." In Kelechi A. Kalu and Peyi Soynka-Airewele, eds., *Socio-Political Scaffolding and the Construction of Change: Constitutionalism and Democratic Governance in Africa.* Trenton: Africa World.

Agüero, Felipe (2001) "Institutions, Transitions, and Bargaining: Civilians and the Military in Shaping Postauthoritarian Regimes." In David Pion-Berlin, *Civil-Military Relations in Latin America: New Analytical Perspectives.* Chapel Hill: University of North Carolina Press.

Alcántara, Manuel, and Mercedes García Montero (2008) "Institutions and Politicians: An Analysis of the Factors That Determine Presidential Legislative Success." Working Paper no. 348. Notre Dame, IN: Helen Kellogg Institute for International Studies.

Alexander, Robert J. (1977) "Caudillos, Coroneis, and Political Bosses in Latin America." In Thomas V. DiBacco, *Presidential Power in Latin American Politics.* New York: Praeger.

Alston, Lee J., Marcus Andre Melo, Bernardo Mueller, and Carlos Pereira (2006) "Political Institutions, Policymaking Processes, and Policy Outcomes in Brazil." Working Paper no. R-509. Washington, DC: Inter-American Development Bank, Research Network.

——— (2008) "On the Road to Good Governance: Recovering from Economic and Political Shocks in Brazil." In Ernesto Stein and Mariano Tommasi, eds., *Policymaking in Latin America: How Politics Shapes Policies.* Washington, DC: Inter-American Development Bank.

Alston, Lee J., and Bernardo Mueller (2005) "Pork for Policy: Executive and Legislative Exchange in Brazil." *Journal of Law, Economics, and Organization* 22:1, 87–114.

Ames, Barry (1987) *Political Survival: Politicians and Public Policy in Latin America.* Berkeley: University of California Press.

——— (1995) "Electoral Rules, Constituency Pressures, and Pork Barrel: Bases of Voting in the Brazilian Congress." *Journal of Politics* 57:2, 324–343.

——— (2001) *The Deadlock of Democracy in Brazil.* Ann Arbor: University of Michigan Press.

——— (2002) "Party Discipline in the Chamber of Deputies." In Scott Morgenstern and Benito Nacif, eds., *Legislative Politics in Latin America.* Cambridge: Cambridge University Press.

Anderson, Leslie E. (2006) "The Authoritarian Executive? Horizontal and Vertical Accountability in Nicaragua." *Latin American Politics and Society* 48:2 (Summer), 141–169.

Aninat, Cristóbal, John Londregan, Patricio Navia, and Joaquín Vial (2008) "Political Institutions, Policymaking Processes, and Policy Outcomes in Chile." In Ernesto Stein and Mariano Tommasi, eds., *Policymaking in Latin America: How Politics Shapes Policies.* Washington, DC: Inter-American Development Bank.

Archer, Ronald P., and Matthew Soberg Shugart (1997) "The Unrealized Potential of Presidential Dominance in Colombia." In Scott Mainwaring and Matthew Soberg Shugart, eds., *Presidentialism and Democracy in Latin America.* Cambridge: Cambridge University Press.

Armah-Attoh, Daniel, E. Gyimah-Boadi, and Annie Barbara Chikwana (2007) "Corruption and Institutional Trust in Africa: Implications for Democratic Development." Afrobarometer Working Paper no. 81. www.afrobarometer.org.

Arter, David (1985) "Government in Finland: A Semi-Presidential System." *Parliamentary Affairs* 38, 472–495.

——— (1991) "Kekkonen's Finland: Enlightened Despotism or Consensual Democracy?" *Western European Politics* 4, 219–234.

Ayala, Maggy (2012) "Ecuador: Court Upholds Prison Term and Fine for Libeling President." *New York Times,* February 17.

Ayittey, George B. N. (1991) *Indigenous African Institutions.* Ardsley-on-Hudson, NY: Transnational.

Bailey, Jeremy D. (2007) *Thomas Jefferson and Executive Power.* New York: Cambridge University Press.

Barber, Benjamin R. (1984) *Strong Democracy: Participatory Politics for a New Age.* Berkeley: University of California Press.

Barber, James David (1985) *The Presidential Character.* Englewood Cliffs, NJ: Prentice-Hall.

Barker, Ernest, ed. and trans. (1962) *The Politics of Aristotle.* New York: Oxford University Press.

Barr, Robert R. (2009) "Populists, Outsiders, and Anti-Establishment Politics." *Party Politics* 15:1, 29–48.

Barrionuevo, Alexei (2009) "Chilean President Rides High As Term Ends." *New York Times,* October 29.

Barros, Robert (2002) *Constitutionalism and Dictatorship.* Cambridge: Cambridge University Press.

Baynham, Simon (2001) "Introduction: Armed Forces in Africa." In Patricio Silva, ed., *The Soldier and the State in South America: Essays in Civil-Military Relations.* New York: Palgrave.

Beck, Linda (2008) *Brokering Democracy in Africa: The Rise of Clientelist Democracy in Senegal.* New York: Palgrave Macmillan.

Bendix, Reinhard (1962) *Max Weber: An Intellectual Portrait.* Garden City, NY: Doubleday Anchor.

Bicheno, E. A. (1992) "Anti-Parliamentary Themes in Chilean History: 1920–1970." *Government and Opposition* 7 (Summer), 351–388.

Bierck, Harold A., Jr., ed. (1951) *Selected Writings of Bolivar.* Compiled by Vicente Lecuna. Vol. 1, *1810–1822.* New York: Colonial.

Blackwell, Christopher W. (2003) *Demos: Classical Athenian Democracy.* www.stoa.org/projects/demos/home.

Blumenthal, Sidney (1982) *The Permanent Campaign.* New York: Simon and Schuster.

Bond, Jon R., and Richard Fleisher (1990) *The President in the Legislative Arena.* Chicago: University of Chicago Press.

Bratton, Michael, and Nicolas van de Walle (1997) *Democratic Experiments in Africa: Regime Transitions in Comparative Perspective.* New York: Cambridge University Press.

Breslauer, George W. (2001) "Boris Yeltsin as Patriarch." In Archie Brown, ed., *Contemporary Russian Politics: A Reader.* Oxford: Oxford University Press.

Breuer, Anita (2007) "Institutions of Direct Democracy and Accountability in Latin America's Presidential Democracies." *Democratization* 14:4 (August), 554–579.

Bryce, James (1971) "The Decline of Legislatures." In Gerhard Loewenberg, ed., *Modern Parliaments: Change or Decline?* Chicago: Aldine Atherton. Originally published in 1921.

Burns, James MacGregor (1973) *Presidential Government: The Crucible of Leadership.* Sentry ed. Boston: Houghton Mifflin.

Calabresi, Steven G., and James Lindgren (2006) "The President: Lightning Rod or King?" *Yale Law Journal* 115, 2611–2622.

Calmes, Jackie (2010) "Obama to Seek More Power to Trim Spending from Bills." *New York Times,* May 7.

Cammack, Paul (2001) "In Permanent Retreat? The Modest Future Role of the Armed Forces in South America." In Patricio Silva, ed., *The Soldier and the State in South America: Essays in Civil-Military Relations.* New York: Palgrave.

Carey, John (1997) "Strong Candidates for a Limited Office: Presidentialism and Political Parties in Costa Rica." In Scott Mainwaring and Matthew Soberg Shugart, eds., *Presidentialism and Democracy in Latin America.* Cambridge: Cambridge University Press.

───── (2003) "Presidentialism and Representative Institutions." In Jorge I. Domínguez and Michael Shifter, eds., *Constructing Democratic Governance in Latin America,* 2nd ed. Baltimore: Johns Hopkins University Press.

Carey, John, and Simon Hix (2009) "The Electoral Sweet Spot: Low-Magnitude Proportional Electoral Systems." Paper prepared for delivery at the seminar "The Legislative Branch in Latin America in Comparative Perspective: Performance and Research Areas." University of Salamanca, December.

Carey, John, and Matthew Soberg Shugart (1998) "Calling Out the Tanks or Filling Out the Forms?" In John Carey and Matthew Soberg Shugart, eds., *Executive Decree Authority.* Cambridge: Cambridge University Press.

Carr, David (2013) "Debating Drones in the Open." *New York Times,* February 11.

Casar, María Amparo (2002) "Executive Legislative Relations: The Case of Mexico (1946–1997)." In Scott Morgenstern and Benito Nacif, eds., *Legislative Politics in Latin America.* Cambridge: Cambridge University Press.

Case, William (2011) "Executive Accountability in Southeast Asia: The Role of Legislatures in New Democracies and Under Electoral Authoritarianism." Policy Study no. 57. Honolulu: East-West Center.

Casper, Gretchen (1995) *Fragile Democracies: The Legacies of Authoritarian Rule.* Pittsburgh: University of Pittsburgh Press.

Ceasar, James (1979) *Presidential Selection.* Princeton: Princeton University Press.

Centeno, Miguel (1994) *Democracy Within Reason: Technocratic Revolution in Mexico.* University Park: Pennsylvania State University Press.

Chazan, Naomi, Robert Mortimer, John Ravenhill, and Donald Rothchild (1992) *Politics and Society in Contemporary Africa.* 2nd ed. Boulder: Lynne Rienner.

Cheibub, José Antonio (2006) "Presidentialism, Electoral Identifiability, and Budget Balances in Democratic Systems." *American Political Science Review* 100:3 (August), 353–368.

───── (2007) *Presidentialism, Parliamentarism, and Democracy.* Cambridge: Cambridge University Press.

Cheibub, José Antonio, Adam Przeworski, and Sebastian Saiegh (2004) "Government Coalitions and Legislative Success Under Presidentialism and Parliamentarism." *British Journal of Political Science* 34:4 (October), 565–587.

Clayman, Steven E., Marc N. Elliott, John Heritage, and Laurie L. McDonald (2006) "Historical Trends in Questioning Presidents, 1953–2000." *Presidential Studies Quarterly* 36 (December), 561–583.

Clayman, Steven E., and John Heritage (2002) "Questioning Presidents: Journalistic Deference and Adversarialness in the Press Conferences of US Presidents Eisenhower and Reagan." *Journal of Communication* 52 (December), 749–775.

Clift, Ben (2005) "Dyarchic Presidentialization in a Presidentialized Polity: The French Fifth Republic." In Thomas Poguntke and Paul Webb, eds., *The Presidentialization of Politics: A Comparative Study of Modern Democracies.* New York: Oxford University Press.

Close, David, and Kalowatie Deonandan (2004) *Undoing Democracy: The Politics of Electoral Caudillismo.* Lanham: Lexington Books.

Cohen, Jeffrey E. (2008) *The Presidency in the Era of 24-Hour News.* Princeton: Princeton University Press.

Cohen, Youssef (1994) *Radicals, Reformers, and Reactionaries: The Prisoner's Dilemma and the Collapse of Democracy in Latin America.* Chicago: University of Chicago Press.

Collier, Ruth B. (1978) "Parties, Coups, and Authoritarian Rule: Patterns of Political Change in Tropical Africa." *Comparative Political Studies* 11:1 (April), 62–89.

Conaghan, Catherine M. (1994) "Loose Parties, 'Floating' Politicians, and Institutional Stress: Presidentialism in Ecuador, 1979–1988." In Juan Linz and Arturo Valenzuela, eds., *The Failure of Presidential Democracy.* Baltimore: Johns Hopkins University Press.

Coppedge, Michael (1994) *Strong Parties and Lame Ducks: Presidential Partyarchy and Factionalism in Venezuela.* Stanford: Stanford University Press.

Corrales, Javier (2009) "The Negotiation of Presidential and Legislative Powers in Bolivia's Constituent Assembly (2006–2008)." Paper prepared for delivery at the seminar "The Legislative Branch in Latin America in Comparative Perspective: Performance and Research Areas." University of Salamanca, December.

Cox, Gary (1987) *The Efficient Secret: The Cabinet and the Development of Political Parties in Victorian England.* Cambridge: Cambridge University Press.

Cox, Gary, and Matthew D. McCubbins (2001) "The Institutional Determinants of Economic Policy Outcomes." In Stephan Haggard and Matthew McCubbins, eds., *Presidents, Parliaments, and Public Policy.* Cambridge: Cambridge University Press.

Cox, Gary, and Scott Morgenstern (2002) "Epilogue: Latin America's Reactive Assemblies and Proactive Presidents." In Scott Morgenstern and Benito Nacif, eds., *Legislative Politics in Latin America.* Cambridge: Cambridge University Press.

Crenson, Matthew, and Benjamin Ginsberg (2007) *Presidential Power: Unchecked and Unbalanced.* New York: Norton.

Crisp, Brian (1997) "Presidential Behavior in a System with Strong Parties: Venezuela, 1958–1995." In Scott Mainwaring and Matthew Soberg Shugart, eds., *Presidentialism and Democracy in Latin America.* Cambridge: Cambridge University Press.

——— (1998) *Democratic Institutional Design: The Powers and Incentives of Venezuelan Politicians and Interest Groups.* Stanford: Stanford University Press.

Croissant, Aurel (2003) "Legislative Powers, Veto Players, and the Emergence of Delegative Democracy: A Comparison of Presidentialism in the Philippine and South Korea." *Democratization* 10:3 (August), 68–98.

Cronin, Thomas E., ed. (1989) *Inventing the American Presidency.* Lawrence: University Press of Kansas.

——— (2009) *On the Presidency: Teacher, Soldier, Shaman, Pol.* Boulder: Paradigm.

Cronin, Thomas E., and Michael E. Genovese (2010) *The Paradoxes of the American Presidency.* 3rd. ed. New York: Oxford University Press.

Davis, Harold E. (1958) *Government and Politics in Latin America.* New York: Ronald Press.

de Gaulle, Charles (1971) *Charles de Gaulle: Memoirs of Hope: Renewal and Endeavor.* Translated by Terence Kilmartin. New York: Simon and Shuster.

de Groot–van Leeuwen, Leny E., and Wannes Rombouts, eds. (2010) *Separation of Powers in Theory and Practice: An International Perspective.* Nijmegen, Netherlands: Wolf Legal.

de Lima, Venicio A. (1993) "Brazilian Television in the 1989 Presidential Campaign: Constructing a President." In Thomas Skidmore, ed., *Television, Politics, and the Transition to Democracy in Latin America.* Washington, DC: Woodrow Wilson Center.

Deonandan, Kalowatie (2004) "The Assault on Pluralism." In David Close and Kalowatie Deonandan, eds., *Undoing Democracy: The Politics of Electoral Caudillismo.* Lanham: Lexington Books.

Dix, Robert H. (1977) "The Colombian Presidency: Continuities and Changes." In Thomas V. DiBacco, *Presidential Power in Latin American Politics.* New York: Praeger.

Dogan, Mattei (2005) "Erosion of Confidence in Thirty European Democracies." In Mattei Dogan, ed., *Political Mistrust and the Discrediting of Politicians.* Leiden: Brill.

Edelman, Murray (1985) *The Symbolic Uses of Politics.* Urbana: University of Illinois Press.

Edwards, George (1989) *At the Margins: Presidential Leadership of Congress.* New Haven: Yale University Press.

Eilperin, Juliet (2010) "U.S. Exempted BP's Gulf of Mexico Drilling from Environmental Impact Study." *Washington Post,* May 5.

Emrich, Cynthia, Holly H. Brower, Jack M. Feldman, and Howard Garland (2001) "Images in Words: Presidential Rhetoric, Charisma, and Greatness." *Administrative Science Quarterly* 46:3, 527–557.

Evans, Diana (2004) *Greasing the Wheels: Using Pork Barrel Projects to Build Majority Coalitions in Congress.* Cambridge: Cambridge University Press.

Fallows, James (2012) "Obama Explained." *The Atlantic,* March.

Farcau, Bruce W. (1996) *The Transition to Democracy in Latin America: The Role of the Military.* Westport: Praeger.

Farrand, Max, ed. (1966) *The Records of the Federal Convention of 1787.* Vols. 1–2. New Haven: Yale University Press.

Fatton, Robert, Jr. (1990) "Liberal Democracy in Africa." *Political Science Quarterly* 105:3 (Autumn), 455–473.

Findley, Roger W. (1980) "Presidential Intervention in the Economy and the Rule of Law in Colombia." *American Journal of Comparative Law* 28:3 (Summer), 423–473.

Fine, Jeffrey A., and Richard W. Waterman (2008) "A New Model of Presidential Leadership: Controlling the Bureaucracy." In Bert A. Rockman and Richard W. Waterman, eds., *Presidential Leadership: The Vortex of Power.* New York: Oxford University Press.

Fish, M. Steven, and Matthew Kroenig (2009) *The Handbook of National Legislatures: A Global Survey.* New York: Cambridge University Press.

Fisher, Louis (1997) *Constitutional Conflicts Between Congress and the President.* 4th rev. ed. Lawrence: University Press of Kansas.

Fitch, J. Samuel (1998) *The Armed Forces and Democracy in Latin America.* Baltimore: Johns Hopkins University Press.

Fombad, Charles Manga (2003) "The Mass Media and Democratization in Africa: Lessons from Cameroon." In John Mukum Mbaku and Julius Omozuanvbo Ihonvbere, eds., *The Transition to Democratic Governance in Africa.* Westport: Praeger.

Foweraker, Joe (1998) "Review Article: Institutional Design, Party Systems, and Governability—Differentiating the Presidential Regimes of Latin America." *British Journal of Political Science* 28:4 (October), 651–676.

Fox, Jonathan (1994) "The Difficult Transition from Clientelism to Citizenship." *World Politics* 46:2 (January), 151–184.

Fromm, Erich (1941) *Escape from Freedom.* New York: Holt, Rinehart, and Winston.

Frye, Timothy (1997) "A Politics of Institutional Choice: Post-Communist Presidencies." *Comparative Political Studies* 30:5 (October), 523–552.

Gamarra, Eduardo A. (2008) "Bolivia: Evo Morales and Democracy." In Jorge I. Domínguez and Michael Shifter, eds., *Constructing Democratic Governance in Latin America,* 3rd. ed. Baltimore: Johns Hopkins University Press.

Ganev, Venelin I. (1997) "Emergency Powers and the New East European Constitutions." *American Journal of Comparative Law* 45:3 (Summer), 585–612.

Gargarella, Roberto (2010) *The Legal Foundations of Inequality: Constitutionalism in the Americas, 1776–1860.* New York: Cambridge University Press.

Geddes, Barbara (1994) *Politician's Dilemma: Building State Capacity in Latin America.* Berkeley: University of California Press.

Gellar, Sheldon (2005) *Democracy in Senegal: Tocquevillian Analytics in Africa.* New York: Palgrave Macmillan.

Gerring, John, and Strom C. Thacker (2004) "Political Institutions and Corruption: The Role of Unitarism and Parliamentarism." *British Journal of Political Science* 34:2 (April), 295–330.

Gerring, John, Strom C. Thacker, and Carola Moreno (2009) "Are Parliamentary Systems Better?" *Comparative Political Studies* 42:3 (March), 327–359.

Gourevitch, Philip (2011) "No Exit: Can Nicolas Sarkozy—and France—Survive the European Crisis?" *New Yorker,* December 12.

Gulati, Girish J. (2010) "No Laughing Matter: The Role of New Media in the 2008 Election." In Larry Sabato, ed., *The Year of Obama: How Barack Obama Won the White House.* New York: Longman.

Haggard, Stephan, Mathew McCubbins, and Matthew Soberg Shugart (2001) "Conclusion: Policy-Making in Presidential Systems." In Stephan Haggard and Matthew McCubbins, eds., *Presidents, Parliaments, and Public Policy.* Cambridge: Cambridge University Press.

Hagopian, Frances (1996) *Traditional Politics and Regime Change in Brazil.* New York: Cambridge University Press.

Hallenberg, Mark, and Patrik Marier (2004) "Executive Authority, the Personal Vote, and Budget Discipline in Latin American and Caribbean Countries." *American Journal of Political Science* 48:3, 571–587.

Hamilton, Alexander, James Madison, and John Jay (1961) *The Federalist Papers*. New York: New American Library. Originally published between 1787 and 1788.

Hammouya, Messaoud (1999) "Statistics on Public Sector Employment: Methodology, Structures, and Trends." Geneva: International Labour Organization.

Hawkins, Kirk A. (2010) *Venezuela's Chavismo and Populism in Comparative Perspective*. New York: Cambridge University Press.

Hayes, Monte (2006) "Leader in Ecuador Presidential Vote Count Looking Toward Radical Reforms." *Associated Press*, November 27.

Hayward, Jack (1993) "The President and the Constitution: Its Spirit, Articles, and Practice." In Jack Hayward, ed., *De Gaulle to Mitterrand: Presidential Power in France*. New York: New York University Press.

Heclo, Hugh (2000) "Campaigning and Governing: A Conspectus." In Norman Ornstein and Thomas Mann, eds., *The Permanent Campaign and Its Future*. Washington, DC: American Enterprise Institute and Brookings Institution.

Hochstetler, Kathryn (2006) "Rethinking Presidentialism: Challenges and Presidential Falls in South America." *Comparative Politics* 38:4 (July), 401–418.

——— (2008) "Organized Civil Society in Lula's Brazil." In Peter R. Kingstone and Timothy J. Power, eds., *Democratic Brazil Revisited*. Pittsburgh: University of Pittsburgh Press.

Howden, Daniel (2009) "Shopaholic Ex-President of Zambia Cleared of Corruption." *The Independent* (London), August 18.

Howell, William G. (2003) *Power Without Persuasion: The Politics of Direct Presidential Action*. Princeton: Princeton University Press.

Howell, William G., and Jon C. Pevehouse (2007) *While Dangers Gather: Congressional Checks on Presidential War Powers*. Princeton: Princeton University Press.

Huber, John D. (1998) "Executive Decree Authority in France." In John M. Carey and Matthew Soberg Shugart, eds., *Executive Decree Authority*. Cambridge: Cambridge University Press.

Hughes, Sallie (2010) "The Latin American News Media and the Policymaking Process." In Carlos Scartascini, Ernesto Stein, and Mariano Tommasi, eds., *How Democracy Works: Political Institutions, Actors, and Arenas in Latin American Policymaking*. Washington, DC: Inter-American Development Bank.

Human Rights Watch (2008) "A Decade Under Chávez: Political Intolerance and Lost Opportunities for Advancing Human Rights in Venezuela." Washington, DC: Human Rights Watch, September 18.

Hunter, Wendy (1996) *State and Soldier in Latin America: Redefining the Military's Role in Argentina, Brazil, and Chile*. Washington, DC: US Institute of Peace.

——— (2008) "The Partido dos Trabalhadores: Still a Party of the Left?" In Peter R. Kingstone and Timothy J. Power, eds., *Democratic Brazil Revisited*. Pittsburgh: University of Pittsburgh Press.

Hunter, Wendy, and Timothy J. Power (2007) "Rewarding Lula: Executive Power, Social Policy, and the Brazilian Elections of 2006." *Latin American Politics and Society* 49:1 (Spring), 1–30.

Huntington, Samuel P. (1968) *Political Order in Changing Societies*. New Haven: Yale University Press.

Huskey, Eugene (1999) *Presidential Power in Russia*. Armonk, NY: Sharpe.

Jackson, Roger H., and Carl G. Rosberg (1982) *Personal Rule in Black Africa: Prince, Autocrat, Prophet, Tyrant*. Berkeley: University of California Press.

Jacobson, Gary C. (2013) *The Politics of Congressional Elections*. 8th ed. Boston: Pearson Education.

Jakubowicz, Karl (1996) "Television and Elections in Post-1989 Poland: How Powerful Is the Medium." In David L. Swanson and Paolo Mancini, eds., *Politics, Media, and Modern Democracy: An International Study of Innovations in Electoral Campaigning and Their Consequences*. Westport: Praeger.

Jarvis, Matthew (2010) "Winning While Backing Down: The Odd History of Bush's Veto Threats." Paper prepared for delivery at the annual meeting of the Western Political Science Association. San Francisco, April.

Jones, Mark (1995) *Electoral Laws and the Survival of Presidential Democracies*. Notre Dame, IN: University of Notre Dame Press.

—— (1996) "Assessing the Public's Understanding of Constitutional Reform: Evidence from Argentina." *Political Behavior* 18:1 (March), 25–49.

—— (2010) "Beyond the Electoral Connection: The Effect of Political Parties on the Policymaking Process." In Carlos Scartascini, Ernesto Stein, and Mariano Tommasi, eds., *How Democracy Works: Political Institutions, Actors, and Arenas in Latin American Policymaking*. Washington, DC: Inter-American Development Bank.

Kalu, Kelechi (2009) "Constitutionalism in Africa: A Conceptual Analysis of Ethnicity and Politics, with Lessons from Nigeria." In Kelechi A. Kalu and Peyio Soyinka-Airewele, eds., *Socio-Political Scaffolding and the Construction of Change: Constitutionalism and Democratic Governance in Africa*. Trenton: Africa World.

Kantor, Harry (1992) "Efforts Made by Various Latin American Countries to Limit the Power of the President." In Arend Lijphart, ed., *Parliamentary v. Presidential Government*. Oxford: Oxford University Press.

Katyal, Neal Kumar (2006) "Internal Separation of Powers: Checking Today's Most Dangerous Branch from Within." *Yale Law Journal* 115:9, 2314–2349.

Kelley, Christopher S., and Ryan J. Barilleaux (2006) "The Past, Present, and Future of the Unitary Executive." Paper prepared for delivery at the annual meeting of the American Political Science Association. Philadelphia, September.

Kernell, Samuel (1986) *Going Public: New Strategies of Presidential Leadership*. Washington, DC: Congressional Quarterly.

Khuri, Faud (1982) "The Study of Civil-Military Relations in Modernizing Societies in the Middle East: A Critical Assessment." In Roman Kolkowicz and Adrzej Korbonski, eds., *Soldiers, Peasants, and Bureaucrats*. London: Allen and Unwin.

Kingstone, Peter R. (1999) *Crafting Coalitions for Reform: Business Preferences, Political Institutions, and Neoliberal Reform in Brazil*. University Park: Pennsylvania State University Press.

Kleinerman, Benjamin A. (2009) *The Discretionary President: The Promise and Peril of Executive Power*. Lawrence: University Press of Kansas.

Koh, Harold Hongju (2006) "Setting the World Right." *Yale Law Journal* 115:9, 2350–2379.

Krastev, Ivan (2006) "Democracy's 'Doubles.'" *Journal of Democracy* 17:2 (April), 52–62.

Krent, Harold J. (2008) "From a Unitary to a Unilateral Presidency." *Boston University Law Review* 88:2 (April), 523–560.

Krupavicius, Algis (2008) "Semi-Presidentialism in Lithuania: Origins, Development, and Challenges." In Robert Elgie and Sophia Moestrup, eds., *Semi-Presidentialism in Central and Eastern Europe.* Manchester: Manchester University Press.

Le Vine, Victor T. (2004) *Politics in Francophone Africa.* Boulder: Lynne Rienner.

Lewis, David E. (2011) "Presidential Appointments in the Obama Administration: An Early Evaluation." In Andrew J. Dowdle, Dirk C. Van Raemdonck, and Robert Maranto, eds., *The Obama Presidency: Continuity and Change.* New York: Routledge.

Lewis, Peter, and Etannibi Alemika (2005) "Seeking the Democratic Dividend: Public Attitudes and Attempted Reform in Nigeria." Afrobarometer Working Paper no. 52. www.afrobarometer.org.

Leys, Colin (1974) *Underdevelopment in Kenya: The Political Economy of Neo-Colonialism.* Berkeley: University of California Press.

Lichfield, John (2007) "Sarkozy More Popular Than Any Leader Since de Gaulle." *The Independent* (London), May 28.

——— (2008) "Struggling Sarkozy to Remind French: I'm a Man of Action." *The Independent* (London), April 24.

Lichtblau, Eric, and Robert Pear (2010) "Washington Rule Makers Out of the Shadows." *New York Times,* December 8.

Lieuwen, Edwin (1962) "Militarism and Politics in Latin America." In John J. Johnson, ed., *The Role of the Military in Underdeveloped Countries.* Princeton: Princeton University Press.

Light, Paul C. (2006) "The New True Size of Government." Organizational Performance Initiative Research Brief Number 2. Robert F. Wagner Graduate School of Public Service, New York University. http://wagner .nyu.edu/performance/files/True_Size.pdf.

Lijphart, Arend (1994) "Presidentialism and Majoritarian Democracy: Theoretical Observations." In Juan Linz and Arturo Valenzuela, eds., *The Failure of Presidential Democracy.* Baltimore: Johns Hopkins University Press.

Lincoln, Abraham (1953) *The Collected Works of Abraham Lincoln.* Roy P. Basler, ed., Abraham Lincoln Association. New Brunswick, NJ: Rutgers University Press.

Linz, Juan (1990) "The Perils of Presidentialism." *Journal of Democracy* 1:1, 51–69.

——— (1994) "Presidential or Parliamentary Democracy: Does It Make a Difference?" In Juan Linz and Arturo Valenzuela, eds., *The Failure of Presidential Democracy.* Baltimore: Johns Hopkins University Press.

Lipton, Eric (2010) "With Obama, Regulations Are Back in Fashion." *New York Times,* May 13.

Locke, John (1955) *Of Civil Government.* Chicago: Henry Regnery. Originally published in 1689.

Logan, Carolyn (2008) "Traditional Leaders in Modern Africa: Can Democracy and the Chief Co-exist?" Afrobarometer Working Paper no. 93. www.afrobarometer.org.

Loss, Richard (1982) "Alexander Hamilton and the Modern Presidency: Continuity or Discontinuity." *Presidential Studies Quarterly* 12:1 (Winter), 6–25.

Lowenstein, Karl (1949) "The Presidency Outside the United States: A Study in Comparative Political Institutions." *Journal of Politics* 11:3 (August), 447–496.

Lowenthal, Abraham, ed. (1976) *Armies and Politics in Latin America.* New York: Holmes and Meier.

Lowi, Theodore (1985) *The Personal President.* Ithaca: Cornell University Press.

Lynch, John (1992) *Caudillos in Spanish America, 1800–1850.* Oxford: Clarendon.

Macey, Jonathan (2006) "Executive Branch Usurpation of Power: Corporations and Capital Markets." *Yale Law Journal* 115:9, 2416–2444.

Machiavelli, Nicolo (1908) *The Prince.* Translated by W. K. Marriott. London: J. M. Dent and Sons.

Madison, James (1793) "Helvidius Paper, Number 4." http://oll.libertyfund.org/index.php?option=com_staticxt&staticfile=show.php&title=1910&search=%22the+prodigy+of+many+centuries%22&chapter=112553&layout=html#a_2335686.

Mahoney, Daniel (1996) *De Gaulle: Statesmanship, Grandeur, and Modern Democracy.* Westport: Praeger.

Mainwaring, Scott (1990) "Presidentialism in Latin America." *Latin American Research Review* 25:1, 157–159.

———— (1993) "Presidentialism, Multipartism, and Democracy: Brazil in Comparative Perspective." *Comparative Political Studies* 26:2 (July), 198–228.

———— (1997) "Multipartism, Robust Federalism, and Presidentialism in Brazil." In Scott Mainwaring and Matthew Soberg Shugart, eds., *Presidentialism and Democracy in Latin America.* Cambridge: Cambridge University Press.

———— (2006) "The Crisis of Representation in the Andes." *Journal of Democracy* 17:3 (July), 13–27.

Mamdani, Mahmood (1996) *Citizen and Subject: Contemporary Africa and the Legacy of Late Colonialism.* Princeton: Princeton University Press.

Mansfield, Harvey G., Jr. (1993) *Taming the Price: The Ambivalence of Modern Executive Power.* Baltimore: Johns Hopkins University Press.

Martinez, Jenny S. (2006) "Inherent Executive Power: A Comparative Perspective." *Yale Law Journal* 115:9, 2480–2511.

Mayer, Kenneth R. (2002) *With the Stroke of a Pen: Executive Orders and Presidential Power.* Princeton: Princeton University Press.

Mayer, Kenneth R., and Kevin Price (2002) "Unilateral Presidential Powers: Significant Executive Orders, 1949–1999." *Presidential Studies Quarterly* 32 (June), 367–386.

Mayhew, David R. (1991) *Divided We Govern: Party Control, Lawmaking, and Investigations, 1946–1990.* New Haven: Yale University Press.

McCubbins, Mathew D., and Thomas Schwartz (1984) "Congressional Oversight Overlooked: Police Patrols Versus Fire Alarms." *American Journal of Political Science* 28:1 (February), 165–179.

McGowan, Patrick J. (2003) "African Military Coups D'état, 1956–2001: Frequency, Trends and Distribution." *Journal of Modern African Studies* 41:3 (September): 339–370.

Meacham, Jon (2008) *American Lion: Andrew Jackson in the White House.* New York: Random.

Meier, Kenneth J. (1979) *Politics and the Bureaucracy.* North Scituate, MA: Duxbury.

Melo, Marcus Andre (2008) "Unexpected Successes, Unanticipated Failures: Social Policy from Cardoso to Lula." In Peter R. Kingstone and Timothy J. Power, eds., *Democratic Brazil Revisited.* Pittsburgh: University of Pittsburgh Press.

Metcalf, Kendall L. (2000) "Measuring Presidential Power." *Comparative Political Studies* 33:5 (June), 660–685.

Mezey, Michael L. (1989) *Congress, the President, and Public Policy.* Boulder: Westview.

——— (2009) "The Political Consequences of Strong Legislatures." Paper prepared for delivery at the seminar "The Legislative Branch in Latin America in Comparative Perspective: Performance and Research Areas." University of Salamanca, December.

Mickiewicz, Ellen, and Andrei Richter (1996) "Television, Campaigning, and Elections in the Soviet Union and Post-Soviet Russia." In David L. Swanson and Paolo Mancini, eds., *Politics, Media, and Modern Democracy: An International Study of Innovations in Electoral Campaigning and Their Consequences.* Westport: Praeger.

Miroff, Bruce (1982) "Monopolizing the Public Space: The President as a Problem for Democratic Politics." In Thomas E. Cronin, ed., *Rethinking the Presidency.* Boston: Little, Brown.

Moe, Terry M., and Scott A. Wilson (1994) "Presidents and the Politics of Structure." *Law and Contemporary Problems* (Spring), 1–44.

Montalvo, Daniel (2009) "Do You Trust Your Armed Forces?" Latin American Public Opinion Project Insights Series no. 27. www.vanderbilt.edu/lapop/studiesandpublicatons.

Montesquieu, Charles Louis de Secondat baron de la Brede et de Montesquieu (1949) *The Spirit of the Laws.* Translated by Thomas Nugent. New York: Hafner.

Mustapic, Ana María (2002) "Oscillating Relations: President and Congress in Argentina." In Scott Morgenstern and Benito Nacif, eds., *Legislative Politics in Latin America.* Cambridge: Cambridge University Press.

Nagourney, Adam, and Marjorie Connelly (2009) "Poll Finds Faith in Obama, Mixed with Patience." *New York Times,* January 18.

Nather, David (2009) "New President, Old Precedent." *Congressional Quarterly Weekly Report,* July 27, 1760–1762.

Neto, Octavio Amorin (2006) "The Presidential Calculus: Executive Policy Making and Cabinet Formation in the Americas." *Comparative Political Studies* 39(4), 415–440.

Neustadt, Richard E. (1980) *Presidential Power.* 2nd ed. New York: Wiley.

Nyamnjoh, Francis B. (2005) *Africa's Media: Democracy and the Politics of Belonging.* London: Zed.

Nye, Joseph S., Jr. (2008) *The Powers to Lead.* New York: Oxford University Press.

O'Donnell, Guillermo (1978) "Reflections on the Patterns of Change in the Bureaucratic-Authoritarian State." *Latin American Research Review* 13:1, 3–38.

———— (1988) *Bureaucratic Authoritarianism: Argentina 1966–1973 in Comparative Perspective.* Berkeley: University of California Press.

———— (1994) "Delegative Democracy." *Journal of Democracy* 5:1 (January), 55–69.

———— (1996) "Illusions About Consolidation." *Journal of Democracy* 7:2, 34–51.

———— (1998) "Horizontal Accountability in New Democracies." *Journal of Democracy* 9:3, 112–126.

Olowu, Dele (1996) "Democratization and the Issue of Neutrality in Nigeria." In Haile I. Asmerom and Elilsa P. Reis, eds., *Democratization and Bureaucratic Neutrality.* London: Macmillan.

Orttung, Robert (2006) "Causes and Consequences of Corruption in Putin's Russia." PONARS Policy Memo no. 430. Washington, DC: Georgetown University, Eurasian Strategy Project.

Packenham, Robert A. (1970) "Legislatures and Political Development." In Alan Kornberg and Lloyd Musolf, eds., *Legislatures in Developmental Perspective.* Durham: Duke University Press.

Paloheimo, Heikki (2005) "Finland: Let the Force Be with the Leader—But Who Is the Leader?" In Thomas Poguntke and Paul Webb, eds., *The Presidentialization of Politics: A Comparative Study of Modern Democracies.* New York: Oxford University Press.

Parrish, Scott (1998) "Presidential Decree Authority in Russia, 1991–95." In John Carey and Matthew Soberg Shugart, eds., *Executive Decree Authority.* Cambridge: Cambridge University Press.

Partlow, Joshua (2009) "As Bolivians Vote on New Constitution, Opposition Finds Itself Divided." *Washington Post,* January 25.

Pereira, Carlos, Timothy Power, and Lucio Renno (2005) "Under What Conditions Do Presidents Resort to Decree Power? Theory and Evidence from the Brazilian Case." *Journal of Politics* 67:1 (February), 178–200.

Perez, Orlando J. (2009) "Crime and Support for Coups in Latin America." Latin American Public Opinion Project Insights Series no. 32. www .vanderbilt.edu/lapop/studiesandpublicatons.

Pérez-Liñán, Aníbal (2007) *Presidential Impeachment and the New Political Instability in Latin America.* New York: Cambridge University Press.

Persson, Torsten, and Guido Tabellini (2003) *The Economic Effects of Constitutions.* Cambridge: Massachusetts Institute of Technology Press.

Peters, B. Guy (1995) *The Politics of Bureaucracy.* 4th ed. New York: Longman.

Peterson, Mark A. (1990) *Legislating Together: The White House and Capitol Hill from Eisenhower to Reagan.* Cambridge: Harvard University Press.

Petukhov, Vladimir, and Andrei Ryabov (2004) "Public Attitudes About Democracy." In Michael McFaul, Nikolai Petrov, and Andrei Ryabov, *Between Dictatorship and Democracy: Russian Post-Communist Political Reform.* Washington, DC: Carnegie Endowment for International Peace.

Pfiffner, James F., and Roger H. Davidson (2009) *Understanding the Presidency.* 5th ed. New York: Pearson, Longman.

Poguntke, Thomas, and Paul Webb (2005) "The Presidentialization of Politics in Democratic Societies: A Framework for Analysis." In Thomas Poguntke and Paul Webb, eds., *The Presidentialization of Politics: A Comparative Study of Modern Democracies.* New York; Oxford University Press.

Power, Timothy (1991) "Politicized Democracy: Competition, Institutions, and 'Civic Fatigue' in Brazil." *Journal of Interamerican Studies and World Affairs* 33 (Fall), 75–112.

Renshon, Stanley A. (2012) *Barack Obama and the Politics of Redemption.* New York: Routledge.

Riggs, Fred (1967) "Bureaucrats and Political Development: A Paradoxical View." In Joseph LaPalombara, ed., *Bureaucracy and Political Development.* Princeton: Princeton University Press.

——— (1988) "The Survival of Presidentialism in America: Para-Constitutional Practices." *International Political Science Review* 9:4 (October), 247–278.

Robinson, David L. (1983) "The Inventors of the Presidency." *Presidential Studies Quarterly* 13:1 (Winter), 8–25.

Rodríguez Raga, Juan Carlos, and Mitchell A. Seligson (2008) "Political Culture of Democracy in Colombia, 2008: The Impact of Governance." Latin American Public Opinion Project. Nashville: Vanderbilt University.

Romero, Simon, and Andres Schipani (2009) "In Bolivia, a Force for Change Endures." *New York Times,* December 5.

Rose-Ackerman, Susan, Diane A. Desierto, and Natalia Volosin (2011) "Hyper-Presidentialism: Separation of Powers Without Checks and Balances in Argentina and the Philippines." *Berkeley Journal of International Law* 29:1, 246–333.

Rubio, Delia Ferreira, and Matteo Goretti (1998) "When the President Governs Alone: The *Decretazo* in Argentina, 1989–93." In John Carey and Matthew Soberg Shugart, eds., *Executive Decree Authority.* Cambridge: Cambridge University Press.

Ryabov, Andrei (2004) "Legislative-Executive Relations." In Michael McFaul, Nikolai Petrov, and Andrei Ryabov, *Between Dictatorship and Democracy: Russian Post-Communist Political Reform.* Washington, DC: Carnegie Endowment for International Peace.

Safran, William (2003) *The French Polity.* 6th ed. New York: Longman.

——— (2009) *The French Polity.* 7th ed. New York: Pearson Longman.

Saiegh, Sebastian M. (2010) "Active Players or Rubber Stamps? An Evaluation of the Policymaking Role of Latin American Legislatures." In Carlos Scartascini, Ernesto Stein, and Mariano Tommasi, eds., *How Democracy Works: Political Institutions, Actors, and Arenas in Latin American Policymaking.* Washington, DC: Inter-American Development Bank.

——— (2011) *Ruling by Statute: How Uncertainty and Vote Buying Shape Lawmaking.* New York: Cambridge University Press.

Sala, Brian R. (1998) "In Search of the Administrative President: Presidential 'Decree' Powers and Policy Implementation in the United States." In John Carey and Matthew Soberg Shugart, eds., *Executive Decree Authority.* Cambridge: Cambridge University Press.

Samuels, David (2008) "Brazil: Democracy Under Lula and the PT." In Jorge I. Domínguez and Michael Shifter, eds., *Constructing Democratic Governance in Latin America,* 3rd ed. Baltimore: Johns Hopkins University Press.

Samuels, David, and Matthew Soberg Shugart (2003) "Presidentialism, Elections, and Representation." *Journal of Theoretical Politics* 15:1 (January), 33–60.

——— (2010) *Presidents, Parties, and Prime Ministers: How the Separation of Powers Affects Party Organization and Behavior.* Cambridge: Cambridge University Press.

Santos, Fabiano, and Marcio Grijo Vilarouca (2008) "Political Institutions and Governability from FHC to Lula." In Peter R. Kingstone and Timothy J. Power, eds., *Democratic Brazil Revisited.* Pittsburgh: University of Pittsburgh Press.

Savage, Charlie (2009) "Obama Looks to Limit Impact of Tactic Bush Used to Sidestep New Laws." *New York Times,* March 10.

Schlesinger, Arthur M., Jr. (1973) *The Imperial Presidency.* Boston: Houghton Mifflin.

Schmidt, Gregory (1998) "Presidential Usurpation or Congressional Preference? The Evolution of Executive Decree Authority in Peru." In John Carey and Matthew Soberg Shugart, eds., *Executive Decree Authority.* Cambridge: Cambridge University Press.

Schumacher, Edward J. (1975) *Politics, Bureaucracy, and Rural Development in Senegal.* Berkeley: University of California Press.

Shklar, Judith N. (1987) *Montesquieu.* New York: Oxford University Press.

Shugart, Matthew Soberg (1995) "Parliaments over Presidents?" *Journal of Democracy* 6:2 (April), 168–172.

——— (1998) "The Inverse Relationship Between Party Strength and Executive Strength: A Theory of Politician's Institutional Choices." *British Journal of Political Science* 28:1 (January), 1–29.

Shugart, Matthew Soberg, and John M. Carey (1992) *Presidents and Assemblies: Constitutional Design and Electoral Dynamics.* Cambridge: Cambridge University Press.

Shugart, Matthew Soberg, and Stephan Haggard (2001) "Institutions and Public Policy in Presidential Systems." In Stephan Haggard and Matthew McCubbins, eds., *Presidents, Parliaments, and Public Policy.* Cambridge: Cambridge University Press.

Shugart, Matthew Soberg, and Scott Mainwaring (1997) "Presidentialism and Democracy in Latin America: Rethinking the Terms of the Debate." In Scott Mainwaring and Matthew Soberg Shugart, eds., *Presidentialism and Democracy in Latin America.* Cambridge: Cambridge University Press.

Siaroff, Alan (2003) "Comparative Presidencies: The Inadequacy of the Presidential, Semi-Presidential, and Parliamentary Distinction." *European Journal of Political Research* 42, 287–312.

Siavelis, Peter (1997) "Executive-Legislative Relations in Post-Pinochet Chile: A Preliminary Assessment." In Scott Mainwaring and Matthew Soberg Shugart, eds., *Presidentialism and Democracy in Latin America.* Cambridge: Cambridge University Press.

———— (2001) *President and Congress in Postauthoritarian Chile*. University Park: Pennsylvania State University Press.

———— (2002) "Exaggerated Presidentialism and Moderate Presidents: Executive-Legislative Relations in Chile." In Scott Morgenstern and Benito Nacif, eds., *Legislative Politics in Latin America*. Cambridge: Cambridge University Press.

Silva, Patricio (2001) "Forging Military-Technocratic Alliances: The Ibanez and Pinochet Regimes in Chile." In Patricio Silva, ed., *The Soldier and the State in South America: Essays in Civil-Military Relations*. New York: Palgrave.

Singer, Matthew M. (2007) "The Presidential and Parliamentary Elections in Bolivia, December, 2005." *Electoral Studies* 26:1 (March), 200–205.

Skidmore, Thomas (1993) "Politics and the Media in Democratizing Latin America." In Thomas Skidmore, ed., *Television, Politics, and the Transition to Democracy in Latin America*. Washington, DC: Woodrow Wilson Center.

Skowronek, Stephen (1993) *The Politics Presidents Make: Leadership from John Adams to George Bush*. Cambridge: Belknap Press of Harvard University.

Smith, Alex Duval (2007) "Chirac Bows Out As France Turns Against Its Past." *The Observer* (United Kingdom), March 11.

Sondrol, Paul C. (1990) "Intellectuals, Political Culture, and the Roots of the Authoritarian Presidency in Latin America." *Governance: An International Journal of Policy and Administration* 3:4 (October), 416–437.

Spiller, Pablo T., and Mariano Tommasi (2008) "Political Institutions, Policymaking Processes, and Policy Outcomes in Argentina." In Ernesto Stein and Mariano Tommasi, eds., *Policymaking in Latin America: How Politics Shapes Policies*. Washington, DC: Inter-American Development Bank.

Stanley, Alessandra (2012a) "On Russian TV, It Isn't All About the Strongman." *New York Times*, February 13.

———— (2012b) "TV in Putin's Russia: Jesters, Strivers, and a Longing for Normalcy." *New York Times*, February 13.

Stanley, Harold W., and Richard G. Niemi (2006) *Vital Statistics on American Politics, 2005–2006*. Washington, DC: Congressional Quarterly.

Suleiman, Ezra N. (1994) "Presidentialism and Political Stability in France." In Juan Linz and Arturo Valenzuela, eds., *The Failure of Presidential Democracy*. Baltimore: Johns Hopkins University Press.

Sunstein, Cass R. (2006) "Beyond Marbury: The Executive's Power to Say What the Law Is." *Yale Law Journal* 115:9, 2580–2610.

Taghiyev, Elguin A. (2006) "Measuring Presidential Power in Post-Soviet Countries." *CEU Political Science Journal* 3, 11–21.

Tanzi, Vito, and Ludger Schuknecht (2000) *Public Spending in the 20th Century: A Global Perspective*. Cambridge: Cambridge University Press.

Tapia-Videla, Jorge (1977) "The Chilean Presidency in Developmental Perspective." *Journal of Interamerican Studies and World Affairs* 19 (November), 451–481.

Thach, Charles C., Jr. (1923) *The Creation of the Presidency, 1775–1789*. Baltimore: Johns Hopkins University Press.

Tordoff, William (1984) *Government and Politics in Africa*. Bloomington: Indiana University Press.

Tsebelis, George, and Eduardo Aleman (2005) "Presidential Conditional Agenda Setting Power in Latin America." *World Politics* 57:3 (April), 396–420.

Tulis, Jeffrey K. (1987) *The Rhetorical Presidency.* Princeton: Princeton University Press.

United Nations Development Programme (2005) *Democracy in Latin America: Towards a Citizen's Democracy.* New York.

Valenzuela, Arturo (1994) "Party Politics and the Crisis of Presidentialism in Chile: A Proposal for a Parliamentary Form of Government." In Juan Linz and Arturo Valenzuela, eds., *The Failure of Presidential Democracy.* Baltimore: Johns Hopkins University Press.

——— (2004) "Latin American Presidencies Interrupted." *Journal of Democracy* 15:4 (October), 5–19.

Valenzuela, Arturo, and A. Wilde (1979) "Presidential Politics and the Decline of the Chilean Congress." In Joel Smith and Lloyd D. Musolf, eds., *Legislatures in Development: Dynamics of Change in New and Old States.* Durham: Duke University Press.

van de Walle, Nicolas (2003) "Presidentialism and Clientelism in Africa's Emerging Party Systems." *Journal of Modern African Studies* 41:2 (June), 297–321.

Vile, M. J. C. (1998) *Constitutionalism and the Separation of Powers.* Indianapolis: Liberty Fund.

Waisbord, Silvio R. (1996) "Secular Politics: The Modernization of Argentine Electioneering." In David L. Swanson and Paolo Mancini, eds., *Politics, Media, and Modern Democracy: An International Study of Innovations in Electoral Campaigning and Their Consequences.* Westport: Praeger.

Wayne, Stephen J. (2012) *The Road to the White House, 2012.* Independence, KY: Wadsworth Cengage Learning.

Welch, Claude E., Jr. (1986) "Military Disengagement from Politics? Incentives and Obstacles in Political Change." In Simon Baynham, ed., *Military Power and Politics in Black Africa.* New York: St. Martin's.

Weldon, Jeffrey (1997) "Political Sources of *Presidencialismo* in Mexico." In Scott Mainwaring and Matthew Soberg Shugart, eds., *Presidentialism and Democracy in Latin America.* Cambridge: Cambridge University Press.

Weyland, Kurt (1996a) *Democracy Without Equity: Failures of Reform in Brazil.* Pittsburgh: University of Pittsburgh Press.

——— (1996b) "Neopopulism and Neoliberalism in Latin America: Unexpected Affinities." *Studies in Comparative International Development* 31:3 (Fall), 3–21.

——— (1998) "The Politics of Corruption in Latin America." *Journal of Democracy* 9:2, 108–121.

——— (2003) "Neopopulism and Neoliberalism in Latin America: How Much Affinity?" *Third World Quarterly* 24:6, 1095–1115.

Whitaker, Jennifer S. (1988) *How Can Africa Survive?* New York: Harper and Row.

Whitehead, Laurence (2001) "High Anxiety in the Andes: Bolivia and the Viability of Democracy." *Journal of Democracy* (April), 6–16.

Woldemariam, Kasahun (2009) *The Rise of Elective Dictatorships and the Erosion of Social Capital: Peace, Development, and Democracy in Africa.* Trenton: Africa World.

Wood, Gordon (1969) *The Creation of the American Republic, 1776–1787.* Chapel Hill: University of North Carolina Press.

Yoo, John (2009) *Crisis and Command: A History of Executive Power from George Washington to George W. Bush.* New York: Kaplan.

Zuleta-Puceiro, Enrique (1993) "The Argentine Case: Television in the 1989 Presidential Election." In Thomas Skidmore, ed., *Television, Politics, and the Transition to Democracy in Latin America.* Washington, DC: Woodrow Wilson Center.

Zuvanic, Laura, and Mercedes Iacoviello, with Ana Laura Rodríguez Gusta (2010) "The Weakest Link: The Bureaucracy and Civil Service Systems in Latin America." In Carlos Scartascini, Ernesto Stein, and Mariano Tommasi, eds., *How Democracy Works: Political Institutions, Actors, and Arenas in Latin American Policymaking.* Washington, DC: Inter-American Development Bank.

Index

About the Book

In countries as diverse as Brazil, Ecuador, France, Russia, South Africa, and the United States, presidents have come to dominate the politics and political cultures of their nations. Michael Mezey offers a comprehensive cross-national study of the presidency, tracing the historical and intellectual roots of executive power and exploring in detail the contemporary forces that have driven a turn toward "presidentialism."

Michael L. Mezey is professor of political science at DePaul University. His books include *Comparative Legislatures, Congress, the President, and Public Policy* and *Representative Democracy: Legislators and Their Constituents*.